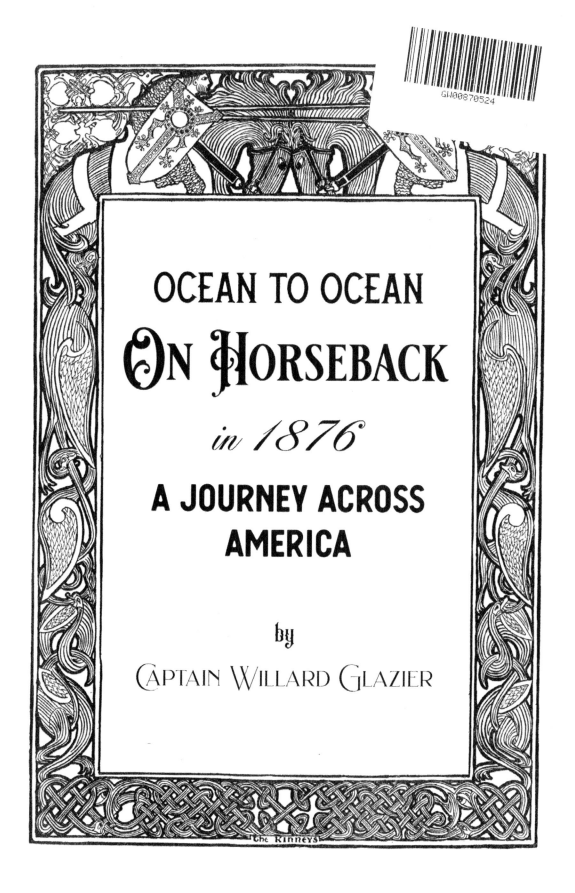

OCEAN TO OCEAN

On Horseback

in 1876

A JOURNEY ACROSS AMERICA

by

CAPTAIN WILLARD GLAZIER

1

Ocean to Ocean on Horseback in 1876:
A Journey Across America
Enlarged Illustrated Special Edition

by Captain Willard Glazier
Originally Printed in 1895

More History Books at
CGRpublishing.com

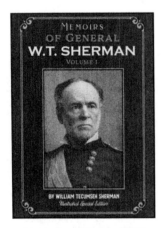

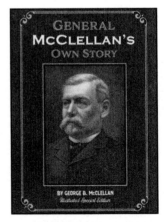

Memoirs of General W.T. Sherman Volume 1: Illustrated Special Edition

The Art Of World War 1

General McClellan's Own Story: Illustrated Special Edition

TO

THE MEMORY

OF

My Beloved Mother,

TO WHOSE

Precepts and Example

I AM INDEBTED FOR WHATEVER I HAVE BEEN
ABLE TO ACCOMPLISH

IN

The Journey of Life,

THIS VOLUME

THE RECORD OF MY LONGEST AMERICAN JOURNEY

IS AFFECTIONATELY

DEDICATED.

OCEAN TO OCEAN

ON

HORSEBACK;

𝕭eing

The Story of a Tour in the Saddle From the Atlantic to the Pacific; with Especial Reference to the Early History and Development of Cities and Towns along the Route; and Regions Traversed beyond the Mississippi; together with Incidents, Anecdotes and Adventures of the Journey.

BY

CAPTAIN WILLARD GLAZIER.

Author of "Capture, Prison-Pen and Escape," "Three Years in the Federal Cavalry," "Battles for the Union," "Heroes of Three Wars," "Peculiarities o. American Cities," "Down the Great River," "Headwaters of the Mississippi," Etc.

———◦◦◦———

Illustrated.

———◦◦———

1900.

PREFACE.

———

T was the intention of the writer to publish a narrative descriptive of his overland tour from the Atlantic to the Pacific
soon after returning from California in
1876, and his excuse for the delay in
publication is that a variety of circumstances compelled him to postpone for a
time the duty of arranging the contents of his journal
until other pressing matters had been satisfactorily
attended to. Again, considerable unfinished literary
work, set aside when he began preparation for crossing
the Continent, had to be resumed, and for these
reasons the story of his journey from "OCEAN
TO OCEAN ON HORSEBACK" is only now ready for
the printer. In view of this delay in going to press,
the author will endeavor to show a due regard for the
changes time has wrought along his line of march, and

while noting the incidents of his long ride from day to day, it has been his aim so far as possible to discuss the regions traversed, the growth of cities and the development of their industries from the standpoint of the present.

ALBANY, NEW YORK,
August 22, 1895.

CONTENTS.

—◆◆◆—

CHAPTER I.

INTRODUCTORY.

Boyhood Longings—Confronted by Obstacles—Trapping Along the Oswegatchie—Enter Gouverneur Wesleyan Seminary—Appointed to State Normal College—Straitened Circumstances—Teach School in Rensselaer County—War of the Rebellion—Enlist in a Cavalry Regiment—Taken Prisoner—Fourteen Months in Southern Prisons—Escape from Columbia—Recaptured—Escape from Sylvania, Georgia—Re-enter the Army—Close of the War—Publish "Capture, Prison-Pen and Escape" and Other Books—Decide to Cross the Continent—Preparation for Journey—Ocean to Ocean on Horseback 19

CHAPTER II.

BOSTON AND ITS ENVIRONS.

Early History and Development—Situation of the Metropolis of New England—Boston Harbor—The Cradle of Liberty—Old South Church—Migrations of the Post Office—Patriots of the Revolution—The Boston Tea Party—Bunker Hill Monument—Visit of Lafayette—The Public Library—House where Franklin was Born—The Back Bay—Public Gardens—Streets of Boston—Soldiers' Monument—The Old Elm—Commonwealth Avenue—State Capitol—Tremont Temple—Edward Everett—Wendell Phillips—William Loyd Garrison—Phillips Brooks—Harvard University — Wellesley College — Holmes, Parkman — Prescott, Lowell, Longfellow—Boston's Claims to Greatness . . 26

CHAPTER III.

LECTURE AT TREMONT TEMPLE.

Subject of Lecture—Objects Contemplated—Grand Army of the

CONTENT.

Republic—Introduction·by Captain Theodore L. Kelly—Reference to Army and Prison Experiences—Newspaper Comment—Proceeds of Lecture Given to Posts 7 and 15—Letter to Adjutant-General of Department 64

CHAPTER IV.

BOSTON TO ALBANY.

First Day of Journey—Start from the Revere House—Escorted to Brighton by G. A. R. Comrades—Dinner at Cattle Fair Hotel—South Framingham—*Second Day*—Boston and Albany Turnpike—Riding in a Rainstorm—Arrival at Worcester—Lecture in Opera House—Pioneer History—Rapid Growth of Worcester—Lincoln Park—The Old Common—*Third and Fourth Days*—The Ride to Springfield—Met by Wife and Daughter—Lecture at Haynes Opera House—*Fifth Day*—Ride to Russell—The Berkshire Hills —*Sixth Day*—Journey to Becket—Rainbow Reflections—*Seventh Day*—Over the Hoosac Mountains—*Eighth Day*—Arrival at Pittsfield—Among the Lebanon Shakers—*Ninth Day*—Reach Nassau, New York 73

CHAPTER V.

FOUR DAYS AT ALBANY.

Nassau to Albany—Among Old Friends in Rensselaer County—Thoughts of Rip Van Winkle—Crossing the Hudson—Albany as Seen from the ·River—Schoolday Associations—Early History—Settled by the Dutch—Henry Hudson—Killian Van Rensselaer—Fort Orange—Peter Schuyler and Robert Livingstone—Lecture at Tweddle Hall—Call at the Capitol—Meet Army Comrades 118

CHAPTER VI.

ALBANY TO SYRACUSE.

Fourteenth Day—On the Schenectady Turnpike—Riding between Showers—Talk with Peter Lansing—Reach Schenectady—Lecture at Union Hall under G. A. R. Auspices—*Fifteenth and Sixteenth Days*—Go over to Troy—Lecture at Harmony Hall—Visit Old Friends—*Seventeenth Day*—Return to Schenectady—*Eighteenth Day*—In the Mohawk Valley—Halt at Amsterdam—Reach Fonda —*Nineteenth Day*—Saint Johnsville—*Twentieth Day*—Little Falls—*Twenty-first Day*—Utica—*Twenty-second Day*—Rome—*Twenty-third Day*—Chittenango 130

CHAPTER VII.

TWO DAYS AT SYRACUSE.

Walks and Talks with the People—Early History—Lake Onondaga—

CONTENTS.

Father Le Moyne—Discovery of Salt Springs—Major Danforth—
Joshua Forman—James Geddes—The Erie Canal—Visit of La
Fayette—Syracuse University—Lecture at Shakespeare Hall 144

CHAPTER VIII.

SYRACUSE TO ROCHESTER.

Twenty-sixth Day—Grand Army Friends—General Sniper—Captain
Auer—Stopped by a Thunder-shower—An Unpleasant Predica-
ment—*Twenty-Seventh Day*—Jordan, New York—Lake Skaneat-
eles—*Twenty-eighth Day*—Photographed—Entertained at Port
Byron—Montezuma Swamp—*Twenty-ninth Day*—Newark, New
York—Journey Continued Along the New York Central Rail-
way—Another Adventure with *Paul*—*Thirtieth Day*—Fairport—
Riding in the Cool of the Day   151

CHAPTER IX.

FOUR DAYS AT ROCHESTER.

Rainstorm Anticipated—Friends of the Horse—Seven-Sealed Wonder
—Newspaper Controversy—Lecture at Corinthian Hall—Colonel
J. A. Reynolds—Pioneer History—Colonel Nathaniel Rochester—
William Fitzhugh—Charles Carroll—Rapid Growth of City—Sam
Patch—Genesee Falls—The Erie Canal—Mount Hope—Lake
Ontario—Fruit Nurseries   161

CHAPTER X.

ROCHESTER TO BUFFALO.

Thirty-fifth Day—Churchville—Cordiality of the People—Dinner
at Chili—*Thirty-sixth Day*—Bergen Corners—Byron Centre—Rev.
Edwin Allen—*Thirty-seventh Day*—Batavia—Meet a Comrade of
the Harris Light Cavalry—*Thirty-eighth Day*—"Croft's"—More
Trouble with Mosquitoes—Amusing Episode—*Thirty-ninth Day*
—Crittenden—Rural Reminiscences—*Fortieth Day*—Lancaster—
Lectured in Methodist Church—Captain Remington   .   172

CHAPTER XI.

THREE DAYS AT BUFFALO.

"Queen City" of the Lakes—Arrival at the Tift House—Lecture
at St. James Hall—Major Farquhar—Aboriginal History—The
Eries—Iroquois—"Cats"—La Hontan—Lake Erie—Black Rock—
War of 1812—The Erie Canal—Buffalo River—Grosvenor Library
—Historical Society—Red Jacket—Forest Lawn—Predictions
for the Future   187

CONTENTS.

CHAPTER XII.

BUFFALO TO CLEVELAND.

Forty-fourth Day—On the Shore of Lake Erie—*Forty-fifth Day*—Again on the Shore of Erie—Bracing Air—Enchanting Scenery—Angola—Big Sister Creek—*Forty-sixth Day*—Angola to Dunkirk—*Forty-eighth Day*—Dunkirk to Westfield—Fruit and Vegetable Farms—Fredonia—*Forty-ninth Day*—Westfield to North East—Cordial Reception—*Fiftieth Day*—North East to Erie—Oliver Hazzard Perry—*Fifty-first Day*—Erie to Swanville—*Fifty-second Day*—Talk with Early Settlers—John Joseph Swan—*Fifty-third Day*—Swanville to Girard—Greeted by Girard Band—Lecture at Town Hall—*Fifty-fourth Day*—Girard to Ashtabula—Lecture Postponed—*Fifty-fifth Day*—Ashtabula to Painesville—The Centennial Fourth—Halt at Farm House—*Fifty-sixth Day*—Reach Willoughby—Guest of the Lloyds 197

CHAPTER XIII.

FIVE DAYS AT CLEVELAND.

An Early Start—School Girls—"Do you Like Apples, Mister?"—Mentor—Home of Garfield—Dismount at Euclid—Rumors of the Custer Massacre—Reach the "Forest City"—Met by Comrades of the G. A. R.—Lecture at Garrett Hall—Lake Erie—Cuyahoga River—Early History—Moses Cleveland—Connecticut Land Company—Job Stiles—The Ohio Canal—God of Lake Erie—"Ohio City"—West Side Boat Building—"The Pilot"—Levi Johnson—Visit of Lorenzo Dow—Monument Square—Commodore Perry—Public Buildings—Euclid Avenue—"The Flats"—Standard Oil Company 224

CHAPTER XIV.

CLEVELAND TO TOLEDO.

Sixty-first Day—Again in the Saddle—Call on Major Hessler—Donate Proceeds of Lecture to Soldiers' Monument Fund—Letters from General James Barnett and Rev. William Earnshaw—Stop for Night at Black River—*Sixty-second Day*—Mounted at Nine A. M.—Halted at Vermillion for Dinner—Lake Shore Road—More Mosquitoes—Reach Huron Late at Night—*Sixty-third Day*—Huron to Sandusky—Traces of the Red Man—Ottawas and Wyandots—Johnson's Island—Lecture in Union Hall—Captain Culver—*Sixty-fourth Day*—Ride to Castalia—A Remarkable Spring—*Sixty-fifth Day*—Reach Fremont—Home of President Hayes—*Sixty-sixth Day*—Reach Elmore, Ohio—Comparison of Hotels 239

CONTENTS.

CHAPTER XV.

FIVE DAYS AT TOLEDO.

Ride from Elmore—Lecture at Lyceum Hall—Forsyth Post, G. A. R.—Doctor J. T. Woods—Concerning General Custer—Pioneer History—Battle of Fallen Timbers—Mad Anthony Wayne—Miami and Wabash Indians—The Toledo War—Unpleasant Complications—Governor Lucas—Strategy of General Vanfleet—Milbourn Wagon Works—Visited by a Detroit Friend . . 253

CHAPTER XVI.

TOLEDO TO DETROIT.

Seventy-second Day—Leave Toledo—Change of Route—Ride to Erie, Michigan—*Paul* Shows His Mettle—*Seventy-third Day*—Sunday—Go to Church—Rev. E. P. Willard—Solicitude of Friends—*Seventy-fourth Day*—Ride to Monroe—Greeted with Music—Hail Columbia—Star-Spangled Banner—Home of Custer—Meet Custer Family—Custer Monument Association—Received at City Hall—Great Enthusiasm—River Rasin—Indian Massacre—General Winchester—Battle of the Thames—Death of Tecumseh—Monroe *Monitor*—*Seventy-seventh Day*—Lecture at City Hall—Personal Recollections of Custer—Incidents of His School Life—*Seventy-eighth Day*—Leave Monroe—Huron River—Traces of the Mound Builders—Rockwood—*Seventy-ninth Day*—Along the Detroit River—Wyandotte—Ecorse—*Eightieth Day*—Letter from Judge Wing—Indorsement of Custer Monument Association . 265

CHAPTER XVII.

FOUR DAYS AT DETROIT.

Leave Ecorse—Met at Fort Wayne—Sad News—Reach Detroit—Met by General Throop and Others—at Russell House—Lecture at St. Andrew's Hall—General Trowbridge—Meet Captain Hampton—Army and Prison Reminiscences—Pioneer History of Detroit—La Motte Cadillac—Miamies and Pottawattomies—Fort Ponchartrain—Plot of Pontiac—Major Gladwyn—Fort Shelby—War of 1812—General Brock and Tecumseh Advance on Detroit—Surrender of General Hull—British Compelled to Evacuate 283

CHAPTER XVIII.

DETROIT TO CHICAGO.

Eighty-fifth Day—Leave Detroit Reluctantly—*Paul* in Good Spirits—Reach Inkster—*Eighty-sixth Day*—Lowering Clouds—Take Shelter under Trees and in a Woodshed—Meet War Veterans—

CONTENTS.

Ypsilanti—*Eighty-seventh Day*—Lecture at Union Hall—Incidents of the Late War—*Eighty-eighth Day*—An Early Start—Ann Arbor—Michigan University—Dinner at Dexter—*Eighty-ninth Day*—Dinner at Grass Lake—Reach Jackson—*Ninetieth Day*—Comment of Jackson *Citizen*—Coal Fields—Grand River—*Ninety-first Day*—A Circus in Town—Parma—*Ninety-second Day*—"Wolverines"—*Ninety-third Day*—Ride to Battle Creek—Lecture at Stuart's Hall—*Ninety-fourth Day*—Go to Church—Goguac Lake—*Ninety-fifth Day*—Arrive at Kalamazoo—Sketch of the "Big Village"—*Ninty-sixth Day*—Return to Albion and Lecture in Opera House—*Ninety-seventh Day*—Lecture at Wayne Hall, Marshall—*Ninety-eighth Day*—Calhoun County—*Ninety-ninth Day*—Letter to Custer Monument Association—*One Hundreth Day*—Colonel Curtenius—*One Hundred and First Day*—Paw Paw—*One Hundred and Second Day*—South Bend, Indiana—Hon. Schuyler Colfax—*One Hundred and Third Day*—Grand Rapids—Speak in Luce's Hall—*One Hundred and Fourth Day*—Return to Decatur—*One Hundred and Fifth Day*—Again in Paw Paw—*One Hundred and Sixth Day*—Lecture at Niles—*One Hundred and Seventh Day*—Go to La Porte by Rail—*One Hundred and Eighth Day*—Return to Michigan City—*One Hundred and Ninth Day*—Go Back to Decatur, Michigan—*One Hundred and Tenth to One Hundred and Twenty-second Day*—Dowagiac—Buchanan—Rolling Prairie 297

CHAPTER XIX.

THREE DAYS AT CHICAGO.

Register at the Grand Pacific Hotel—Lecture at Farwell Hall—Visit McVicker's Theatre—See John T. Raymond in "Mulberry Sellers"—The Chicago Exposition—Site of City—Origin of Name—Father Marquette—First Dwelling—Death of Marquette—Lake Michigan—Fort Dearborn—First Settlement Destroyed by Indians—Chicago as a Commercial City—The Great Fire—An Unparalleled Conflagration—Rises from her Ashes—Financial Reorganization—Greater than Before—Schools and Colleges—Historical Society—The Palmer House—Spirit of the People—*One Hundred and Twenty-sixth Day*—Again at Michigan City—Attend a Political Meeting—Hon. Daniel W. Voorhees—"Blue Jeans" Williams—*One Hundred and Twenty-eighth Day*—Leave Michigan City—Hobart—"Hoosierdum"—*One Hundred and Twenty-ninth Day*—Weather Much Cooler 357

CONTENTS.

CHAPTER XX.

CHICAGO TO DAVENPORT.

One Hundred and Thirtieth Day—Followed by Prairie Wolves—
Reach Joliet, Illinois—Lecture at Werner Hall—*One Hundred
and Thirty-first Day*—Ride on Tow Path of Michigan Canal—
Morris—*One Hundred and Thirty-second Day*—Corn and Hogs
—Arrive at Ottawa—*One Hundred and Thirty-third Day*—Reach
La Salle—*One Hundred and Thirty-fourth Day*—Colonel Stephens
—*One Hundred and Thirty-fifth Day*—Visit Peru—*One Hundred
and Thirty-sixth Day*—Mistaken for a Highwayman—*One Hun-
dred and Thirty-seventh Day*—Fine Stock Farms—Wyanet—*One
Hundred and Thirty-eighth Day* — Annawan — Commendatory
Letter—*One Hundred and Thirty-ninth Day*—A Woman Farmer—
One Hundred and Fortieth Day—Reach Milan, Illinois .   372

CHAPTER XXI.

FOUR DAYS AT DAVENPORT.

Cross the Mississippi—Lecture at Moore's Hall—Colonel Russell—
General Sanders—Early History of the City—Colonel George
Davenport—Antoine Le Claire—Griswold College—Rock Island
—Fort Armstrong—Rock Island Arsenal—General Rodman—Col-
onel Flagler—Rock Island City—Sac and Fox Indians—Black
Hawk War—Jefferson Davis—Abraham Lincoln—Defeat of Black
Hawk—Rock River—Indian Legends 398

CHAPTER XXII.

DAVENPORT TO DES MOINES.

One Hundred and Forty-fifth Day—Leave Davenport—Stop over
Night at Farm House—*One Hundred and Forty-sixth Day*—Reach
Moscow, Iowa—Rolling Prairies—*One Hundred and Forty-seventh
Day*—Weather Cold and Stormy—Iowa City—*One Hundred and
Forty-eighth Day*—Description of City—*One Hundred and Forty-
ninth Day*—Lectured at Ham's Hall—Hon. G. B. Edmunds—*One
Hundred and Fiftieth Day*—Reach Tiffin—Guests of the Tiffin
House—*One Hundred and Fifty-first Day*—Marengo—*One Hun-
dred and Fifty-second Day*—Halt for the Night at Brooklyn—*One
Hundred and Fifty-third Day*—Ride to Kellogg—Stop at a School
House—Talk with Boys—*One Hundred and Fifty-fourth Day*—
Reach Colfax—*One Hundred and Fifty-fifth Day*—Arrive at Des
Moines—Capital of Iowa—Description of City—Professor Bowen
—Meet an Army Comrade 410

CONTENTS.

CHAPTER XXIII.
DES MOINES TO OMAHA.

One Hundred and Fifty-seventh Day—Leave Des Moines with Pleasant Reflections—Reach Adel—Dallas County—Raccoon River—*One Hundred and Fifty-eighth Day*—Ride through Redfield—Reach Dale City—Talk Politics with Farmers—*One Hundred and Fifty-ninth Day*—A Night with Coyotes—Re-enforced by a Friendly Dog—*One Hundred and Sixtieth Day*—Cold Winds from the Northwest—All Day on the Prairies—*One Hundred and Sixty-first Day*—Halt at Avoca—*One Hundred and Sixty-second Day*—Riding in the Rain—Reach Neola—*One Hundred and Sixty-third Day*—Roads in Bad Condition—Ride through Council Bluffs—Arrive at Omaha 425

CHAPTER XXIV.
A HALT AT OMAHA.

The Metropolis of Nebraska—First Impressions—Peculiarity of the Streets—Hanscom Park—Poor House Farm—Prospect Cemetery—Douglas County Fair Grounds—Omaha Driving Park—Fort Omaha—Creighton College—Father Marquette—The Mormons—"Winter Quarters"—Lone Tree Ferry—Nebraska Ferry Company—Old State House—First Territorial Legislature—Governor Cummings—Omaha in the Civil War—Rapid Development of the "Gate City" 439

CHAPTER XXV.
OMAHA TO CHEYENNE.

Leave *Paul* in Omaha—Purchase a Mustang—Use Mexican Saddle—Over the Great Plains—Surface of Nebraska—Extensive Beds of Peat—Salt Basins—The Platte River—High Winds—Dry Climate—Fertile Soil—Lincoln—Nebraska City—Fremont—Grand Island—Plum Creek—McPherson—Sheep Raising—Elk Horn River—In Wyoming Territory—Reach Cheyenne—Description of Wyoming—"Magic City"—Vigilance Committee—Rocky Mountains—Laramie Plains—Union Pacific Railroad 452

CHAPTER XXVI.
CAPTURED BY INDIANS.

Leave Cheyenne—Arrange to Journey with Herders—Additional Notes on Territory—Yellowstone National Park—Sherman—Skull Rocks—Laramie Plains—Encounter Indians—Friendly Signals—Surrounded by Arrapahoes—One Indian Killed—Taken Prisoners—Carried toward Deadwood—Indians Propose to Kill

CONTENTS.

their Captives—Herder Tortured at the Stake—Move toward
Black Hills—Escape from Guards—Pursued by the Arrapahoes—
Take Refuge in a Gulch—Reach a Cattle Ranch—Secure a
Mustang and Continue Journey 471

CHAPTER XXVII.

AMONG THE MORMONS.

Ride Across Utah—Chief Occupation of the People—Description of
Territory — Great Salt Lake — Mormon Settlements — Brigham
Young—Peculiar Views of the Latter Day Saints—"Celestial
Marriages"—Joseph Smith, the Founder of Mormonism—The Book
of Mormon—City of Ogden—Pioneer History—Peter Skeen Ogden
—Weber and Ogden Rivers—Heber C. Kimball—Echo Canyon—
Enterprise of the Mormons—Rapid Development of the Terri-
tory 487

CHAPTER XXVIII.

OVER THE SIERRAS.

The Word Sierra—At Kelton, Utah—Ride to Terrace—Wells,
Nevada—The Sierra Nevada—Lake Tahoe—Silver Mines—The
Comstock Lode—Stock Raising—Camp Halleck—Humboldt River
—Mineral Springs—Reach Palisade—Reese River Mountain—
Golconda—Winnemucca—Lovelocks—Wadsworth—Cross Truckee
River—In California 503

CHAPTER XXIX.

ALONG THE SACRAMENTO.

Colfax—Auburn—Summit—Reach Sacramento — California Boun-
daries—Pacific Ocean—Coast Range Mountains—The Sacramento
Valley—Inhabitants of California—John A. Sutter—Sutter's Fort
—A Saw-mill—James Wilson Marshall—Discovery of Gold—
"Boys, I believe I have found a Gold Mine"—The Secret Out—First
Days of Sacramento—A "City of Tents"—Capital of California 510

CHAPTER XXX.

SAN FRANCISCO AND END OF JOURNEY.

Metropolis of the Pacific Coast—Largest Gold Fields in the World—
The Jesuits—Captain Sutter—Argonauts of "49"—Great Excite-
ment—Discovery of Upper California—Sir Francis Drake—John
P. Lease—The Founding of San Francisco—The "Golden Age"
—Story of Kit Carson—The Golden Gate—San Francisco Deserted
—The Cholera Plague—California Admitted to the Union—Cran-
dall's Stage—Wonderful Development of San Francisco—United
States Mint—Handsome Buildings—Trade with China, Japan,
India and Australia—Go Out to the Cliff House—Ride into the
Pacific—End of Journey 525

OCEAN TO OCEAN
ON
HORSEBACK.

CHAPTER I.

INTRODUCTORY.

FROM earliest boyhood it had been my earnest desire to see and learn from personal observation all that was possible of the wonderful land of my birth. Passing from the schoolroom to the War of the Rebellion and thence back to the employments of peace, the old longing to make a series of journeys over the American Continent again took possession of me and was the controlling incentive of all my ambitions and struggles for many years.

To see New England—the home of my ancestors; to visit the Middle and Western States; to look upon the majestic Mississippi; to cross the Great Plains; to scale the mountains and to look through the Golden Gate upon the far-off Pacific were among the cherished desires through which my fancy wandered before leaving the Old Home and village school in Northern New York.

The want of an education and the want of money were two serious obstacles which confronted me for a time. Without the former I could not prosecute my journeys intelligently and for want of the latter I could not even attempt them.

Aspiring to an academic and collegiate course of study, but being at that period entirely without means for the accomplishment of my purpose, I left the district school of my native town and sought to raise the necessary funds by trapping for mink and other fur-bearing animals along the Oswegatchie and its tributary streams. This venture proving successful I entered the academy at Gouverneur in August, 1857, from which institution I was appointed to the State Normal College at Albany in the fall of 1859.

I had been in Albany but six weeks when it became apparent that if I continued at the Normal I would soon be compelled to part with my last dollar for board and clothing.

The years 1859-60 were spent alternately at Albany as student and in the village schools of Rensselaer County as teacher—the latter course being resorted to whenever money was needed with which to meet current expenses at the Normal School.

Then came our great Civil Conflict overriding every other consideration. Books were thrown aside and the pursuits of the student and teacher supplanted by the sterner and more arduous duties of the soldier.

During my three years of camping and campaigning with the cavalry of the Army of the Potomac I was enabled to gratify to some extent my desire for travel and to see much of interest as the shifting scenes of war led Bayard, Stoneman, Pleasonton, Gregg, Custer,

Davies and Kilpatrick and their followers over the hills and through the valleys of Virginia, Maryland and Pennsylvania.

Being captured in a cavalry battle between Kilpatrick and Stuart in October, 1863, I was imprisoned successively at Richmond, Danville, Macon, Savannah, Charleston and Columbia, from which last prison I escaped in November, 1864; was recaptured and escaped a second and third time, traversing the States of South Carolina and Georgia in my long tramp from Columbia to Savannah.

The marches, raids, battles, captures and escapes of those days seem to have increased rather than diminished my ardor for travel and adventure and hence it is possibly not strange that on leaving the army I still looked forward to more extended journeys in the East and exploratory tours beyond the Mississippi.

With the close of the war and mustering out of service came new duties and responsibilities which I had hardly contemplated during my school days. The question of ways and means again confronted me. I desired first to continue the course of study which had been interrupted by my enlistment, and secondly to carry out my cherished plans for exploration. Having a journal kept during my incarceration in and escapes from Southern prisons, I was advised and decided to amplify and publish it if possible with a view to promoting these projects.

Going to New York, I at once sought the leading publishers. My manuscript was submitted to the Harpers, Appletons, Scribners, and some others, but as I was entirely unknown, few cared to undertake the publication and none seemed disposed to allow a royalty which to me at least seemed consistent with the time and labor expended in preparation. I had now spent my last dollar in the Metropolis in pursuit of a publisher, and in this dilemma it was thought best to return to Albany, where I had friends and perhaps some credit, and endeavor to bring out the book by subscription. This course would compel me to assume the cost of production, but if successful would prove much more lucrative than if issued in the usual way through the trade.

Fully resolved upon retracing my steps to Albany, I was most fortunate in meeting an old comrade and friend to whom I frankly stated my plans and circumstances. He immediately loaned me twenty dollars with which to continue my search for a publisher and to meet in the meantime necessary current expenses.

On reaching Albany an attic room and meals were secured for a trifling sum, arrangements made with a publisher, and the work of getting out the book begun. While the printer was engaged in composing, stereotyping, printing and binding the work, I employed my spare time in a door-to-door canvass of the city for subscriptions, promising to deliver on the orders as soon as the books came from the press. In this way the start was made and before the close of the year hundreds of agencies were established throughout the country.

The venture proved successful beyond my most sanguine expectations, and where I had expected to dispose of two or three editions and to realize a few hundred dollars from the sale of " Capture, Prison-Pen and Escape," the book had a sale of over 400,000 copies and netted me $75,000. This remarkable success, rivalling in its financial results even " Uncle Tom's Cabin," which had just had a run of 300,000 copies, was most gratifying and led to the publication, at intervals, of "Three Years in the Federal Cavalry;" "Battles for the Union," and "Heroes of Three Wars."

The temptation to make the most of my literary ventures lured me on from year to year until 1875, when I laid down the pen and began preparation for my long contemplated and oft deferred journey across the Continent. Being now possessed of ample means, I proposed to ride at leisure on a tour of observation from OCEAN TO OCEAN ON HORSEBACK.

My preference for an equestrian journey was in a great measure due to early associations with the horse, in jaunts along country highways and over the hills after the cows, as well as numerous boyhood adventures in which this noblest of animals frequently played a conspicuous part. Then, too, my experience in the cavalry largely influenced me to adopt the saddle as the best suited to my purpose.

Reflecting further upon the various modes of travel, I was led to conclude as the result of much experience that he who looks at the country from the windows of a railway car, can at best have only an imperfect idea of the many objects of interest which are constantly brought to his notice. Again, a journey in the saddle, wherein the rider mounts and dismounts at will as he jogs along over the highway, chatting with an occasional farmer, talking with the people in town and gazing upon rural scenes at his pleasure, presents many attractive features to the student and tourist who wishes to view the landscape, to commune with nature, to see men and note the products of their toil and to learn something of their manners and customs.

Having therefore decided to make my journey in the saddle, I at once set about to secure such a horse as was likely to meet the requirements of my undertaking. As soon as my purpose was known, horses of every grade, weight and shade were thrust upon my attention and after some three weeks spent in advertising, talks with horse fanciers and in the livery and sale stables of Boston, my choice fell upon a Kentucky Black Hawk, one of the finest animals I had ever seen and, as was subsequently established, just the horse I wanted for my long ride from sea to sea.

His color was coal black, with a white star in the forehead and four white feet; long mane and tail: height fifteen hands; weight between ten and eleven hundred pounds, with an easy and graceful movement under the saddle; his make-up was all that could be desired for the objects I had in view. The price asked for this beautiful animal was promptly paid, and it was generally conceded that I had shown excellent judgment in the selection of my equine companion.

A few days after my purchase I learned that my four-legged friend had been but a short time before the property of an ex-governor of Massachusetts and that the reason he had but recently found his way into a livery stable on Portland street, was that he had acquired the very bad habit of running away whenever he saw a railway train or anything else, in short, that tended to disturb his naturally excitable nature. This information led to no regrets, however, nor did it even lessen my regard for the noble animal which was destined soon to be my sole companion in many a lonely ride and adventure.

The unsavory reputation he had made, and possibly of which he was very proud, of running away upon the slightest provocation, smashing up vehicles and scattering their occupants to the four winds, was considered by his new master a virtue rather than a fault, so long as he ran in the direction of San Francisco, and did not precipitate him from his position in the saddle.

As soon as I was in possession of my horse the question of a suitable name arose and it was agreed after some discussion among friends that he should be christened *Paul Revere*, after that stirring patriot of the Revolution who won undying fame by his ride from Boston and appeals to the yeomanry the night before the Battle of Lexington.

CHAPTER II.

BOSTON AND ITS ENVIRONS.

THE month of April, 1876, found myself and horse fully equipped and ready to leave Boston, but I will not ride away from the metropolis of New England without some reference to its early history and remarkable development, nor without telling the reader of my lecture at Tremont Temple and other contemplated lectures in the leading cities and towns along my route.

Boston, standing on her three hills with the torch of learning in her hand for the illumination of North, South, East and West, is not one of your ordinary every-day cities, to be approached without due introduction. Like some ancient dame of historic lineage, her truest hospitality and friendliest face are for those who know her story and properly appreciate her greatness, past and present. Before visiting her, therefore, I recalled to memory those facts which touch us no more nearly than a dream on the pages of written history, but when studied from the living models and relics gain much life, color and verisimilitude.

Boston Harbor, with its waters lying in azure

placidity over the buried boxes of tea which the hasty hands of the angered patriots hurled to a watery grave; Boston Common, whose turf grows velvet-green over ground once blackened by the fires of the grim colonial days of witch-burning, and again trampled down by innumerable soldierly feet in Revolutionary times; the Old State House, from whose east window the governor's haughty command, "Disperse, ye rebels!" sounded on the occasion of the "Boston Massacre," the first shedding of American blood by the British military; and the monument of Bunker Hill—these, with a thousand and one other reminders of the city's brilliant historical record, compose the Old Boston which I was prepared to see. The first vision, however, of that many-sided city was almost bewilderingly different from the mental picture. Where was the quaint Puritan town of the colonial romances? Where were its crooked, winding streets, its plain uncompromising meeting-houses, darkened with time, its curious gabled houses, stooping with age? Around me everything was shining with newness—the smooth wide streets, beautifully paved, the splendid examples of *fin de siècle* architecture in churches, public buildings, school houses and dwellings.

Afterwards I realized that there was a New Boston, risen Phœnix-like from the ashes of its many conflagrations, and an Old Boston, whose "outward and visible signs" are best studied in that picturesque, shabby stronghold of ancient story, now rapidly degenerating into a "slum" district—the North End.

Boston, viewed without regard to its history, is indeed "Hamlet presented without the part of

Hamlet." It would be interesting to conjecture what the city's present place and condition might be, had Governor Winthrop's and Deputy-Governor Dudley's plan of making " New-towne "—the Cambridge of to-day—the Bay Colony's principal settlement, been executed. Instead, and fortunately, Governor Winthrop became convinced of the superiority of Boston as an embryo " county seat." " Trimountain," as it was first called, was bought in 1630 from Rev. William Blackstone, who dwelt somewhere between the Charles River and what is now Louisburg Square, and held the proprietary right of the entire Boston Peninsula —a sort of American Selkirk, " monarch of all he surveyed, and whose right there was none to dispute." He was " bought off," however, for the modest sum of £30, and retired to what was then the wilderness, on the banks of the Blackstone River— named after him—and left " Trimountain " to the settlers. Then Boston began to grow, almost with the quickness of Jack's fabled beanstalk. Always one of the most important of colonial towns, it conducted itself in sturdy Puritan style, fearing God, honoring the King—with reservations—burning witches and Quakers, waxing prosperous on cod-fish, and placing education above every earthly thing in value, until the exciting events of the Revolution, which has left behind it relics which make Boston a veritable "old curiosity shop " for the antiquarian, or indeed the ordinary loyal American, who can spend a happy day, or week, or month, prowling around the picturesque narrow streets, crooked as the proverbial ram's horn, of Old Boston

He will perhaps tur ⸿ first, as I did, to the

"cradle of Liberty"—Faneuil Hall. A slight shock will await him, possibly, in the discovery that under the ancient structure, round which hover so many imperishable memories of America's early struggles for freedom, is a market-house, where thrifty housewives and still more thrifty farmers chaffer, chat and drive bargains the year round, and which brings into the city a comfortable annual income of $20,000. But the presence of the money-changers in the temple of Freedom does not disturb the "solid men of Boston," who are practical as well as public-spirited. The market itself is as old as the hall, which was erected by the city in 1762, to take the place of the old market-house, which Peter Faneuil had built at his own expense and presented to the city in 1742, and which was burned down in 1761.

The building is an unpretending but substantial structure, plainly showing its age both in the exterior and the interior. Its size—seventy-four feet long by seventy-five feet wide—is apparently increased by the lack of seats on the main floor and even in the gallery, where only a few of these indispensable adjuncts to the comfort of a later luxurious generation are provided. The hall is granted rent free for such public or political meetings as the city authorities may approve, and probably is only used for gatherings where, as in the old days, the participants bring with them such an excess of effervescent enthusiasm as would make them unwilling to keep their seats if they had any. The walls are embellished by portraits of Hancock, Washington, Adams, Everett, Lincoln, and other great personages, and by Healy's immense painting—sixteen by thirty feet—of "Webster Replying to Hayne."

For a short time Faneuil Hall was occupied by
the Boston Post Office, while that institution, whose
early days were somewhat restless ones, was seeking
a more permanent home. For thirty years after the
Revolution, it was moved about from pillar to post,
occupying at one time a building on the site of Boston's first meeting-house, and at another the Merchants' Exchange Building, whence it was driven by
the great fire of 1872. Faneuil Hall was next
selected as the temporary headquarters, next the Old
South Church, after which the Post Office—a veritable
Wandering Jew among Boston public institutions—
was finally and suitably housed under its own roof-
tree, the present fine building on Post Office Square.

To the Old South Church itself, the sightseer next
turns, if still bent on historical pilgrimages. This
venerable building of unadorned brick, whose name
figures so prominently in Revolutionary annals, stands
at the corner of Washington and Milk streets. Rows
of business structures, some of them new and clean as
a whistle and almost impertinently eloquent of the importance of this world and its goods, cluster around
the old church and hem it in, but are unable to jostle
it out of the quiet dignity with which it holds its
place, its heavenward-pointing spire preaching the
sermons against worldliness which are no longer
heard within its ancient walls. To every window the
fanciful mind can summon a ghost—that of Benja-
min Franklin, who was baptized and attended service
here; Whitfield, who here delivered some of the
soul-searching, soul-reaching sermons, which swept
America like a Pentecostal flame; Warren, who here
uttered his famous words on the anniversary of the

VIEWS IN BOSTON.

Copp's Hill Burying Ground

THE COMMON

THE SUBWAY ENTRANCE

SOLDIERS' MONUMENT.

Boston Massacre; of the patriot-orators of the Revolution and the organizers of the Boston Tea-Party, which first took place as a definite scheme within these walls. Here and there a red-coated figure would be faintly outlined—one of the lawless troop of British soldiers who in 1775 desecrated the church by using it as a riding-school.

At present the church is used as a museum, where antique curiosities and historical relics are on exhibition to the public, and the Old South Preservation Committee is making strenuous efforts to save the building from the iconoclastic hand of Progress, which has dealt blows in so many directions in Boston, destroying a large number of interesting landmarks. Its congregation left it long ago, in obedience to that inexorable law of change and removal, which leaves so many old churches stranded amid the business sections of so many of our prominent cities, and settled in the " New Old South Church " at Dartmouth and Boylston streets.

It is curious and in its way disappointing to us visitors from other cities to see what "a clean sweep" the broom of improvement has been permitted in a city so intensely and justly proud of its historical associations as Boston. Year by year the old landmarks disappear and fine new buildings rise in their places and Boston is apparently satisfied that all is for the best. The historic Beacon, for which Beacon Hill was named and which was erected in 1634 to give alarm to the country round about in case of invasion, is not only gone, but the very mound where it stood has been levelled, this step having been taken in 1811. The Beacon had disappeared ten years before and a shaft

sixty feet high, dedicated to the fallen heroes of
Bunker Hill, had been erected on the spot and of
course removed when the mound was levelled. The
site of Washington's old lodgings at Court and Han-
over street—a fine colonial mansion, later occupied by
Daniel Webster and by Harrison Gray Otis, the celebrated lawyer—is now taken up by an immense
wholesale and retail grocery store; the splendid Hancock mansion, where the Revolutionary patriot entertained Lafayette, D'Estaing, and many other notabili-
ties of the day, was torn down in 1863, despite the protests of antiquarian enthusiasts. The double house,
in one part of which Lafayette lived in 1825, is still
standing; the other half of it was occupied during his
lifetime by a distinguished member of that unsurpassed group of *literati* who helped win for Boston so
much of her intellectual pre-eminence—George
Ticknor, the Spanish historian, the friend of Holmes,
Lowell, Whittier and Longfellow, from whom the
latter is supposed to have drawn his portrait of the
"Historian" in his "Tales of a Wayside Inn." The
Boston Public Library, that magnificent institution,
which has done so much to spread "sweetness and
light," to use Matthew Arnolds' celebrated definition
of culture, among the people of the "Hub," counts
Mr. Ticknor among the most generous of its bene-
factors.

One interesting spot for the historical pilgrim is the
oldest inn in Boston, the "Hancock House," near
Faneuil Hall, which sheltered Talleyrand and Louis
Philippe during the French reign of terror.

In addition to the fever for improvement, Boston
owes the loss of many of her time-hallowed buildings

to a more disastrous agency—that of the conflagrations which have visited her with strange frequency.
A fire in 1811, which swept away the little house on
Milk street where Franklin was born—and which is
now occupied by the Boston *Post*—another in 1874, in
which more than one hundred buildings were destroyed; and the "Great Boston Fire" of 1872, followed by conflagrations in 1873, 1874, 1877 and 1878,
seemed to indicate that the fire fiend had selected
Boston as his especial prey. To the terrible fire of
1872 many precious lives, property valued at eighty
millions of dollars, and the entire section of the city
enclosed by Summer, Washington, Milk and Broad
streets were sacrificed. The scene was one a witness
never could forget. Mingled with the alarum of the
fire-bells and the screams and shouts of a fear-stricken
people came the sound of terrific explosions, those of
the buildings which were blown up in the hope of
thus "starving out" the fire by making gaps which
it could not overstep, and to still further complete the
desolation, the gas was shut off, leaving the city in
a horror of darkness; but the flames swept on like a
pursuing Fury, wrapping the doomed city still closer
in her embrace of death, and who was not satisfied until she had left the business centre of Boston a charred
and blackened ruin.

This same district is to-day, however, the most prosperous and architecturally preposessing of the business
sections of the city, practically illustrating another
phase of that same spirit of improvement and civic
pride which has overturned so many ancient idols and
to-day threatens others. Indeed, it would be a churl-
ish disposition which would lament the disappearance

of the old edifices, the straightening of the thoroughfares, the alterations without number which have
taken place, and which have resulted in the Boston
of to-day, one of the most beautiful, prosperous
and public-spirited cities in the world. The intelligence and local loyalty, for which her citizens are
renowned, have been set to work to attain one object—
the modest goal of perfection. Obstacles which
some cities might have contentedly accepted as un-
avoidable have been swept away; advantages with
which other cities might have been satisfied have
been still further extended and improved. The 783
acres originally purchased by the settlers of Boston
from William Blaxton for £30 has been increased
over thirty times, until the city limits comprise
23,661 acres; this not by magic as it would seem,
but by annexation of adjoining boroughs—Roxbury,
Dorchester, Charlestown, and others—and by recla-
mation of the seemingly hopeless marshy land to the
north and south of the city. The "Back-Bay" district,
the very centre of Boston's wealth, fashion and refinement, the handsomest residence quarter in
America, is built upon this "made land," which it
cost the city about $1,750,000 to fill in and otherwise
render solid.

All good Bostonians, like the rest of their countrymen, may wish to go to Paris when they die—that point
cannot be settled; but it is certain that they all wish to
go to the Back-Bay while they live. And who can
wonder? To drive at night down Commonwealth
avenue, the most aristocratic street in this aristocratic
quarter, is to view a scene from fairyland. "The
Avenue" itself is 250 feet wide from house to house

PUBLIC GARDENS AND TRINITY CHURCH.

and 175 feet wide from curb to curb, and in the centre a picturesque strip of parkland, adorned with statues and bordered with ornamental trees and shrubs, follows its entire length. On either side of the street stand palatial hotels and magnificent private residences, from whose innumerable windows twinkle innumerable lights, which, mingling with the quadruple row of gas-lamps which look like a winding ribbon of light, make the vista perfectly dazzling in its beauty. By day, when the Back Bay Park, the Public Garden, the fine bridge over the park water-way extension and the handsome surrounding and intersecting streets can be seen, the view is even more attractive.

In the newer parts of Boston the reproach of crooked streets, which has given her sister cities opportunity for so much good-natured "chaff," is removed, and the thoroughfares are laid out with such precision that "the wayfaring man, though a fool," can hardly "err therein." In the business district much money has been spent on the straightening process, a fact whose knowledge prompts the bewildered stranger to exclaim, "Were they ever worse than this?" Stories aimed at this little peculiarity of the "Hub" are innumerable, the visitor being told with perfect gravity that if he follows a street in a straight line he will find himself at his original starting-point—a statement the writer's experience can pretty nearly verify. The best, if not the most credible, of these tales relates how a puzzled pedestrian, becoming "mixed up in his tracks," endeavored to overtake a man who was walking ahead of him, and inquire his way. The faster he walked, however, the faster the other man walked, until it became a regular chase, and the now thoroughly confused stranger had but one idea—to catch his fellow-pedestrian by the coat-tails, if need be, and demand to be set on his homeward way. Finally, by making a frantic forward lurch, he succeeded—and discovered that the coat-tails he was grasping were his own!

The true Bostonian is secretly rather proud, however, of this distinguished trait of his beloved city, and is willing to go "all around Robin Hood's barn" to get to his destination.

But the thing of which the Bostonian is proudest of all is his famous Common, whose green turf and noble shade-trees have formed a stage and background for so many of the most exciting scenes of Colonial and Revolutionary history. Among the troops which have been mustered and drilled upon it were a portion of the forces which captured Quebec and Louisburg ; and the rehearsals for the grim drama of war, which later was partly performed on the same ground by red-coat and continental, took place here. It was at the Common's foot that the hated "lobster-backs" assembled before embarking for Lexington ; on the Common that they marshalled their forces for the conflict at Bunker Hill. It has been covered with white tents during the British occupation of Boston ; dotted with earthworks behind which the enemy crouched, expecting an attack by Washington upon their stronghold. It was on Boston Common that the school-boys constructed their snow-men, whose destruction by the insolent red-coats sent an indignant deputation of young Bostonians to complain to General Gage, who, stunned by what the young Bostonian of to-day would designate as "the cheek of the thing," promised them redress, and exclaimed, "These boys seem to take in the love of liberty with the very air they breathe."

There are other interesting historical incidents, recorded in connection with the Common, but space forbids their narration. I would rather describe it as it first appeared to me, a beautiful surprise, a gracious spot of greenness and of silvery waters and splendid shade-trees, in the heart of the busy brick-bound city. Here the children play and coast, as they did in the days of General Gage; here the lovers walk, on the five beautiful broad pathways, the Tremont street, Park street, Beacon street, Charles street and Boylston street malls. Here the invalids and old folks rest on the numerous benches; here the people congregate on summer evenings to enjoy the free open-air concerts, which are given from the band-stand. "Frog Pond," a pretty lakelet, near Flagstaff Hill, and a fine deer-park in the vicinity of the Boylston street mall, are great attractions. The Common covers forty-eight acres, with 1000 stately old shade-trees, and the iron fence by which it is inclosed measures 5932 feet.

In addition to its natural beauties, the Common has two fine pieces of statuary, the Soldiers' and Sailors' Monument on Flagstaff Hill, and the Brener Fountain. The former was erected in 1871 at a cost of $75,000. It is a majestic granite shaft in the Roman-Doric style, seventy feet high, surmounted by a bronze figure of the Genius of America, eleven feet in height. At the base of the shaft are grouped alto-relievo figures representing the North, the South, the East, and the West. Four other bronze figures, representing Peace, History, the Army and the Navy, stand on projecting pedestals around the foundation. The monument, which was executed by Martin Milmore, was Boston's tribute to her fallen heroes of the Civil War. The Brener Fountain is a beautiful bronze casting designed by Lienard, of Paris, with bronze figures representing Neptune, Amphitrite, Acis, and Galatea grouped round the base. The late Gardner Brener presented it to the city in 1868.

To forget the Old Elm in describing the Common, would be rank disrespect to that hoary "oldest inhabitant," albeit nothing remains of it now but its memory. An iron fence surrounds the spot where once it stood, and a vigorous young sapling has providentially sprung up in its place, as a successor. The Old Elm was ancient in 1630, when the town was settled, and was one of its most interesting landmarks up to 1876, when it was blown down.

The Public Garden, from which the beautiful Commonwealth avenue begins, the Back-Bay Park, which cost a million of dollars, and the Arnold Arboretum, where Harvard University has planted and maintained a fine horticultural collection for the pleasure of the public, are lovely spots on whose beauty the mind would fain linger, but whose descriptions must be omitted, for all Boston's splendid public buildings wait in stately array their share of attention. Nowhere has the skilled artist-architect been so freely permitted to carry out his designs unhampered by stupidity and stinginess as in Boston, and the result has been a collection of public buildings unsurpassed by those of any modern city. The Boston State House comes first, of course— did not the "Autocrat of the Breakfast Table" term it, with loving exaggeration, the "Hub of the Solar System?" From Beacon Hill, the most prominent coign of vantage which could be selected for it, its gilded dome rises majestically against the blue sky and imperiously beckons the visitor to come and pay his respects to this most venerated of Boston institutions. The State House stands, at a height of 110 feet, at the junction of Beacon and Mt. Vernon streets and Hancock avenue, on a lot which Governor Hancock once used for pasturing his cows, and was erected in 1795, beginning its existence in a blaze of glory, with the corner-stone laid by Paul Revere, then Grand Master of the Masons, and an oration by Samuel Adams. The building contains Doric Hall, which is approached by a fine series of stone terraces from Beacon street; Hall of Representatives, the Senate Chamber, the Goverment Room, and the State Library.

It abounds in relics, among which are the tattered shreds of flags brought back by Massachusetts soldiers from Southern battlefields—a sight which must stir every loyal heart, to whatsoever State it owes allegiance ; the guns carried by the Concord minute-men in the Revolutionary conflict ; and duplicates of the gift to the State by Charles Sumner, of the memorial tablets of the Washington family in England. Doric Hall contains busts of Sumner, Adams, Lincoln, and other great men, and several fine statues—one of Washington, by Chantrey, and one by Thomas Ball ; a speaking likeness in marble of John A. Andrew, the indomitable old War Governor of Massachusetts.

On the handsome terraces in front of the building stand two superb bronzes, one is the Horace Mann statue, by Emma Stebbins, which was erected in 1865, and paid for by contributions from teachers and school children all over Massachusetts; the other Hiram Powers' statue of Daniel Webster, which cost $10,000. It was erected in 1859, and was the second statue of Webster which the famous sculptor wrought, the first, the prod· uct of so much toil and pains and the embodiment of so much genius, having been lost at sea.

Last, but very far from least in importance, may be mentioned the historic codfish, which hangs from the ceiling of Assembly Hall, dangling before the eyes of the legislators in perpetual reminder of the source of Massachusetts' present greatness, for the codfish might by a stretch of Hibernian rhetoric be described as the patron saint of the Bay State.

I must confess to having been one of the 50,000 curious ones who, it is computed, annually ascend into the gilded cupola and " view the landscape o'er." The spectacle unrolled panorama-like before the sight is indeed a feast to the eyes.

The Old State House of 1748, built on the site of Boston's earliest town hall, is now used as a historical museum under the auspices of the Bostonian Society. Careful restoration has perpetuated many of the old associations which hallow the ancient fane, sacred to loyalty and to liberty. The old council-chambers have been given much of their original appearance, and the great carving of the Lion and the Unicorn, which savored of offence to patriotic nostrils and so was taken down from its gables in Revolutionary times, has been replaced. To visit this building is a liberal education in local history.

The Boston Post Office, of whose migrations I have spoken earlier, is now settled for good and all in a magnificent structure of Cape Ann granite, built in Renaissance style, whose corner-stone was laid in 1871 and which was just ready for the addition of the roof when the Great Fire of 1872 descended upon it and beat upon it so fiercely that even to-day the traces of the intense heat are visible on parts of the edifice. Damage to the amount of $175,000 was done. The Sub-Treasury, the United States courts, the pension and internal revenue offices are domiciled here, and it is considered the handsomest public building in all New England, having cost $6,000,000. The interior furnishings are sumptuous in the extreme, the doors and windows in the Sub-Treasury apartments being of solid mahogany, beautifully polished. The " marble cash-room " is a splendid hall, decorated in Greek style, with wall-slabbing of dark and light shades of Sienna marble and graceful pilasters of Sicilian marble.

The City Hall, on School street, is the seat of the municipal housekeeping. Here the departments of streets, water, lighting, police, and public printing have their offices, and Common Council sits in august assemblage. It is a commanding structure of granite, fireproof, and in the Renaissance style. Its cost was $500,000. Two fine bronze statues, one by Greenough, of Franklin, one by Ball, of Josiah Quincy, ornament the grassy square in front of the building.

No picture of Boston would be complete without that old landmark, Tremont Temple. It occupies the former site of the Tremont Theatre and contains one of the largest halls in the city. The building itself, however, sinks into insignificance before the crowd of associations that stir the blood at its very name. For years it has been the rallying point of Boston's most notable gatherings—political, intellectual, and religious. If, instead of colorless words, we could photograph upon this page the pictures those old walls have looked upon, we might revel in a gallery of famous portraits such as the world has rarely seen. Edward Everett, Wendell Phillips, William Lloyd Garrison, Joseph Cook, Phillips Brooks, and other master-spirits of the age, would be there. And there, too, would be a sprinkling of that other sex, no longer handicapped by the epithet "gentler."

But, could we press the phonograph as well as the camera into our service, and hear again the thunders of stormy oratory, the clash of political warfare, and the pleading tenderness of religious eloquence that has often resounded under that old roof, then indeed we might well forget the world of to-day in the fascination of this drama of the past.

Architecturally, Boston combines in the happiest way all that is beautiful and dignified in the classic models and all that is fresh and original in modern canons of building. A magnificent group of buildings, in the vicinity of Boylston and Huntingdon streets and Copley Square, fairly takes the breath away with its beauty. Trinity Church and the Museum of Fine Arts, the "New Old South Church" and the new Boston Public Library, form such a quartet of splendid edifices as even the travelled eye seldom sees. The Public Library is an embodied Triumph—the symbol of that great heritage of culture which the city pours out on her denizens as lavishly and as freely as water, and which, like "the gentle dew from heaven, blesseth him that gives and him that takes," returning to enrich the community with its diffused presence, like the showers which return to the bosom of the river, the moisture the sun only borrowed for a space.

SKETCHES IN THE FENS & FRANKLIN PARK

ENVIRONS OF BOSTON.

Bostonians have always been proud of their Public Library, from its foundation in 1852. By 1885, the Boylston street building, with accommodations for 250,000 volumes, was too contracted a space to hold the largest public library in the world, and with characteristic promptness the city rose to the occasion and embodied its thought that "nothing can be too good for the people" in the beautiful new library in Copley Square, which cost the royal sum of $2,600,000.

The long chapter of description which this splendid enterprise merits must be reluctantly crowded into a few lines. Nothing, however, save personal observation, can give an adequate perception of its outward loveliness; its exterior of soft cream-gray granite, with a succession of noble arched windows ranged along its fine façades; its arches, pillars and floorings of rare marbles, and its mosaics, panels and carvings. The grand staircase of splendid Sienna marble, opposite the main entrance, is one of the finest in the world; and scholar, or philosopher could ask no more attractive spot for thoughtful promenade than the beautiful open court, with its marble basin and MacMonnies fountain in the centre, the soft green of its surrounding turf affording grateful rest to book-wearied eyes, and the pensive beauty of the cloister-like colonnade forming an ideal retreat.

The foremost artists of the world are represented in the interior decoration. The famous St. Gaudens seal, designed by Kenyon Cox and executed by Augustus St. Gaudens, ornaments the central arch of the main vestibule; the bronze doors are by Daniel G. French; the splendid marble lions in the staircase hall—erected as memorials to their martyred comrades by two regiments of Massachusetts volunteers—are by Louis St.

Gaudens; and Puvis de Chavannes, James McNeil Whistler, Edwin A. Abbey and John S. Sargent are among the celebrated artists who have contributed to the mural decorations, friezes and ceiling frescoes.

Six hundred and fifty thousand volumes at present constitute the stock of the library—a vast treasure-house of information, instruction and pleasure to which any citizen of Boston can have access by simply registering his name, and which among other valuable special collections includes the Brown musical library of 12,000 volumes and rare autograph manuscripts; the Barton Shaksperian library, one of the finest collections of Shakesperiana extant, valued at $250,000; the Bowditch mathematical library and the splendid Chamberlain collection of autographs, which is worth $60,000 and represents a lifetime of work on the part of the donor. The wonderful pneumatic and electric system of tubes and railways which connects the delivery and stackrooms and keeps this vast collection of books, pamphlets and magazines in circulation, smacks almost of the conjurer's craft. Whatever else must be crowded out of a visit to Boston, the Public Library assuredly should not be passed by.

Trinity Church stands within hailing distance of the Public Library, on Boylston and Clarendon streets —an imposing and beautiful edifice of granite and freestone, built in French Romanesque style, with a tower 211 feet high. Far outside of Boston has the fame of Trinity Church penetrated, owing not to the fact that it is one of the most splendid, costly and fashionable churches in the country, but to its ever-revered and ever-mourned rector, the late Phillips Brooks, Bishop of Massachusetts, whose massive figure will stand out against the horizon for many a year as the most striking speaker and deeply spiritual thinker America has ever known.

From Copley Square, not far from Trinity, rise the spires of the "New Old South" Church, a superb structure in North Italian Gothic style, rich in beautiful stone-work, carvings and stained glass. It was erected at a cost of over half a million of dollars to take the place of the disused "Old South" on Washington street. Another prominent church is the First Church, at Marlborough and Berkeley streets, the lineal descendant of the humble little mud-walled meeting-house which was the first consecrated roof under which the good folk of Boston gathered for divine worship. The congregation of that day could scarce believe their sober Puritan eyes could they behold the $325,000 church which was built in 1868 to continue the succession which had begun with the little mud meeting-house of 1632.

King's Chapel, with its ancient burying-ground, is one of the most famous churches in Boston, having been the chapel of the royal governor, officers of the army and navy, and other official representatives of the "principalities and powers" of the mother country. Massive, almost sombre, in its exterior, and quaint and picturesque within, the old church stands, with few changes, as erected in 1749, with its old-fashioned pulpit and sounding-board, prim, straight pillars, and antique high-backed pews which recall the remark of the little girl, that when she went to church she "went into a cupboard and climbed up on the shelf." Its burying-ground is believed to be the oldest in the city. Christ Church, built in 1723, is the oldest church edifice in the city. Its age-mellowed chime of bells was the first ever brought into this country, and the first American Sunday-school was established there in 1816. To-day its tall steeple, which on the eve of Lexington's conflict bore the signal lanterns of Paul Revere, is the most conspicuous object in the North End, where the old-time aristocrats who worshipped in Christ Church have given place to a poverty-stricken foreign population to whom the church is little and its traditions less. Churches which well deserve more extended mention, could space permit, are the beautiful Gothic Cathedral of the Holy Cross, with its fine organ and splendid high-altar of onyx and marble; Tremont Temple, whose hall is the largest in Boston; and the South Congregational Church, presided over by Rev. Edward Everett Hale, author of " The Man without a Country " and other world-famous literary productions, and originator of the equally famous " Ten Times One " clubs.

Boston's religious history is most interesting, although almost kaleidoscopic in its changes. From being the stronghold of Puritan orthodoxy it has become the headquarters of liberal Unitarianism. King's Chapel is a curious instance; originally an Episcopal church and congregation, it became Unitarian in 1787, retaining the Episcopal liturgy with necessary changes, and now doctrines are preached over the tombs of the dead dignitaries interred beneath the church floor, diametrically opposed to those in which they lived, died and were buried. Though all denominations of course flourish within her walls, Boston is still strongly Congregational in her leanings.

From the churches to the schools is a natural transition. The founders of Boston's greatness placed the two influences side by side in importance, and their wisdom in doing so has had its justification. The current "poking of fun" at the "Boston school-ma'am," her glasses, her learning and her devotion to Browning; and the Boston infant, who converses in polysyllables almost from his birth, has its foundation in the fact, everywhere admitted, that nowhere are intelligence and culture so widely diffused in all ranks of life as in Boston. The free-school system, an experiment which she was the first American city to inaugurate, is considered by educators to lead the world. The city's annual expenditures for her public schools, of which there are over 500, amount to about $2,000,000, and from the kindergarten to the High School, where the pupils can be prepared for college, the youth of the city are carefully watched, trained, instructed, and all that is best in them drawn out. Even in summer, "vacation schools" are held, where the children who would otherwise be running wild in the streets can learn sewing, box-making, cooking and other useful branches.

The English High and Latin School is the largest free public school building in the world, being 423 feet long by 220 feet wide. It is a fine structure in Renaissance style, with every advantage and improvement looking to health and convenience that even the progressive Boston mind could think of. It would be a sluggish soul indeed that would not be thrilled by the sight of the entire school-battalion going through its exercises in the immense drill-room, and realize the hopeful future for this vast army of coming citizens.

who are thus early and thus admirably taught the priceless lesson of discipline.

The Boston Normal School, the Girls' High School and the Public Latin School for girls, fully cover the demand for the higher education of women. The latter institution is the fruit of the efforts of the Society for the University Education of Women, and its graduates enter the female colleges with ease. Wellesley, the " College Beautiful," as its students have fondly christened it, is situated close to Boston in the beautiful village of Wellesley, where feminine education is conducted almost on ideal lines. No woman's college in the world has so many students, or so beautiful a home in which to shelter the fair heads, inwardly crammed and running over with knowledge, and outwardly adorned, either in fact or in prospective, with the scholastic cap of learning. Since its opening in 1875, Wellesley has almost created a new era in woman's education, and its curriculum is the same as those of the most advanced male colleges. The College Aid Society, which at an annual cost of from $6000 to $7000 helps ambitious girlhood, for whom straitened means would otherwise render a university education impossible, is an interesting feature of the college.

What Wellesley has for twenty years been to American girlhood, Harvard University has for 150 years been to American young manhood, and though its chief departments are located at Cambridge, it may still be fairly ranked with Bostonian institutions. The tie which connects the Cambridge University and the capital of Massachusetts is closer than that existing between mere neighbors—it is a veritable bond of kin-

COMMONWEALTH AVENUE, BOSTON.

ship. It might be said that from the opening of the University in 1638, Boston made Harvard and Harvard Boston. Its illustrious founder, John Harvard, was a resident of Charlestown, now a part of Boston— and his monument, erected by subscriptions of Harvard graduates, is one of the principal "sights" of that district, where it stands near the Old State Prison. To its classic groves Boston has sent, and from them received again, the noblest of her sons; and three of her departments, the Bussey Institution of Agriculture, the Medical School and the Dental School, are situated within the limits of Boston proper. Harvard University at present owns property valued at $6,000,000, and accommodates nearly 2000 pupils. In addition to the departments already mentioned and which are located in Boston, the principal sections are Harvard College, the Jefferson Laboratory, the Lawrence Scientific School, the new Law School, the Divinity School, the Harvard Library, Botanical Gardens, Observatory, Museum of Comparative Zoölogy, Peabody Museum of Archæology and Ethnology, Agassiz Museum, Hemenway Gymnasium and Memorial Hall. To wander through its ancient halls, the oldest of which dates back to 1720, and which have been used by Congress, is to visit the cradle of university education in America.

Boston University, the Massachusetts Institute of Technology, one of the best scientific colleges on the continent, Tufts College and the celebrated Chauncy Hall School, are among the finest of Boston's many admirable educational institutions.

Mention has been made of the Harvard Monument, but not of the others among the scores of fine examples of the sculptor's art which are scattered throughout the city in generous profusion for the delight and the education of the public eye. The famous Bunker Hill Monument was naturally one of the first objects sought out by the writer on the occasion of his first visit to Boston. This splendid shaft of granite was dedicated to the fallen patriots of Bunker Hill in 1841, the corner-stone having been laid in 1825 by General Lafayette—Daniel Webster delivering the orations on both occasions. Its site, on Monument Square, Breed's Hill, is the spot where the Americans threw up the redoubt on the night before the memorable battle, and a tablet at its foot marks the place where the illustrious Warren fell.

The monument is $221\frac{1}{8}$ feet high—a fact fully realized only by climbing the 259 steps of the spiral staircase of stone in the interior of the shaft which leads to a small chamber near the apex, from which four windows look out upon the surrounding country—a superb vista. The cost of this monument was $150,000.

In the Public Gardens, in the Back Bay district, across from Commonwealth avenue, may be seen one of the largest pieces of statuary in America, and, according to some connoisseurs, the handsomest in Boston. This is Ball's huge statue of Washington, which measures twenty-two feet in height. The statue was unveiled in 1869, and it is said that not a stroke of work was laid upon it by any hand of artisan or artist outside of Massachusetts. The Beacon street side of the Public Gardens contains another famous statue— that of Edward Everett, by W. W. Story. Other great citizens whose memory has been perpetuated in life-like marble are Samuel Adams, William Lloyd Garrison and Colonel William Prescott. The Emancipation Group is a duplicate of the "Freedman's Memorial" statue in Washington. The soldiers' monuments in Dorchester, Charlestown, Roxbury, West Roxbury and Brighton commemorate the unnamed, uncounted, but not unhonored dead who laid down their lives on the battlefields of the Civil War.

> "The bravely dumb who did their deed,
> And scorned to blot it with a name;
> Men of the plain, heroic breed,
> Who loved Heaven's silence more than fame."

An interesting object is the Ether Monument on the Arlington street side of the Public Gardens erected in recognition of the fact that it was in the Massachusetts General Hospital—in the face of terrible opposition and coldness and discouragement, as history tells us, though the marble does not—that Dr. Sims first gave the world his wonderful discovery of the power of ether to cause insensibility to pain.

That there should be so many of these fine pieces in Boston's parks and public places is matter for congratulation but scarcely for surprise. As a patron of music, literature, art and all the external graces of civilization she has so long and so easily held her supremacy that one is half inclined to believe that at least a delegation of the Muses, if not the whole sisterhood, had exchanged the lonely and unappreciated grandeur of Parnassus for a seat on one of Boston's three hills. The Handel and Haydn Society, the oldest musical society in the United States; the Harvard Musical Association; the famous Boston

Symphony Orchestra and the Orpheus Club, speak— and right musically—of Boston's love for the art of which Cecilia was patron saint. Music Hall, an immense edifice near Tremont street, is the home of music in Boston. Here the symphony concerts are held weekly, and here all the musical "stars" whose orbit includes Boston make their first appearance before a critical "Hub" audience. Its great organ, with over 5,000 pipes, is one of the largest ever made.

The idea of a national university of music—sneered at and scouted when a few enthusiasts first talked and dreamed of it—took shape in 1867 in the now famous New England Conservatory of Music, founded by Eben Tourjée. It is a magnificent school in a magnificent home—the old St. James' Hotel on Franklin Square—with a hundred teachers from the very foremost rank of their profession. The conservatory has possibly done more for New England culture than any other influence save Harvard University.

The literary life of Boston needs neither chronicler nor comment. Such men as Thomas Bailey Aldrich, Oliver Wendell Holmes, Francis Parkman, Prescott, the historian, Longfellow, Lowell and countless others who, living, have made the city their home, or, dead, sleep in its chambers of Peace, have cast a glamour of books and bookmen and book-life around her until her title of "The Athens of America" has passed from jest to earnest. The earliest newspaper in America was the Boston *News Letter;* and to-day its many newspapers maintain the highest standard of "up-to-date" journalism in the dignified, not the degrading sense of the word. Boston is indeed a "bookworm's paradise," with its splendid free lending library and low-priced book-stores, making access to the best authors possible to the poorest. The *Atlantic Monthly*, which for so many years has occupied a place unique and unapproachable among American magazines, is published here.

Art is represented by the magnificent Museum of Fine Arts, with its beautiful exterior and interior decorations and fine collection of antiques and art objects; the Art Club, the Sketch and the Paint and Clay clubs, as well as by the innumerable paintings and statues appearing in public places; by the Athenæum, the American Academy of Arts and Sciences, the Boston Society of Natural History, the Warren Museum and the Lowell Institute free lectures.

To draw this brief study of Boston to a close without mentioning her countless charities would be a grave omission, since these form so large a part of the city's life and activities. As is always the case in great towns, two hands are ever outstretched—that of Lazarus, pleading, demanding, and that of Dives— more unselfish now than in the days of the parable— giving again and yet again. Boston's philanthropists flatter themselves that *there* the giving is rather more judicious, as well as generous, than is frequently the case; and that "the pauperizing of the poor," that consummation devoutly to be avoided, is a minimized danger. The "Central Charity Bureau" and the "Associated Charities" systematize the work of relief, prevent imposture and duplication of charity, and do an invaluable service to the different organizations. Private subscriptions of citizens maintain the work, which is carried on in three fine buildings of brick and stone on Chardon street, one of which is used as a temporary home for destitute women and children. The Massachusetts General Hospital—which, save for the Pennsylvania Hospital, is the oldest in the country —the Boston City Hospital, the New England Hospital for Women and Children, and a number of other finely-organized institutions care efficiently for the city's sick and suffering. Orphan asylums, reform schools, missions of various sorts, and retreats for the aged and indigent, are numerous.

One of the most unique and interesting among these charities is "The Children's Mission to the Children of the Destitute," which aims to bring the little ones of these two sadly separated classes, the poor and the well-to-do, in contact for their mutual benefit. By its agency the forlorn little waifs of the streets are provided with home and friends, religious and secular instruction, and employment whenever necessary or advisable. Still more unique is the Massachusetts Charitable Mechanics' Association, whose vast building and hall on Huntingdon avenue occupies an area of over 110,000 square feet. As early as 1795 this association was founded to extend a helping hand to mechanics in difficulties, to establish libraries and classes for apprentices, offer premiums for inventions and improvements in trades, and give every encouragement to the tradesman. The building is a beautiful as well as a vast structure, and eight thousand people can be seated in the grand hall. The mechanics' festivals, fairs, and exhibitions of industry are held here from time to time, when there is much awarding of medals, prizes and honors.

On Boston's commercial greatness there is no space to touch. Nor is it needed. Could her schools, her churches, her charities, her institutions, public and private, which have here been outlined, flourish without the backbone of Puritan thrift and the framework of prosperity which have made her one of the wealthiest of cities? The solid business foundation is apparent to all who visit her teeming marts and exchanges. But the "power behind the throne" is kept with rare judgment in the background; and when the visitor comes to kiss the hand of the "Queen of the Commonwealth" he sees only her chosen handmaids—Ambition, Culture, Philanthropy, Religion. On these, finally, she rests her claims to greatness.

CHAPTER III.

LECTURE AT TREMONT TEMPLE.

ECTURING in the towns I purposed visiting was an after consideration of secondary importance—a sort of adjunct to the journey and the objects I had in view. It was thought that it might afford some facilities for meeting large numbers of people face to face in the different sections of the country through which I designed to pass, and thus enable me the better to learn something of their social customs, industries and general progress in the arts of civilization.

The subject decided upon for the lecture was "Echoes from the Revolution," and was intended to be in keeping with the spirit of the Centennial year. The fact that I had been a cavalryman during the War of the Rebellion and the novelty of an equestrian journey of such magnitude would, I estimated, very naturally awaken considerable interest and a desire on the part of many to hear what I had to say of the heroes of "76."

My lecture was a restrospective view of the leading incidents of the Revolution, with especial reference to some of the sturdy heroes and stirring scenes of that

(66)

most eventful period in American History. Briefly referring to the causes which led up to the war, I started with the Ride of Paul Revere from Boston the night before the Battle of Lexington, and closed with the Surrender of Cornwallis at Yorktown.

It was not my wish or intention to derive any pecuniary benefit from my lectures ; but being a member of the Grand Army of the Republic, and thoroughly in sympathy with the aims and benevolent projects of my soldier friends, it was proposed to donate the proceeds to the Relief Fund of that patriotic organization.

Fully equipped, the weather favorable and roads in good condition, I was anxious to begin my journey early in May. It was therefore arranged, as previously suggested, that I should lecture at Tremont Temple on the evening of May eighth under the auspices and for the benefit of the G. A. R. Relief Fund.

The subjoined fraternal and highly complimentary letter of introduction from Captain Frank M. Clark of New York was received by the committee of arrangements soon after my arrival in Boston.

4 IRVING PLACE,
New York, April 20, 1876.

To COMRADES OF THE G. A. R. :

I have been intimately acquainted with Captain Willard Glazier, a comrade in good standing of Post No. 29, Department of New York, Grand Army of the Republic, for the past eight years, and know him to be worthy the confidence of every loyal man. He is an intelligent and courteous gentleman, an author of good repute, a soldier whose record is without a stain, and a true comrade of the "Grand Army." I bespeak for him the earnest and cordial support of all comrades of the Order.

Yours very truly in F., C. and L.,
FRANK M. CLARK,
Late A. A. G. Department of New York, G. A. R

I may add that, as this was the first occasion of any importance on which I had been expected to appear before a public assemblage, I was strongly recommended to deliver my initial lecture before a smaller and less critical audience than I was likely to confront in Boston, and thus prepare myself for a later appearance in the literary capital ; but I reasoned from the standpoint of a soldier that, as lecturing was a new experience to me, my military training dictated that if I could carry the strongest position in the line I need have but little, if any, concern for the weaker ones, and hence resolved to deliver my first lecture at Tremont Temple. I was introduced by Captain Theodore L. Kelly, commander of Post 15, Department of Massachusetts, G. A. R., and was honored by the presence on the platform of representatives from nearly all of the Posts of Boston and adjacent cities. In presenting me to my audience Captain Kelly spoke in the following terms :

"LADIES AND GENTLEMEN : It gives me pleasure to have the honor of introducing to you one who, by his services in the field and by the works of his pen, is entitled to your consideration, and the confidence of all comrades of the 'Grand Army of the Republic.' I desire to say that he comes well accredited, furnished with the proper vouchers and documents, and highly endorsed and recommended by the officers of the Department of the State of New York. Though young in years, his life has been one of varied and exciting experience. Born in the wilds of St. Lawrence County, New York, his education was drawn from the great book of Nature; and from his surroundings he early imbibed a love of liberty. His early associations naturally invested him with a fondness for adventure and excitement and when the call of war was heard he at once responded, and enlisted in the Harris Light Cavalry, with which corps he passed through many exciting scenes of march and fray. His experience amid the various vicissitudes of the war, in camp and field and prison, have been vividly portrayed by his pen in his various publications. Still inspired by this love of adventure, he proposes to undertake the novelty of a journey across the Continent in the saddle. His objects are manifold. While visiting scenes and becoming more familiar with his own country, he will collect facts and information for a new book, and at his various stopping-places he will lecture under the auspices and for the benefit of the 'Grand Army of the Republic,' to whose fraternal regard he is most warmly commended. Allow me then, ladies and gentlemen, without further ceremony, to present to you the Soldier-Author, and our comrade, Willard Glazier.''

I was much gratified on the morning of the ninth to find commendatory reference to my lecture in the leading journals of Boston, for I will frankly admit that I had had some misgivings as to the verdict of the critics, and rather expected to be " handled without gloves" in some of the first cities on the programme. Of the dailies which came to my notice the *Globe* said :—

"A very fair audience considering the unfair condition of the elements, was gathered in Tremont Temple last night to hear Captain Willard Glazier's lecture upon 'Echoes from the Revolution.' The frequent applause of the audience evinced not only a sympathy with the subject, but an evident liking of the manner in which it was delivered. The lecture itself was a retrospective view of the leading incidents of the Revolution. It would have been unfair to expect to hear anything very new upon a subject with which the veriest school-boy is familiar ; but Captain Glazier wove the events together in a manner which freed the lecture from that most unpardonable of all faults, which can be committed upon the platform—dulness. He passed over, in his consideration of the Revolution, the old scenes up to the time when Cornwallis surrendered up his sword and command to George Washington. 'The year 1876,' said Captain Glazier, 're-echoes the scenes and events of a hundred years ago. In imagination we make a pilgrimage back to the Revolution. We visit the fields whereon our ancestors fought for liberty and a republic. We follow patriots from Lexington to Yorktown. I see them pushing their way through the ice of the Delaware—I see them at Saratoga, at Bennington, at Princeton, and at Monmouth. I follow Marion and his daring troopers through the swamps of Georgia and the Carolinas;' and in following them up, the lecturer interspersed his exciting narrative with sundry droll episodes. Treating of the battles of Trenton and Princeton, he expatiated upon the devoted heroism of John Stark, and briefly traced his career until, at Bennington, Burgoyne's victor announced to his comrades, 'We must conquer to-day, my boys, or to-night Molly Stark's a widow.' One battle after another was handled by the lecturer in a pleasing manner, showing that he was thoroughly familiar with the subject he had chosen for his theme. After speaking in a most zealous manner of the troops on land, Captain Glazier remarked : ' Our victories on the ocean during the war of the Revolution were not less decisive and glorious than those achieved on land. John Paul Jones and the gallant tars who, under his leadership, braved the dangers of the deep, and wrested from proud Britain, once queen of the sea, that illustrious motto which may be seen high on our banner beside the stars and stripes.'

"Captain Glazier made special mention of the naval engagement between the Bon Homme Richard and the British man-of-war Serapis, which took place in September, 1789. He described in glowing words the fierce nature of that memorable contest, until the captain of the Serapis, with his own hand, struck the flag of England to the free Stars and Stripes of young America. Captain Glazier has elements in him which, carefully matured and nurtured, will make him successful on the platform, as he has already proved himself in the field of literature. He has a strong and melodious voice, a gentlemanly address, and unassuming confidence. He was presented to the audience by Commandant Kelly, of Post 15, Grand Army of the Republic, in a brief but eloquent speech. Captain Glazier will start on his long ride to San Francisco, from the Revere House, this morning, at 9.30, and will be accompanied to Bunker Hill and thence to Brighton, by several distinguished members of the 'Grand Army,' and other gentlemen, who wish the Captain success on his long journey from Ocean to Ocean."

The lecture proved a success financially, and in ful-

LEAVING THE REVERE HOUSE, BOSTON.

69

filment of my purpose I donated the entire proceeds to the Relief Fund of Posts 7 and 15, as I was largely indebted to the comrades of these organizations for the hearty co-operation which insured a full house at Tremont Temple. The letter below was addressed to the Assistant Adjutant-General of the Department.

REVERE HOUSE,
Boston, Massachusetts,
May 9, 1876.

CAPTAIN CHARLES W. THOMPSON,
A. A. G. DEPARTMENT OF MASS., G. A. R.

COMRADE: I find pleasure in handing you the net proceeds of my lecture, delivered at Tremont Temple last night, which I desire to be divided equally between Posts 7 and 15, G. A. R., of Boston, for the benefit of our disabled comrades, and the needy and destitute wards of the "Grand Army." Gratefully acknowledging many favors and courtesies, extended to me in your patriotic city.
I am yours in F., C. and L.,
WILLARD GLAZIER.

My letter to Captain Thompson elicited responses from the Posts to which donations were made, and the following from the Adjutant of John A. Andrew, Post 15, is introduced to show their appreciation of my efforts in behalf of their Relief Fund.

HEADQUARTERS,
POST 15, DEPARTMENT OF MASSACHUSETTS, G. A. R.,
Boston, May 12, 1876.

CAPTAIN WILLARD GLAZIER:

COMRADE: In obedience to a vote of this Post, I am pleased to transmit to you a vote of thanks for the money generously donated by you, through our Commander, as our quota of the proceeds of your lecture in this city; and also the best wishes of the comrades of this Post for you personally, and for the success of your lecture tour from sea to sea.
Yours in F., C. and L.,
EDWARD F. ROLLINS,
Adjutant of Post.

It is only justice to the comrades of Posts 7 and 15 to say that on my arrival in Boston they were most cordial in their reception, most zealous in their co-operation with my advance agents and most solicitous for the success of my journey and its objects. In short they were true comrades in the best sense of the term, and my delightful sojourn in their generous and patriotic city was largely due to their numerous courtesies.

CHAPTER IV.

BOSTON TO ALBANY.

First Day.

South Framingham House,
SOUTH FRAMINGHAM, MASSACHUSETTS,
May 9, 1876.

THE initial step in my journey from Ocean to Ocean was taken at ten o'clock on the morning of the above date when I mounted my horse in front of the Revere House, Boston, and started for Worcester, where it had been announced I would lecture on the following evening. The Revere House was fixed upon by comrades of the G. A. R. as a rendezvous before starting. Here I found a large gathering of the Order. A rain storm setting in as I put my foot into the stirrup, hasty adieus were said to the Boys in Blue and others as I was about riding away from the " Revere."

I was escorted to Bunker Hill and thence to Brighton by many comrades and friends, among them Colonels John F. Finley and E. A. Williston, who were mounted; and Captain Charles W. Thompson, adjutant-general Department of Massachusetts; Cap-

5

73

tain Theodore L. Kelly, commander of Post 15; Grafton Fenno, adjutant, Post 7, G. A. R., and many others in carriages.

Our route from Boston was by way of Charlestown and Cambridge to Brighton. A short halt was made at Bunker Hill. After a hurried look at the Monument we rode around it and then headed for Brighton. The rain was now falling in torrents and quickening our pace we passed rapidly through Cambridge, glancing hastily at the University Buildings as we galloped down the main thoroughfare of the city.

Brighton was reached between twelve and one o'clock. Owing to the storm our short journey to this place was anything but agreeable and when we dismounted at the Cattle Fair Hotel all who were not in covered conveyances were drenched to the skin. Here the entire party had dinner, after which I took leave of my friendly escort, who one and all took me by the hand and wished me Godspeed.

Pushing on through Newton and some smaller towns and villages I pulled up in front of the South Framingham House a few minutes after five o'clock in the evening. My clothing was thoroughly soaked and my cavalry boots filled to overflowing. Having secured accommodations for the night, *Paul* was fed and groomed; clothing and equipments hung up to dry and the first day of my long ride from sea to sea was off the calendar.

Second Day.

Bay State House,
WORCESTER, MASSACHUSETTS,
May Tenth.

I slept soundly at the South Framingham House

RIDING THROUGH CAMBRIDGE.

and was up and out to the hotel stable at an early hour in the morning. I found *Paul Revere*, my equine companion, in good spirits and fancied that the significant look he gave me was an assurance that he would be ready for the road when called for.

After a hearty breakfast and a few questions concerning the beautiful little city in which I had spent the first night of my journey, I mounted *Paul* and rode out towards the Boston and Albany Turnpike. Being impressed with the appearance and enterprise of the place, while passing through some of its streets especial inquiry was made concerning its population, schools and industries. I learned that South Framingham is twenty-one miles from Boston, at the junction of the Boston and Albany and Old Colony Railways. Its population at that time was about 10,000. Its graded schools are among the first in the State. It supports several banks and newspapers and is engaged in the manufacture of woollens, rubber goods, boots and shoes, harness and machinery.

The ride from South Framingham to Worcester was uneventful if I except the pelting rain which from drizzle to down-pour followed me from start to finish. Indeed, it really seemed as though the first days of my journey were to be baptismal days and I regret exceedingly that these early stages of the trip were not more propitious; for, had the weather been less disagreeable, I should have seen Eastern Massachusetts under much more favorable circumstances.

The city limits of Worcester were reached at four o'clock in the afternoon and a half hour later I was registered at the Bay State House. Many relatives called upon me here, most of whom were residents of the city and vicinity. Lectured at the Opera House in the evening, being introduced to my audience by Colonel Finley of Charlestown, to whom previous reference has been made, and with whom I had arranged to accompany me as far as Syracuse, New York, and further if my advance agents should think it advisable for him to do so.

The fact that both my father and mother were natives of Worcester County and that most of our ancestors for several generations had been residents of Worcester and vicinity made that city of unusual interest to me, and I trust the reader will be indulgent if I allot too much space or seem too partial in my description of this early landmark in my journey.

Worcester, nestling among the hills along the Blackstone River, the second city in Massachusetts, the heart of the Commonwealth, has a population of about 85,000.

Shut in by its wall of hills, it seemed, as I first came into it, something like a little miniature world in itself. It possesses some share of all the good we know. Nature, that "comely mother," has laid her caressing hand upon it. Art has made many a beautiful structure to adorn its streets. Commerce smiles upon it. While its wonderful manufactures seem to form a a great living, throbbing heart for the city.

Sauntering up from the depot, through Front street, five minutes' walk brought me to the Old Common. There I found, what one so frequently finds in Massachusetts towns and cities—namely, a War Monument. Apparently that mighty five years' struggle, that brilliant victory, bringing freedom to two million

VIEW IN WORCESTER MASSACHUSETTS.

fellow-creatures, bringing power, union, glory to the nation, has burned itself into the very heart of the Old Bay State; and lest posterity might forget the lessons she learned from 1861 to 1865, everywhere she has planted her war monuments, to remind her children that

> "Simple duty has no place for fear."

In the shade of Worcester Common is another object of interest. A little plot of ground, wherein stands a grand old tomb. It is the resting-place of Timothy Bigelow, the early patriot of Worcester. Here in the sunshine and the twilight, in the bloom of summer, and under the soft falling snows of winter, he perpetually manifests to the world

> "How sleep the brave, who sink to rest
> By all their country's wishes blest."

A sturdy old New Englander was Colonel Bigelow. "When the news of the destruction of the tea in Boston Harbor reached him, he was at work in his blacksmith shop, near the spot now called Lincoln Square. He immediately laid aside his tools, proceeded directly to his house, opened the closet, and took from it a canister of tea, went to the fire-place, and poured the contents into the flames. As if feeling that everything which had come in contact with British legislative tyranny should be purified by fire, the canister followed the tea; and then he covered both with coals.

"Before noon on the nineteenth of April, 1775, an express came to town, shouting, as he passed through the street at full speed, 'To arms! to arms!—the war's begun.' His white horse, bloody with spurring, and dripping with sweat, fell exhausted by the church. Another was instantly procured, and the tidings went on. The bell rang out the alarm, cannon were fired, and messengers were sent to every part of the town to collect the soldiery. As the news spread, the implements of husbandry were thrown by in the field; and the citizens left their homes, with no longer delay than to seize their arms. In a short time, the ' minute-men ' were paraded on the green, under Captain Timothy Bigelow. After fervent prayer by Rev. Mr. Maccarty, they took up their line of march to the scene of conflict." Such was Bigelow's zeal and ardor in the great cause of the times, that he appeared on the following morning, at the head of his "minute-men," in the square at Watertown, having marched them there, a distance of over thirty miles, during that one short night.

On the nineteenth of April, 1861, the Bigelow Monument was dedicated. At the very hour of the consecration exercises, the Massachusetts Sixth Regiment was engaged in its memorable struggle and triumphant passage through the blockaded streets of Baltimore at the beginning of the Civil War.

Along the west side of the Old Common runs Main street, just out of which, in Pearl street, is the Post Office. I have seen a curious computation with regard to that Post Office development, which aptly illustrates the rapid growth of Worcester. The number of letters sent out in 1809 was about 4,400. The number of letters taken out fifty years later was 523,808. Main street reaches Lincoln Square, where stand the two court houses. The old one has been removed a

A NEW ENGLAND PAPER MILL.

few feet, and refitted. In it the criminal courts are held; there too are the offices of the court of probate and insolvency.

The New Court House was built in 1845 of Quincy granite, at a cost of about one hundred thousand dollars. In it the civil terms of the courts are held, with numerous ante-rooms for the jurors and for consultation. The lower floor is occupied by the office of the register of deeds, and by the clerk's and treasurer's offices.

Close neighbor to the court houses is the building containing the rooms of the American Antiquarian Society, one of the leading learned bodies of our country. It was founded in 1812. It possesses a very valuable library, especially rich on subjects of local interest to Americans. The newspapers filed here include over four thousand volumes, beginning with the Boston *News Letter* of 1804, and closing with the great journals of to-day. This same society also possesses a very interesting collection of pre-historic American relics.

In Lincoln Square stands the old Salisbury mansion, an interesting specimen of a colonial house, which has been standing a century or so, since the time when those substantial buildings, with their wide halls, high ceilings, and strong walls, were built on honor. There it has stood in its dignity, more flimsy, more showy architecture springing up around it, until now the *fin de siecle* eye discovers that nothing is more to be desired than one of these same sturdy old colonial houses.

Main street contains many churches. On it is the large, ugly-looking, but justly celebrated, Clark University, which is devoted to scientific research, with its wonderfully equipped chemical laboratory.

Any one who wants a bird's-eye view of Worcester and its environments, can easily have it by strolling out Highland street to Newton Hill. It is only about a mile from Lincoln Park, but it is six hundred and seventy feet above the sea level, and from it "the whole world, and the glory thereof," seems spread out at one's feet.

On Salisbury street, one mile from the square, stands the house in which George Bancroft, the historian, dear to American hearts, was born.

A mile and a half from the square, on Salisbury Pond, are located the famous Wire Works of Washburn and Moen.

There are many buildings to interest the visitor in Worcester. The State Lunatic Asylum, with its one thousand patients; the free Public Library on Elm street, containing eighty thousand volumes; the High School on Walnut street; the Museum of the National Historical Society, on Foster street; All Saint's Church; the Polytechnic Institute; the College of the Holy Cross, six hundred and ninty feet above the sea, and many another place of interest, calling on the passers-by to look, and learn of the world's advancement.

Standing on one of the heights overlooking the little river, the surrounding hills, the busy city, throbbing with its many manufactories, it seemed to me I had before my eyes an object lesson of the wonderful resources, the vim, the power of making "all things work together for good," which I take to be the vital characteristic of American manhood.

I remembered reading that in 1767 a committee was appointed to decide whether it would be wise to attempt to locate a village on the present site of Worcester.

They reported that the place was one day's journey from Boston, and one day's journey from Springfield, that the place was well watered by streams and brooks, and that in eight miles square there was enough meadow to warrant the settling of sixty families, adding these words: "We recommend that a prudent and able committee be appointed to lay it out, and that due care be taken by said committee that a good minister of God's Word be placed there, as soon as may be, that such people as be there planted may not live like lambs in a large place."

That was only a little more than a century ago. As I stood overlooking it all, "thickly dotted with the homes of the husbandmen, and the villages of the manufacturer, traversed by canal and railway, and supporting a dense population," proving so strong a contrast between the past generation's humble anticipations, and our overflowing prosperity, I asked myself what those old Puritans would have thought of our railroads, our electric cars, our modern machines, our telephones; and I said, with a spirit of self-gratulation,

> "We are living, we are dwelling,
> In a grand and awful time;
> In an age on ages telling,
> To be living is sublime."

There is little doubt that future generations will look back upon this age as the brightest in the world's history.

Third and Fourth Days.

Bates House,
SPRINGFIELD, MASSACHUSETTS,
May Eleventh.

Lowering clouds and a slight fall of rain again confronted me as I mounted *Paul* at seven o'clock on the morning of the Third Day in front of the Bay State House, Worcester, and rode out to the Boston and Albany Turnpike. The prospect of meeting my wife and daughter, whom I had not seen for several months, and the lecture appointment for Springfield made this one of the memorable days of my journey for speed and endurance. Fifty-four miles were whirled off in eight hours and the fact established that *Paul* could be relied upon to do all that was required of him.

I had hardly dismounted in front of the Bates House when Mrs. Glazier and Alice came running from the hotel to greet me. They had been visiting in Hartford and had come up to Springfield early in the morning, reaching the city several hours before my arrival. This visit with my family at Springfield was one of the pleasant episodes of my journey and long to be remembered in connection with my ride across the Bay State.

My lecture was delivered at the Haynes Opera House, whither I was escorted by comrades of the G. A. R. The introduction was by Captain Smith, Commander of the Springfield Post, who spoke pleasantly of my army and prison experiences and of the objects of my lecture tour.

Hastening back to the Bates House after the lecture,

OLD TOLL BRIDGE, SPRINGFIELD.

the remainder of the evening was spent with my wife and daughter and a few friends who had called for a social talk and to tell me something of the early history of Springfield and vicinity.

As the lecture appointment for Pittsfield was set for the fifteenth I readily discovered by a simple calculation that I could easily spend another day with Hattie and Alice and still reach Pittsfield early in the afternoon of the fifteenth. The leisure thus found was devoted to strolls in and around Springfield and a careful study of the city and its environs.

When King Charles the First had dissolved his third parliament, thus putting his head on the bleeding heart of puritanism, there lived in Springfield, England, a warden of the established church. " He was thirty-nine years of age, of gentle birth, acute, restive, and singularly self-assertive. He had seen some of the stoutest men of the realm break into tears when the King had cut off free speech in the Commons; he had seen ritualism, like an iron collar, clasped upon the neck of the church, while a young jewelled courtier, the Duke of Buckingham, dangled the reputation of sober England at his waistcoat. A colonial enterprise, pushed by some Lincolnshire gentlemen, had been noised abroad, and the warden joined his fortunes with them, and thus became one of the original incorporators mentioned in the Royal Charter of the Massachusetts Bay Company in America. This was William Pinchon." After reaching this country he became treasurer of the colony, and a member of the general court. He formed plans for a coast trade, and for a trade with the Indians.

Such was the man of mark, who in 1636, with a

colony of friends, made a settlement on the fertile meadows of the Indian Agawam. The spot was obtained by a deed signed by thirteen Indians, and Pinchon, in loving remembrance of his old English home, christened the new settlement Springfield. From the little we can glean of them, the ancient inhabitants of the village must have been a grim old race.

Hugh Parsons, and Mary, his wife, were tried for witchcraft.

Goodwife Hunter was gagged and made to stand in the stocks for "Sundry exhorbitance of ye toung."

Men were fined for not attending town meeting and voting.

In August, 1734, the Rev. Robert Breck was called to the church in Springfield.

Shortly before that he had used the following words in one of his sermons: "What will become of the heathen who never heard of the gospel, I do not pretend to say, but I cannot but indulge a hope that God, in his boundless benevolence, will find out a way whereby those heathen who act up to the light they have may be saved."

The news of this alarming hope came to Springfield, and a few other so-called unorthodox utterances were attributed to him. " In the minds of the River Gods heterodoxy was his crime. For this the Rev. gentleman was not only tried by a council of the church, but a sheriff and his posse appeared and arrested Mr. Breck in his Majesty's name, and the prisoner was taken first to the town-house, and afterward to New London for trial."

The early Springfield settlers had few of the

A MASSACHUSETTS MILL STREAM.

articles which we consider the commonest comforts of life.

Hon. John Worthington, "One of the Gods of the Connecticut Valley," owned the first umbrella in Springfield. He never profaned the article by carrying it in the rain, but used it as a sun-shade only.

In 1753 there was but one clock in Springfield. It was considered a great curiosity, and people used to stop to hear it strike.

As early as about 1774 that wonderful innovation, a cooking-stove, made its appearance in Springfield. The stove was made in Philadelphia, and weighed eight or nine hundred pounds.

It was 1810 when David Ames brought the first piano into the little settlement.

We are furnished with a description of Springfield in 1789 by the journal of the Great Washington. Under the date of October twenty-first he wrote, "There is a great equality in the people of this State. Few or no opulent men, and no poor. Great similitude in their buildings, the general fashion of which is a chimney—always of brick or stone—and a door in the middle, with a staircase fronting the latter, and running up by the side of the former; two flush stories, with a very good show of sash and glass windows; the size generally from thirty to fifty feet in length, and from twenty to thirty in width, exclusive of a back shed, which seems to be added as the family increases."

Much later in our national history, Springfield became one of the most important stations of the " Underground Railroad."

In a back room on Main street can still be seen a fireplace, preserved as a memento of stirring days, when many a negro was pushed up through it, to be secreted in the great chimney above.

Springfield has had many noted citizens. The historian Bancroft lived there at one time; so did John Brown, of Harper's Ferry fame.

George Ashman, a brilliant member of the local bar, was made chairman of the famous Chicago convention of 1860 which nominated Abraham Lincoln for President. Mr. Ashman also had the honor to convey the formal notice of the nomination to Lincoln in Springfield, Illinois.

Dr. J. G. Holland lived in Springfield, where all of his prose works first made their appearance, in the columns of the *Springfield Republican.*

No spot in Springfield is more interesting to those fortunate enough to see it than the United States Arsenal.

Springfield Armory was established by act of Congress, April, 1794, its site having been accepted by by Washington in 1789. The plant consists of the Armory and Arsenal on the hill, and the water shops, distant about two miles, on Mill River. Main Arsenal is on a bluff overlooking the city, and is one hundred and sixty feet above the river. It is a partial copy of East India House in London. From its tower there is a wonderful view of the surrounding country, and one which was greatly admired by Charles Dickens during his visit to America.

The Main Arsenal is two hundred feet by seventy, and is three stories high, each floor having storage capacity for one hundred thousand stand of arms.

THE SPRINGFIELD ARMORY.

Longfellow's lines have made this a classic spot:

> "This is the Arsenal. From floor to ceiling,
> Like a huge organ, rise the burnished arms;
> But from the silent pipes no anthem pealing
> Startles the villages with strange alarms.
>
> "Oh! what a sound will rise, how wild and dreary,
> When the death angel touches those swift keys!
> What loud lament and dismal miserere
> Will mingle with those awful symphonies!
>
> "Peace! and no longer from its brazen portals
> The blast of War's great organ shakes the skies;
> But beautiful as songs of the immortals,
> The holy melodies of love arise."

Beside the Main Arsenal, two other buildings are used for the storage of arms.

In 1795 Uncle Sam made his first musket. That year forty or fifty men were employed, and 245 muskets were made. Between that and the present time over 2,000,000 weapons have been turned out. During that time $32,500,000 have been expended. When Sumter was fired on about 1,000 weapons per month were being made. Three months later, 3,000 were made each month. In 1864, 1,000 muskets were completed each day, and 3,400 men were employed, with pay roll sometimes amounting to $200,000 per month. At present only 400 men are employed.

From Springfield stock have come eight college presidents, namely of Yale, Harvard, Columbia, Amherst, Princeton, Trinity, Beloit, and Dickinson.

Springfield of to-day is a thriving city of about 50,000, and is the county seat of Hampden County. Some one, I think, has called it the "city of homes." Its streets are broad, and well shaded by elms and maples; many of its residences are detached, and as a whole it bears the stamp of taste and refinement.

Springfield is within easy reach of many points of interest. It is ninety-eight miles from Boston, one hundred and twenty miles from New York, and twenty-six miles from Hartford.

The growth of the Springfield Street Railroad Company has been phenomenal. In 1869 this company started out with only $50,000 capital stock. Its length was only about two miles. It had only four cars and twenty-five horses. Three years ago horses were displaced by electricity. Now, in the busy season, the daily mileage of transit on the thirty-five miles of track is equal to the distance from Springfield to San Francisco and half-way back. During the fiscal year closing October first, 1892, 7,500,000 fares were taken.

The stores of Springfield are remarkably large and tasteful. Haynes & Company have the largest clothing house in Massachusetts, out of Boston.

In 1875 Meakins & Packard started in business with only one boy to help them. Now their building is one hundred feet square, and seven stories high, while they now have over one hundred employees.

Springfield has three great manufactories, Smith & Wesson Pistol Works; R. F. Hawkins Iron Works; and the Wesson Car Manufactory. Smith & Wesson employ about 500 men, with an annual output of 80,000 weapons. They ship goods to Russia and other countries. The Wesson Car Company in 1860 sent $300,000 worth of goods to the Egyptian government. They have also done considerable work for South America. They have done $150,000 worth for

A MILL IN THE BERKSHIRE HILLS.

the New Jersey Central Railroad, and $1,700,000 worth for the Central Pacific Railroad.

The City Library was built at a cost of $100,000, and contains 80,000 books. Adjoining the library is the beautiful new art building, containing a rare and costly collection of curiosities.

The City Hall is a building in the Romanesque style. It contains a public hall with a seating capacity of 2,700.

The Court House is an imposing structure, is built of granite, and cost $200,000.

The city has many a lovely spot in which to recreate. Imagine four hundred acres, woodland alternating with highly cultivated lawns, and stretches of blooming plants. Imagine in the midst of this a deep ravine, with a brawling little brook through it. Imagine five lakelets covered by Egyptian lotus, and the different varieties of water-lilies. Through all this loveliness, think of seven miles of charming drives, winding in and out like a ribbon, and you have in your mind a picture of Springfield's enchanting Forest Park.

Fifth Day.

Russell House,
RUSSELL, MASSACHUSETTS,
May Thirteenth.

My wife and daughter were not easily reconciled to my leavetaking of Springfield, but yielding to the inevitable, adieus were quickly said, *Paul* was mounted and I rode slowly away from the Bates House, turning occasionally in the saddle until entirely out of sight of my loved ones, then putting spurs to my horse

6

galloped out to the turnpike and headed for Russell, the evening objective.

Considerable rain fell during the day and the roads at this time through Western Massachusetts were in a wretched condition. With clothing thoroughly soaked and mud anywhere from ankle to knee deep, the trip from Springfield to Russell was anything but what I had pictured when planning my overland tour in the saddle. Some consolation was found, however, in recalling similar experiences in the army and I resolved to allow nothing to depress or turn me from my original purpose. A halt was made for dinner during this day's ride, at a country inn or tavern ten miles west of Springfield.

Notwithstanding the fact that I did not leave Springfield until nearly ten o'clock in the morning, and that I was out of the saddle over an hour on account of dinner, and compelled to face a pelting storm throughout the day, I did well to advance eighteen miles by four o'clock, the time of dismounting at the Russell House.

Russell is one of the most beautiful of the numerous villages of Hampden County, and is picturesquely situated among the Berkshire Hills in the western part of the State. It stands on the banks of the Westfield River, upon which it relies for water-power in the manufacture of paper, its only industry. It has direct communication with Eastern and Western Massachusetts through the Boston and Albany Railway, and while it is not likely that it will ever come to anything pretentious, it will always be, in appearance at least, a rugged and romantic-looking little village.

A HAMLET IN THE BERKSHIRE HILLS.

Sixth Day.

Becket House,
BECKET, MASSACHUSETTS,
May Fourteenth.

Mounted *Paul* in front of the hotel at Russell at nine o'clock in the morning to ride towards Chester, along the bank of the Westfield River. This swift branch of the Connecticut runs along between its green banks fertilizing the meadows and turning the factory wheels that here and there dip down into its busy current. The Indian name "Agawam," by which it is known nearer its mouth, seems more appropriate for the wild little stream, and often, while I was following its course, I thought of the banished Red Men who had given it this musical name and who had once built their wigwams along its shores.

On this morning the air was fresh and the view pleasing under the magical influence of spring, and both were none the less enjoyed by the assurance that dinner could be had at our next stopping-place. Upon dismounting, I found that the ride could not have been as agreeable to *Paul* as to his master, for his back was in a very sore condition. Everything was done for his comfort; cold water and castile soap being applied to relieve the injured parts, and the cumbersome saddle-cloth which had been doing duty since we left Boston was discarded for a simple blanket such as I had used while in the cavalry service. This was a change for the better and was made at the right time, for, as I afterwards had some difficulty in keeping the direct road, the equipment of my horse relieved what might have proved a fatiguing day's ride.

As it was, the novelty of being lost, which was my experience on this occasion, had its advantages, for a wanderer in the Berkshire Hills finds much to suit the fancy and to please the eye. At six o'clock, notwithstanding the delay, we came into Becket, where Edwin Lee, the proprietor of the hotel of the place, told me I was the only guest.

Becket is an enterprising little village, thirty-seven miles northwest of Springfield, having a graded school and several manufactories. The scenery throughout the region is rugged and attractive · a charming characteristic of the Bay State. ·

Seventh Day.

Berkshire House,
PITTSFIELD, MASSACHUSETTS,
May Fifteenth.

Rode away from Becket at eight o'clock in the morning, and on the way found it necessary to favor *Paul* in this day's ride; so I dismounted and walked several miles. This was not a disagreeable task, for my journey lay over the picturesque Hoosac Mountains whose wooded sides and fertile valleys were almost a fairyland of loveliness at this season. Owing to this delay, Pittsfield was not reached until one o'clock. Here I delivered my fourth lecture at the Academy of Music, Captain Brewster, commander of the Pittsfield Post, G. A. R., introducing me.

Eighth Day

Berkshire House,
PITTSFIELD, MASSACHUSETTS,
May Sixteenth.

Spent the morning at the "Berkshire," posting my journal and attending to private and business corre-

SUBURB OF PITTSFIELD.

spondence. The afternoon was passed in a stroll through the town, where I saw much that was of interest and gathered some information concerning its early history, progress and present condition.

Of the fourteen counties of Massachusetts, the most strongly marked and highly favored is Berkshire, with its four cardinal boundaries, formed by four different states. To one who sees, for the first time, the luxuriance of its vegetation, the beauty of its forest-covered hills, the broad shady avenues of its villages, with their palatial homes, it seems as if Nature and wealth had combined to make this spot a veritable " Garden of the Gods."

In the exact centre of all this loveliness, more than 1,000 feet above the level of the sea, lies the little city of Pittsfield, containing about 16,000 inhabitants. Its principal streets form a cross, North, South, East, and West streets meeting at an elliptical grove of stately elms forming a small park. Here in old days stood one central tree, its height one hundred and twenty-eight feet, its bare shaft ninety feet, with many a memory of the French and Indian wars attached to it. In 1841, it was struck by lightning. In 1861 it was cut down, even stern men weeping at its fall. It was replaced by a fountain, whose stream may be raised to the height of the old tree. This park also holds a huge shaft of granite, upon which stands the bronze figure of a soldier, flag in hand. On the granite are cut the words, " For the dead a tribute, for the living a memory, for posterity an emblem of devotion to their country's flag." To the west of the park is Pittsfield's large brownstone Post Office, it being the first building on North street, a small business thoroughfare, whose stores, with their dainty wares and tasteful fabrics, would do credit to many a large city.

On the south of the park stands the Athenæum, a building of rough stone, erected at the cost of $100,000 as a "tribute to art, science, and literature," and presented to his fellow-townspeople by Thomas Allen. It contains a large free library, an art gallery, and a very entertaining museum of curiosities. Next door to the Athenæum is the large white Court House, said to have cost $400,000. Across from the Court House, in a little corner of the park, is a tiny music house, gay with colored electric lights, where open air evening concerts are given all through the summer.

On the north of the park stand two of the handsomest of Pittsfield's eleven churches.

The city's manufactories are large and thrifty, but they, and the operatives who manipulate them, are tucked away in a corner, so to speak, where they may not offend the eyes of the opulent inhabitants. Only in the riotous jostle of Saturday night in the store is one brought face to face with the fact that beauty, leisure and wealth do not hold a monopoly of the sweet Berkshire air. For everything appears so lovely. The streets are very wide, great stately avenues, where beautiful strips of the finest lawn border each edge of the sidewalk. Society is the choicest, for the summer residences of New York's four hundred intermingle with the magnificent old mansions owned by the staunchest of Massachusetts' old blue-blooded sons and daughters. Cropping out through the elegance of this little city are some queer old Yankee traits. Lawlessness there is none. No policemen guard the park, with its ideal lawns, but a polite

A SCENE IN THE BERKSHIRE HILLS.

notice informs passers-by that this being no thoroughfare, trespassing will not be tolerated, and there is
none. When the concerts are in full blast, people
gather in the walks and drives only. Whole rows of
little street Arabs may be seen on these occasions,
drawn up with their little bare toes touching the very
edge of the precious grass. The open music house is
always left full of chairs, which no one steals, nay,
which no one uses. The entrance to the Court House is
filled with blooming plants. No child, no dog even,
is ill-bred enough to break one.

But the peculiarities of the people, the beauty of
the dwellings, the magnificence of the equipages, the
tide of fashionable life which pours in, summer and
fall, *all*, ALL is forgotten as, from some point of vantage, the spectator takes in the beauty surrounding
him. "On the west sweep the Taconics, in that
majestic curve, whose grace travelers, familiar with the
mountain scenery of both hemispheres, pronounce un-
equaled. On the east the Hoosacs stretch their unbroken battlements, with white villages at their feet,
and, if the sunlight favors, paths of mingled lawn and
wood, enticing to their summits; while from the
south, 'Greylock, cloud-girdled on his purple throne"
looks grandly across the valley to the giant heights,
keeping watch and ward over the pass where the
mountains throw wide their everlasting gates, to let
the winding Housatonic flow peacefully toward the
sea."

Thus, in taking leave of Massachusetts, I looked
back to the starting-point, and thought with pleasure
of the many beautiful links in the chain connecting
Boston with Pittsfield, none more beautiful than the
last.

Ninth Day.

Nassau House,
NASSAU, NEW YORK,
May Seventeenth.

Ordered my horse at ten in the morning, and before riding on stopped at the office of the *Berkshire Eagle* to talk a few minutes with the editor. The route from Pittsfield lay over the Boston and Albany Turnpike, one of the villages on the way being West Lebanon. Here we had dinner. While quietly pursuing my journey afterwards, in crossing the Pittsfield Mountain, I overtook Egbert Jolls, a farmer, with whom I had a long and interesting conversation. He amused me with stories of the Lebanon Shakers, among whom he had lived many years, and whose peculiar belief and customs have always set them widely apart from other sects. Perhaps the most singular point in their doctrine is that God is dual, combining in the One Person the eternal Father and Mother of all generated nature. They believe that the revelation of God is progressive, and in its last aspect the manifestation was God revealed in the character of Mother, as an evidence of Divine affection. Ann Lee, the daughter of a Manchester blacksmith, is the founder of the sect, and considered from her holy life to be the human representation of this Divine duality. This is a strange belief, and one that is not generally known, but its adherents have among other good traits one which commends them to the respect of those who know anything of them, and that is their sober and industrious habits.

Soon after crossing the State line between Massachusetts and New York, we passed the home of Governor Samuel J. Tilden. Two years before, this popular Democrat was elected governor, by a plurality of 50,000 votes above his fellow-candidate, John A. Dix. He won popular attention by his strong opposition to certain political abuses; notably the Tweed Charter of 1870; and by incessant activity he was, in 1876, beginning to reap the laurels of a career which began while he was a student at Yale.

CHAPTER V.

STARTED from Nassau at eleven o'clock, still following the Boston and Albany Turnpike, and soon reached the Old Barringer Homestead. It was with this family that I spent my first night in Rensselaer County sixteen years before, when a lad of seventeen, I was looking for a school commissioner and a school to teach. Brockway's was another well-known landmark which I could not pass without stopping, for it was here that I boarded the first week after opening my school at Schodack Centre in the autumn of 1859. At the school, too, I dismounted, and found that the teacher was one of my old scholars. The Lewis family, at the hotel just beyond, were waiting my approach with wide-open door; for Oscar Lewis had gone to Albany and had said before he left: " Keep a sharp lookout for Captain Glazier, as he will surely pass this way." It was very pleasant to be met so cordially, although the sight of well-known faces and landmarks brought back the past and made me feel like another Rip Van Winkle.

In crossing the river between Greenbush and Albany,

THE ROAD TO ALBANY.

119

Paul seemed disinclined to stay on board, so the bars had to be put up and every precaution taken. It may have been that the shades of the ferrymen who had run the little craft for the last two hundred years came back to vex us. Perhaps the particular ghost of Hendrick Albertsen, who, two hundred and eight years ago bargained with Killian Van Rensselaer for the privilege of running his boat; but whatever the cause of the disturbance we reached *terra firma* without accident, and were soon in the familiar streets of the old Dutch town ; the day's journey agreeably ended with our trip across the Hudson by the oldest ferry in the United States.

From the river the view of Albany is picturesque in the extreme, where the eye catches the first glimpse of the city, rising from the water's edge, and surmounted then by its brown-domed Capitol. It was a sight that had always had a singular charm for me, for many of the pleasantest hours of my early life were spent here, where my sisters and I were educated. Here I left school to enlist at the opening of the Civil War, and here I published my first book, "Capture, Prison-Pen and Escape." But even if the city had no claim other than its own peculiar attractiveness it would hold an enviable place among its sister cities. The irregularity of its older streets, the tone of its architecture, the lack of the usual push and bustle of an American town, give it an old-world air that makes it interesting. There is a Common in the centre of the city, shaded by old elms, and around this stand the public buildings —the State Hall for state offices and the City Hall for city offices—both of marble and fronting on the Common. The Albany Academy, where Joseph

Henry, one of its professors from 1826 to 1832, first demonstrated his theory of the magnetic telegraph. A few squares west of the Common was the stretch of green that has since been set apart for a public park, where the good people of Albany may find an agreeable change of scene and an hour's pleasant recreation.

The New Capitol, on the site of the Old Capitol, is a magnificent edifice in the renaissance style, built of New England granite, at a cost to the State of many millions. On passing quaint bits of architecture or the suggestive aspect of some out-of-the way corner, one turns naturally to the days of wigs and kneebreeches, before the capital of the Empire State was thought of, and when the forests of fair Columbia were overrun by the bronzed warriors who still held undisputed sway. It was back in these days that Henry Hudson, sent from Holland by the Dutch East India Company, in sailing up the "Grande" River in search of a passage to India and China, found that he could not send his ship beyond the point where the city of Hudson now stands. This was discouraging, but sure that the desired passage was found, he and a few of his men pushed farther on in a small craft, landing, it is believed, on the present site of Albany. Later, Hudson and his men returned, assured that the noble river could not take them where they had hoped it might. After them came Dutch traders, led by an enterprising Hollander who had been with Hudson on his first voyage, and who saw a promising field in the red man's country. They established a trading-post where the "Half Moon" had been moored before, and from here carried on their barter with the Indians, exchanging attractive trifles for furs. Other traders followed these, and then came the colo-

STATE STREET AND CAPITOL, ALBANY, NEW YORK.

nists; a brave little band full of hope and eager to try their fortune in the New World. Their leader was none other than Killian Van Rensselaer, the wealthy pearl merchant of Amsterdam, and one of the directors of the West India Company, who had received a grant from the Prince of Orange for a large tract of land about the Upper Hudson, including the present site of Albany. Here he established his "patroonship," guarding the affairs of the colony, and providing his tenants with comfortable houses and ample barns. And more than this, their spiritual welfare was promoted through the services of the Reverend Doctor Joanes Megapolensis. From his personal accounts we read that the good Dominie found his life among the ' wilden ' as full of peril and unceasing labor as that of his flock; for he undertook not only the guidance of his own people, but the enlightenment and conversion of the Indians. To this end he threw himself into the task of mastering their language with true missionary zeal; a task which in those days meant not only difficulty but danger.

Under the shelter of the handsome churches that grace the streets of the Albany of to-day, we see a striking contrast in the primitive house where this pioneer clergyman preached; and from the security of long-established peace, we look back upon those sturdy people of Rensselaerwyck who sowed and reaped and went to church under the protection of the Patroon's guns.

But there came a day when English ships sailed up to the harbor at Manhatoes, and demanded the surrender of the Dutch colonies in the name of the Duke of York and Albany. The terrified people at sight of the guns refused to withstand an attack, and the English quietly came into possession. Van Rensselaer sent down his papers, and Fort Orange surrendered on the twenty-fourth of September, 1664, soon after receiving its new name in honor of the Duke's second title. Twenty-two years later, Albany had the satisfaction of sending two of her representatives, Peter Schuyler and Robert Livingston, to New York to claim her charter as a city ; which, upon their return, was received, according to the old chronicler, " with all ye joy and acclamation imaginable."

Through the strength of their new dignity and influence we can trace the spirit of independence which was beginning to rise in opposition to the unjust English rule ; and it was here in 1754 that the first General Congress was held to discuss arrangements for the national defence, when Franklin and his compatriots " signed the first plan for American Union and proclaimed to the colonies that they were one people, fit to govern and able to protect themselves." Later, when the storm of the Revolution broke, this place, where the first threatenings were heard, was the most impoverished by the contest and the most persevering in the fight ; but she came out triumphant, with a record well meriting the honors received in 1797, when she was made the capital of the Empire State. After peace was again established and the routine of business taken up, Albany became the centre of the entire trade of Western New York.

Fulton's steamboats began to run between Albany and New York as early as 1809, and this commercial activity and contact with the world gave an impulse to the city which has made itself felt all along the Hudson. Since then it has grown rapidly, and has in

RIVER STREET, TROY, NEW YORK.

its steady advancement an influential future to which its citizens may look forward with pardonable pride.

My arrival in Albany and lecture at Tweddle Hall on the evening of the eighteenth were to me among the notable events of my journey. Colonel J. M. Finley, who accompanied me from Boston, a veteran of the late war and manager of my lecture course from Boston to Buffalo, introduced me.

Called at the Capitol on the nineteenth to see the adjutant-general in relation to my lecturing in the interest of the fund for the erection of a Soldiers' Home which at that time interested persons had pro-posed to build at Bath, New York. I was presented to General Townsend by Colonel Taylor, assistant ad-jutant-general, whom I had known for several years. Found that General Townsend was not, as I had been informed, the treasurer of the fund. Colonel Taylor then went with me up Washington avenue in search of Captain John Palmer, Past Department Commander, G. A. R., whom I was advised to consult on the subject.

These matters attended to, I went in pursuit of Captain William Blasie and Lieutenant Arthur Richardson—acquaintances of many years and both of whom had been the companions of my capitivity in Southern prisons during the War of the Rebellion.

My stay in Albany was prolonged by preparation for lectures at Troy and Schenectady, and by needed in-formation concerning the early history and development of the former city. The second Sunday of my journey found me here and I went in the morning to the Presbyterian Church at the corner of Hudson and Philip streets.

CHAPTER VI.

ALBANY TO SYRACUSE.

Fourteenth Day.

Given's Hotel,
SCHENECTADY, NEW YORK
May 22, 1876,

LEFT Albany at eleven o'clock. My journey to this city led me over the Schenectady Turnpike. Was compelled to ride between showers all day as a rainstorm had set in just as I was leaving Albany. Stopped for dinner at Peter Lansing's, whose farm is about midway between the two cities. This genial gentleman of old Knickerbocker stock greatly amused me with his blunt manner and dry jokes. I was sorry to leave the shelter of his hospitable roof, especially as the weather was exceedingly disagreeable, but my engagement to lecture in Schenectady obliged me to go on. I found it necessary to ride the last three miles at a gallop in order to avoid an approaching shower. Reached my hotel at four o'clock in the afternoon, and lectured in the evening at Union Hall under the auspices of Post 14, G. A. R. Several representatives of the city press were with me

VIEW IN SCHENECTADY, NEW YORK.

on the platform, and among them was Colonel S. G. Hamlin, a fellow-prisoner in " Libby " during the war, and now editor of the *Union*. In the morning Colonel Finley went over to Troy to assist Mr. Farrington, my advance agent, in arranging for my lecture in that city.

Fifteenth and Sixteenth Days.

> 91 *Centre Street,*
> SCHENECTADY, NEW YORK,
> *May Twenty-third–Twenty-fourth.*

Accepting an invitation to spend a day or two with friends, I went to 91 Centre street after my lecture. While here I was occupied chiefly in posting my journal and in attending to business and private correspondence. A telegram from Colonel Finley told me that he had fixed upon the next evening for my lecture at Harmony Hall, Troy. Acting upon this plan I went over to Troy the following afternoon by way of Albany. Called on Captain Palmer in the latter city. and handed him the proceeds of my lecture at Schenectady, which he at once transmitted to the fund in aid of the Soldiers' Home. While in Troy I met R. H. Ferguson, Hon. Martin I. Townsend, the Mc-Coys and many other friends and acquaintances of Auld Lang Syne. I may add that this was the only instance in my journey thus far in which I had deviated from a direct line of march.

Seventeenth Day.

> 91 *Centre Street,*
> SCHENECTADY, NEW YORK,
> *May Twenty-fifth.*

Returned to Schenectady by way of Albany after

my lecture at Troy. Was very busy at this time in organizing for my lecture campaign between Schenectady and Buffalo. There was rather a surprising announcement in the afternoon's *Union* to the effect that I had left for Little Falls. I did not learn from what source Comrade Hamlin of that paper received his information. Colonel Finley went on to Utica, where he was joined by Mr. Farrington.

During my stay here I became interested in the place and found that Schenectady was as rich in legends and story as her neighbors. She counts her birthday among the historic dates of America, having begun her career in 1620, when the Mohawks were still holding their councils of war and spreading the terror of their name. Here in their very haunts a band of courageous Dutchmen established a trading-post and began the work of civilization. This brave colony did not find life as peaceful as the innocent aspect of Nature would suggest, however, for in the winter of 1690 the French and Indians began their terrible work, burning the houses and massacreing the inhabitants. It was only through a baptism of blood that the small trading-post developed into a city. Now it was one of the most flourishing and important towns in the valley; and the transformation was so complete that it is almost impossible to realize that this was the scene of so many struggles. The Schenectady of to-day is a busy manufacturing town, with a prosperous farming district about it, whose cornfields and orchards attest the richness of the soil. It is the seat of Union College, a well-known institution of rich endowments and possessing a handsome library of 15,000 volumes. The college was founded in 1795 by a union of several religious sects. Its buildings are plain and substantial, their stuccoed walls suggestive of the good solid work that is accomplished within them from year to year.

Eighteenth Day.

Union Hotel,
FONDA, NEW YORK,
May Twenty-sixth.

Moved from Schenectady at eight o'clock in the morning. Found the weather delightful and the scenery charming. On either side were the meadows dotted with spring flowers and fertilized by the river, whose shore line of willows and elms was bright with new green. If I were to except the Berkshire Hills, I saw nothing in Massachusetts to surpass, or even equal, the Valley of the Mohawk. It surprised me that poet and novelist had apparently found so little here for legendary romance.

Had dinner at Amsterdam, sixteen miles from Schenectady, and while halted here had *Paul* shod for the first time since leaving Boston. Resumed my journey at four o'clock and reached Fonda two hours later. Made twenty-six miles during the day and was now 243 miles from the "Hub." Through the courtesy of Mr. Fisher, my landlord at this place, I was given a verbal sketch of Fonda which made a pleasant addition to my own small store of information. There were no striking characteristics here to attract the traveller's eye and history had not chronicled its modest advancement, but for those who enjoy the sight of peace and prosperity, Fonda has a charm of its own. Around it on all sides the grain fields were under excellent cultivation, with here and there a well-stocked farm, suggesting an agricultural and dairying centre. I found a good night's rest here, envied the people their peaceful existence, and rode away with a sense of complete refreshment.

Nineteenth Day.

Briggs House,
SAINT JOHNSVILLE, NEW YORK,
May Twenty-seventh.

Called for *Paul* at eight o'clock, and after halting a moment at the office of the *Mohawk Valley Democrat*, crossed the river to Fultonville, which is connected with Fonda by a substantial iron bridge. Passing through this town, an enterprising one for its size, I continued my journey along the south bank of the Mohawk until I reached Canajoharie, where I stopped at the Eldridge House for dinner.

Here I met another Socrates who had a "favorite prescription" for healing the sore on *Paul's* back. Spent an hour very pleasantly in the office of the *Mohawk Valley Register* at Fort Plain, where I learned that Charles W. Elliott of this paper is a son of George W. Elliott, author of "Bonnie Eloise." For many years this song was a great favorite, not only along the Mohawk, but all over the country, and is certainly one of the sweetest ballads of America. There is a swing to the rythm and charm in the lines which keeps it in memory, and in riding along through the scenes it describes, my thoughts go back to the old days in Rensselaer County, where as a boy I first heard the words.

A MILL STREAM IN THE MOHAWK VALLEY.

"O sweet is the vale where the Mohawk gently glides,
   On its clear winding way to the sea;
And dearer than all storied streams on earth besides,
   Is this bright rolling river to me.

         But sweeter, dearer, yes, dearer far than these,
            Who charms when others all fail,
         Is blue-eyed, bonnie, bonnie Eloise,
            The belle of the Mohawk vale.

"O sweet are the scenes of my boyhood's sunny years
   That bespangle the gay valley o'er;
And dear are the friends, seen through memory's fond tears,
   That have lived in the blest days of yore.

         But sweeter, dearer, yes, dearer far than these, etc.

"O sweet are the moments when dreaming I roam
   Through my loved haunts now mossy and gray;
And dearer than all is my childhood's hallowed home
   That is crumbling now slowly away.

         But sweeter, dearer, yes, dearer far than these, etc."

Reached this place at seven o'clock in the evening and will go on to Little Falls after dinner to-morrow. In the morning I had an opportunity to look about me and admire the unusually fine scenery whose romantic aspect was heightened by a rugged tip of the Adirondacks which runs down into the valley at that point. At the foot of the mountain lies the brisk little town of Saint Johnsville, whose manufacturing interests have given it a reputation for miles around.

Twentieth Day.

Girvan House,
LITTLE FALLS, NEW YORK,
May Twenty-eighth.

Rode to this place from Saint Johnsville after five o'clock in the afternoon, taking the north bank of the river. The effect of the scene in front of me as I traced my way along the valley was most striking. Nearer the town my eye caught the picturesque masses of rock lifting their rugged sides to a height of five hundred feet, the swift waters of the Mohawk rushing along between them. The homes perched all along on the steep hills suggested Swiss scenes and Alpine journeys, but the busy hum and characteristic American push soon dissipated these fancies. The rapid fall of the river here is of great benefit to the manufacturers who are making good use of their excellent water-power in the paper and woollen mills.

Soon after my arrival, several citizens came into the hotel to learn the particulars of my journey, but before I had time to register, Postmaster Stafford made himself known and introduced me to several of his friends and acquaintances, among them General Curtis and Major Lintner. A laughable story was related which afforded considerable amusement soon after I rode into town. It seems that a credulous old lady from the country had been led to believe that a cavalryman would ride through the place that night on the horse which General Washington rode during the Revolution. A story suggested, no doubt, by the subject of my lecture. She had come in to sell her firkin of butter and had waited until long after dark for the rider and his ancient steed, while the objects of her misguided interest were resting in Saint Johns-ville unconscious of the disappointment they were causing.

Let us hope that she never discovered her mistake, for the old are often sensitive on such points. It is better at times to suffer keen disappointment than to find we have been too credulous.

Twenty-first Day.

12 Cornelia Street,
UTICA, NEW YORK,
May Twenty-ninth.

After considerable trouble in finding a saddle blanket for *Paul*, to take the place of the saddle cloth used until we reached Little Falls, I started from that romantic town at nine o'clock, halting at Ilion for dinner. This village, well known through the firm of the Remingtons, is on the south bank of the Mohawk, twelve miles from Utica. From here the famous Remington machines and rifles are sent all over the world.

Farrington met me two miles east of Utica and escorted me back to the city, conducting Colonel Finley and myself to rooms which had been engaged for us through the hospitality of J. C. Bates.

Left my pleasant quarters here to make a few observations about town, and found much to arrest my attention. A century ago Utica was known as " Old Fort Schuyler " from a small stockade of that name, built on the site in 1750. As the country grew more peaceful, and the life of the future city began, the name was changed. A gradual slope of the land from the river gave from the more elevated parts some very fine views; and the public parks with their shade trees and gay flowers made a rich adornment to a naturally attractive city. The great Erie Canal passes through the centre of the city and is joined by the Chenango Canal at this point. Among the landmarks are the homes of Roscoe Conkling and Horatio Seymour.

Twenty-second Day.

Stanwix Hall,
ROME, NEW YORK,
May Thirtieth.

Was compelled to remain in Utica until four o'clock in the afternoon in order to have my saddle padded. This brief delay, while favoring my equine friend, was in some particulars also favorable to his rider, as it afforded me an excellent opportunity to gather information I desired concerning the growth of this enterprising town.

Rode up to Rome on the south bank of the Mohawk. Soon after my arrival at the Stanwix I met a large number of Grand Army comrades. Room " 14 " had been engaged and made a rendezvous, and here until a late hour the experiences of the late war were told over again and our battles re-fought. This gathering of comrades to celebrate Memorial Day was marked by deep and enthusiastic feeling; and, although my day's journey had somewhat fatigued me, I felt this was no time to show a lack of spirit; so I cheerfully yielded to the old maxim, "When in Rome do as the Romans do." Through the courtesy of Captain Joseph Porter, then Commander of Skillen Post 47, I was introduced to Hon. H. J. Coggeshall, of Waterville; Colonel G. A. Cantine, Hon. W. F. Bliss, Mr. Taylor, editor of the *Sentinel,* and many others.

Rome lies on a level stretch of land at the head of the valley, whence I could see its spires as I approached. On its site once stood old Fort Stanwix, of Revolutionary fame, which cost the British £60,000 sterling. It was built as a defence against the French in Canada, and was the first settlement before the French War. From that time until the close of the Revolution it was an important frontier post. Rome is the centre of a large dairying interest, the cheese factory system having originated here.

Twenty-third Day.

Chittenango House,
CHITTENANGO, NEW YORK,
May Thirty-first.

Had a late breakfast at the Stanwix and, after a stroll through the streets of Rome, called for my horse at ten o'clock, and bidding adieu to Grand Army comrades who had assembled to see me start from their city, mounted and rode out of town. The journey, as usual, since leaving Albany, lay along the New York Central. The roads were dry and favorable, the weather settled, and the scenery through this section of the Empire State such as to make my journey most enjoyable. Chittenango was not reached until ten o'clock, as the distance from Rome made this one of the longest rides noted in a single day. The twinkling lights of the village looked very pleasant as I neared my destination, marking here and there the homes of its hundreds of inhabitants. I found upon inquiry at the Chittenango House that I was the only guest, which augured well for a good night's sleep.

CHAPTER VII.

TWO DAYS AT SYRACUSE.

HAD an early breakfast at Chittenango and calling for *Paul* at eight o'clock mounted and rode forward, with the city of Syracuse as my evening destination. Nothing of especial interest occurred to vary the day's journey. Syracuse was reached at four o'clock in the afternoon, and the remainder of the day was spent in walks and drives through the city which I had visited several times in former years, and of whose history I had a fair knowledge. Long before the white man came, a band of Iroquois had built their wigwams in the low basin, almost entirely surrounded by hills, that lies to the south of Lake Onondaga, and from here followed the pursuits of war and peace. We first hear of this Indian village in 1653 through the Jesuit missionary, Father Le Moyne, who had come to establish good feeling between the Iroquois and other Indian tribes; and we see strange evidences of a counteracting influence made probably by his own countrymen in the discovery of European weapons and ammunition, that were distributed among the red men about the same time. For more than a hundred years after

this, the present site of Syracuse, then an un-
promising stretch of swamps, was the home of the
wolf and bear. Over its dreary waste the cry of
the wild cat, the warning of the rattlesnake and the
hooting of the owl lent their sounds to the weird chorus
of Nature, and it was here that the wily Indian came to
seek his game. It was through Father Le Moyne,
too, that we hear of the great Salt Springs, which he
visited at the southern end of the lake in company
with some Huron and Onondaga chiefs. The Indians,
unable to comprehend the strange effect of salt and
clear water bubbling from the same fountain, had a
superstition that the springs were possessed by an evil
spirit and were afraid to drink from them ; but when
the white man began to share their old haunts, we hear
of the bewitched water being fearlessly used, and the
evil spirit converted into a propitious one. It was
Major Asa Danforth and his companion, Colonel Comfort Tyler, who began early in the present century the
enterprise which has since proved such a splendid success. These two pioneers started out afoot for the
springs with no other implements than an axe, chain
and kettle, which seem primitive enough to us who
know of the means that are now employed in the making of this great staple. Arrived at the springs, two
young trees were cut, a stout branch placed in their
crochets and on this the kettle was hung. When the
work was finished, the men hid their implements in the
bushes for safety, shouldered their rich possession and
started home over the ground that in a few years was
to be the scene of such striking and sudden changes.

Joshua Forman was the first man who saw a promising field in the unhealthy land south of Lake Onon-

daga, and it was he who first thought of a plan for its improvement.

With characteristic persistency he carried out his ideas, and with the co-operation of James Geddes, a surveyor and fellow-townsman, did more to convince men of the practicability of laying a canal route through central New York than any other man. At that time the advocate of such an undertaking was considered mad. Even the President shared the public view of the matter, and when the zealous member from Onondaga laid the plans before this incredulous gentleman, Jefferson remarked: "It is a splendid project, and may be executed a century hence." It must have been a satisfaction to Judge Forman to see this inland water-course completed a few years later, and to realize the success of the great enterprise.

When the breaking up of the unhealthy soil caused so much sickness and so many deaths during the building of the canal at Syracuse—then "Corinth"—this thoughtful benefactor began to devise a way for improving the ground, which resulted in the passage of a bill, a year later, for lowering the lake by means of drains. This stopped the injurious overflow that occurred during the spring months and eventually put an end to the "Corduroy" and "gridiron" roads by which the "dreary waste of swamp" had been hitherto approached.

It seems strange enough now, to one riding through the beautiful and regular streets of the present city, to realize that only a few years ago its pioneers either followed these rough routes, or went around by the hills to avoid them.

In April, 1820, Syracuse had grown sufficiently

to merit the distinction of a Post Office, and with
this new acquisition a discussion arose about its
name. It had been called successively "Webster's
Landing," "South Salina," "Bogardus Corners,"
"Cossit's Corners" and "Milan;" but, as there was
another "Milan" in the State, its last title had to be
abandoned. For awhile it was known as "Corinth,"
but finally by an odd coincidence it was named by its
first Postmaster, John Wilkinson, after the old Sicilian capital, to which it was supposed to bear a slight
resemblance. Mr. Wilkinson, it is said, in reading a
poetical description of the ancient city, was singularly
impressed by its name, and by the fact that there was
a fountain of mythological origin just beyond its
walls, from which sprang clear and salt water.

At a meeting held to decide the matter, he among
others eloquently discussed his choice, and it was
unanimously accepted. At this time, the government
official at Syracuse had charge of such vast communi-
cations from "Uncle Sam," that when the Post Office
was transferred later to the office of John Durford,
printer, Mr. Wilkinson carried the entire concern,
"mail matter, letter bags and boxes on his shoulders!"
Still, when the Marquis de La Fayette visited Syracuse,
five years later, it had made such rapid advancement
that it called forth his warmest congratulations. On
this occasion, truly a great one among the city's records,
her founder and benefactor, Joshua Forman, was chosen
to express the gratitude of her people. It must have
been a pleasant moment for the brave General and a
proud one for the Syracusans when, in response to their
hospitality, he returned Mr. Forman's courtesy in the
following words: "The names of Onondaga and Syra-

cuse, in behalf of whose population you are pleased so kindly to welcome me, recall to my mind at the same time the wilderness that, since the time I commanded on the Northern frontier, has been transformed into one of the most populous and enlightened parts of the United States; and the ancient Sicilian city, once the seat of republican institutions, much inferior, however, to those which in American Syracuse are founded upon the plain investigation, the unalloyed establishment of the rights of men, and upon the best representative forms of government. No doubt, sir, but that among the co-operators of the Revolution, the most sanguine of us could not fully anticipate the rapidity of the improvements which, on a journey of many thousand miles—the last tour alone from Washington to this place amounting to five thousand miles— have delighted me; and of which this part of the country offers a bright example. Be pleased to accept my personal thanks and in behalf of the people of Onondaga and Syracuse to receive this tribute of my sincere and respectful acknowledgments. "

Could the Marquis have lived longer, and made his tour hither at this time, he would scarcely have found words to express his surprise. Perhaps no city in New York has made such great strides in so few years.

Handsome buildings have sprung up on all sides, each one adding to the sightliness of the place; and on the surrounding hills wealthy residents have built their charming homes. The University of Syracuse, a Methodist institution, built upon one of these hills in 1870, looks down invitingly upon the knowledge-seekers of the city, and with the State Armory, that stands in the park near Onondaga Creek, would furnish a brilliant equipment for some modern Minerva, were she to visit this interesting namesake of Sicilian Syracuse.

To the stranger looking out for characteristics, the Salt Works are the most prominent among them. The sheds stretch along like enormous stock-yards at one end of the city, but looking into them one discovers great vats and troughs filled with salt in every stage of evaporation. There are two ways by which the article is manufactured, one by solar and the other by artificial heat, with thirty or forty companies employing their chosen method.

Another striking feature is the unusual number of public halls. This is due to the central location which makes Syracuse a favorite point for conventions. It was my pleasure to lecture in one of these, "Shakespeare Hall," on my first evening in the city, where I was introduced by General Augustus Sniper. After this engagement, I went by rail to Buffalo, on business connected with my proposed lecture in that city, and returned the following afternoon. This was very unusual, as it was contrary to the practice of my journey to avail myself of the railway under any circumstances. My advance agents having completed preparations for my lecture at Rochester, I made arrangements to resume my journey on the following day. My short stay here gave me another opportunity to look about this interesting town, and to realize its charms at the prettiest season of the year. Some have believed that its situation, importance and beauty would win for Syracuse the honor, so long bestowed upon the good old town on the Hudson, of being the capital of the Empire State. Whether or not it will ever be known as such, it will receive the flattering acknowledgment of being one of the loveliest cities in New York.

CHAPTER VIII.

SYRACUSE TO ROCHESTER.

Twenty~sixth Day.

Camillus House,
CAMILLUS, NEW YORK,
June Third.

OUNTED in front of the Vanderbilt House, Syracuse, at four o'clock in the afternoon. A large number of friends and acquaintances had assembled to see me off, among them many G. A. R. comrades, including General Sniper and Captain Auer; the latter a companion in Libby Prison during the late war. Thomas Babcock, who had been acting as an assistant to my advance agents, accompanied me as far as Geddes, and arranged to co-operate with my brother and Mr. Farrington in preparation for my lecture. In passing through this little suburb of Geddes, whose name by the way, keeps in memory one of the prominent men of Onondaga County, my attention was drawn to a fine building standing on a hill, overlooking Syracuse. I learned that it was the New York Asylum for Imbeciles and that the site, a magnificent sweep of upland, measur-

8

ing fifty-five acres, was donated by the city. I was stopped just west of here by a thunder shower and took refuge under a tree. *Paul* and I had waited for storms to pass over before, and made excellent rainy-day friends. We rather enjoyed resting under some shelter until the dust was well laid and the air freshened. On our arrival at Camillus, myself and horse were literally covered with mud, the result of *Paul's* fright on the approach of a train at a point where it was impossible to leave the turnpike. We were trotting along quietly and had just turned a bend in the road when the quick ear of the horse caught the distant rumbling of wheels. In an instant he was on the alert, and when the swift express came round the curve, made a sudden spring to the right, leaped a rail-fence, and landed in a bog where the mud was two or three feet deep. I managed to keep the saddle, but could not avoid the mire in which we had haplessly fallen.

Twenty-seventh Day.

Jordan House,
JORDAN, NEW YORK,
June Fourth.

By an hour's close application to my bespattered garments, after reaching the Camillus House, I found that I was ready to "turn in" for the night. Started forward in the morning, the ride on this perfect June day proving false the old saying that "Jordan is a hard road to travel." This village was reached about noon and I was quite prepared for the generous meal which was placed before me.

When the gnawings of hunger had been appeased I

A FLOURISHING FARM.

153

gave myself up to the agreeable quiet of Sunday afternoon.

There was ample encouragement for such a course in this cosy little retreat at the head of Lake Skaneateles, for there was not a sound from store or mill while the people were taking their Sabbath rest.

This brief halt in the march forward was very agreeable, for it gave me an opportunity to try my own powers of locomotion, so little used since leaving Boston. It was a real luxury to stroll about the quiet lanes, and scan the outlying fields from the standpoint of a modest pedestrian. In the course of my rambles I came across some photographers from Auburn who had been taking views of the scenery about here. Some of their pictures were excellent.

Twenty-eighth Day.

Montezuma Hotel,
MONTEZUMA, NEW YORK,
June Fifth.

The Auburn photographers whom I saw yesterday met me as I was riding out of Jordan, and proposed photographing myself and *Paul.* Some time was passed and several ruses resorted to in attempting to quiet the restless animal, but he skilfully avoided the camera.

At last some men who happened to be near offered their assistance, and attempted to attract the attention of the horse from a distance, by jumping up and down in a neighboring field. *Paul* threw his head forward, quietly and curiously watching their manœuvres. He was evidently amused, but there was no spirit to the picture. Unfortunately the "spirited" part of the scene was out of range.

This delay for vanity's sake prevented us from getting farther than Weedsport by noon, where a brief halt was made for dinner. I was met here by W. H. Ransom and the proprietor of the Howard House of Port Byron, who came over to Weedsport and escorted me to their village, where I had tea and was very courteously entertained for a few hours. On leaving Port Byron, these gentlemen rode forward with me towards Montezuma Swamp, which lies between the two towns. Here we parted company, there being no reason why they should "run the gauntlet" with me. I had heard wonderful tales of the dreaded monsters of this swamp, who were reputed to be the very worst mosquitoes on record, not excepting their famous kinsmen of the Hackensack Flats, New Jersey.

Unable to bear patiently the torture of my assailants who were swarming around me by thousands, I put spurs to *Paul*, and went through at a gallop; but notwithstanding this attempt to put the enemy to rout, superior numbers gave them the advantage and their victim came out covered with scars.

When Montezuma was reached we were glad to rest, for our late adventure had quite exhausted both horse and rider.

Twenty-ninth Day.

Newark House,
NEWARK, NEW YORK,
June Sixth.

The journey along the line of the New York Central

AN OLD LANDMARK.

from Montezuma to Newark, was an exciting one to me and *Paul*. I had long since learned that whenever the route brought us in close proximity with the railroad, the quiet pursuit of our way was often varied by exciting moments, owing to *Paul's* suspicion of the "iron horse." The climax of these escapades was reached this morning, when *Paul*, becoming frightened by an approaching train repeated the experience of three days ago by plunging into a slough, about two miles from Newark, and completely covering himself and rider with mud. When I had recovered sufficiently to realize the situation, my thoughts were not as amiable, I fear, as those of Bunyan's good Christian, tried in like manner. The "slough of despond" was so very literal in this case.

I had made every effort to control the excited animal, but found the attempt useless; and I verily believe if he were between the infernal regions and a coming train, he would choose the former at a bound. It was rather trying to appear before people of the town in such a lamentable condition, to say nothing of the discomforts arising from damp clothing; but there was no alternative, so I followed my course; the unfortunate victim of circumstances.

Thirtieth Day.

Fairport House,
FAIRPORT, NEW YORK,
June Seventh.

Resumed march at eight o'clock in the morning, but the weather was so oppressively warm and sultry, that I was obliged to wait over from noon until six o'clock.

Riding in the cool of the day was much more agree-able, yet, notwithstanding the physical comfort, I must confess that the lonely and unknown road gave rather a gloomy forecast to my thoughts. Beside this, I found some difficulty in obtaining necessary directions, and lost the chief charm of the journey— a view of the beautiful country through which I was passing.

It had not been my intention to do any travelling after sundown unless the heat made it absolutely necessary, but in this instance I felt justified in changing the original plan. Moving along through the unfamiliar scenes, I missed the pleasant coloring of woods and fields under the broad light of day, the noisy hum the sunshine calls forth, and the sound of the birds, always the sweetest music to me. Instead of these there was the mystical silence of night, broken only by the clatter of *Paul's* hoofs over the dusty road. Four hours' steady travel brought us in sight of the straggling lights of the little post-village of Fairport, where we stopped for the night. Found several Rochester papers awaiting me here, which contained pleasant reference to my proposed lecture at Corinthian Hall.

CHAPTER IX.

FOUR DAYS AT ROCHESTER.

ANTICIPATING rain during the forenoon and fearing that my journey might be interrupted in consequence, I started at an early hour on the morning of June eighth from Fairport, and riding at a brisk pace came into Rochester at eleven o'clock.

Just before reaching the city, a halt was made at a little hamlet, two or three miles out, for the purpose of treating *Paul's* back. Heretofore the necessity of meeting my lecture appointments along the route had given me no opportunity to attend to the painful bruise, although I had been studying the various modes of treatment recommended by veterinary surgeons from the time I left Boston until now. The peculiar nature of my journey gave me an excellent opportunity to follow this especial course, and I felt confident of my ability to do all that was possible for my faithful horse, yet at every stopping-place some kindly disposed admirer of the horse had some favorite prescription which he had found a never-failing cure for the particular affliction that daily confronted me. The enterprising little hamlet in question had its famed savant, who thought it would be highly imprudent of me to proceed farther without his advice—and a bottle of his "Seven-Sealed Wonder."

Anxious to make Rochester at the earliest moment possible, I had no time to discuss the merits of this great elixir, so, noting the price on the face of the bottle, I handed this modest disciple of Æsculapius the amount due, although he generously protested, and congratulating myself upon being the most highly favored traveller between Boston and San Francisco, rode away.

On a hill just beyond the village and well out of sight, I came upon an old barn standing to the left of the road, on whose front I noticed a huge door with a knothole in the centre. Now was my opportunity for unsealing the "Wonder." In an instant I brought *Paul* to a standstill and rising in the saddle, tried my luck. The "Wonder" fell short of the mark, but it met a resistance from the old door which effectually tested its powers, and in my humble opinion placed the good doctor high up in his profession. This momentary diversion over, I again resumed the march, vowing that this would be my last experiment with "sealed wonders" and that hereafter I would confine my treatment to bathing *Paul's* back with warm water and castile soap, whose virtue I had learned in the cavalry service during the war.

Found that the Rochester papers had been discussing my military record before my arrival, and that the *Express* and *Sunday Morning Times* had upheld my cause against the *Union*, which had ventured some falsehoods on the ground that my "youthful appearance" belied my experience as a soldier. With this pleasant criticism came another greeting from the city press. It had been announced that I would probably arrive at the Osburn House at four in the afternoon, hence it was not strange that my sudden appearance at an earlier hour caused some surprise and led to the impression that I had come forward by rail, and that my horseback journey was possibly not an entirely genuine affair. I may add that it had not occurred to me that my trip across country was of sufficient importance to warrant any criticism upon my methods so long as I met my lecture appointments promptly. The sharp comment had no more serious result than that of increasing the lecture receipts in the cities which followed.

My tenth lecture was delivered in Corinthian Hall, at the usual hour in the evening, the introduction being made by Colonel J. A. Reynolds.

Next day, June ninth, gave me an opportunity to look up the familiar places and to note the changes that had occurred since my last visit to the city. The cleanliness and beauty of the streets, now in their summer glory of tree and flower, made such a tour of inspection anything but unpleasant.

East avenue, where the " flour and coal kings " are at home, is an attractive place in which to see individual taste carried out in architecture and horticulture. Down town, where the " kings " are at work, there is a brisk activity which pervades everything, like an unending accompaniment to the Falls, whose sounds always mingle with those of the busy life around them. Perhaps it was this continual encouragement from the river, offered to her early pioneers, that has given Rochester such a notable career and made her the metropolis of the Genesee Valley : for with that first mill-wheel set into the stream by old " Indian Allen," the faithful waters have kept up a continual flow of good fortune.

Her characteristic enterprise, milling, begun by this same Allen, has been an unfailing source of wealth ; the golden grain with almost magic transformation filling the coffers of her merchants and giving her the security that a healthy financial condition brings. Besides this, she owes much to that liberal-minded gentleman, Colonel Nathaniel Rochester, who came with his family from Maryland when the settlement was in its infancy, and made his home in " the pleasant valley." It is amusing to fancy the unique procession, headed by the Colonel and his sons on horseback, that started out towards " the wild west " in the summer of 1802. There were carriages for the ladies and servants, and wagons for provisions and household goods, stretched out in formidable array : for railroads were out of the question then.

We hear that the travellers met with cordial hospitality at the villages and towns along their route, and that their arrival created quite a sensation. In fact it was an historical event. Two friends of the Rochesters, William Fitzhugh and Charles Carroll, cast in their fortunes with them; and in 1802 bought together the three hundred acres at the Upper Falls, which were laid out for a settlement ten years later. In those times the prestige of a name went far towards establishing a reputation, and the one chosen by the people of the settlement was afterward proudly placed **upon** the municipal banner. Soon after the advent of Colonel Rochester and his friends, the scheme for making a water communication between the Lakes and the Sea began to be eagerly discussed, and there were not a few energetic representatives from "Rochesterville" who lent their efforts towards the carrying out of the plan. When the canal was completed there was the wildest enthusiasm in Rochester, which would perhaps have a greater benefit than any other place along the route: for with her big grain and coal interests, her future prosperity seemed assured.

The natural course of events followed. Improvement and embellishment began on all sides. New buildings and enterprises started up on solid foundations, and provision was made for those who might "drop out of the ranks," in the selection of beautiful Mount Hope, one of the loveliest cemeteries in point of natural charm in this country. It lies on a wooded slope between the lake and the city, and its pathways, shadowed by the great trees from the "forest primeval," are the playgrounds for the wild little creatures who make their homes there unmolested.

Back again into the town where the sound of the Falls is heard, and one thinks of the odd touch a simple character has added to the traditions of the place, and whose name, to a stranger, is so often associated with that of Rochester. This quaint figure is none other than "Sam Patch, the jumper," who met his fate by leaping into the Genesee at the "Falls," and who left as a legacy the warning maxim, "Be careful, or, like Sam Patch, you may jump once too often." History has chronicled Sam's last speech, delivered from the platform, just before his fatal leap; which, as a sample of rustic oratory, is amusing.

He said : "Napoleon was a great man and a great general. He conquered armies, and he conquered nations, but *he couldn't jump the Genesee Falls.* Wellington was a great man and a great soldier. He conquered armies, and he conquered nations, and he conquered Napoleon, but *he couldn't jump the Genesee Falls.* That was left for *me* to do, and I can do it, and will."

Rochester, the capital of Monroe County, New York, was first settled in 1810, and incorporated as a city in 1834. It is situated on both sides of the Genesee River, seven miles from Lake Ontario, two hundred and fifty miles from Albany and sixty-nine from Buffalo by railway. An aqueduct of stone carries the Erie Canal across the river, the cost of which amounted to over half a million dollars. The city is well laid out with wide and handsome streets, lined with shade trees.

Within the city limits the Genesee undergoes a sudden descent of two hundred and sixty-eight feet, falling in three separate cataracts within a distance of two miles. The roar of these falls is heard continually all over the city, but no one is inconvenienced by it in the slightest degree. The cataracts are believed to have formed, at one time, a single fall, but the different degrees of hardness of the rocks have caused an unequal retrograde movement of the falls, until they have assumed their present position. At the Upper Falls, the river is precipitated perpendicularly ninety-six feet. It then flows between nearly perpendicular walls of rock, for about a mile and a quarter to the Middle Falls, where it has another descent of twenty-five feet. One hundred rods below, at the Lower

VIEW OF ROCHESTER.

Falls, it again descends eighty-four feet, which brings the stream to the level of Lake Ontario, into which it enters.

The immense water-power thus afforded in the centre of one of the finest wheat-growing regions in the world, with the facilities of transportation afforded by the Erie Canal, Lake Ontario, and the several railways, have given a vast impulse to the prosperity of Rochester and it has, in consequence, become one of the most important manufacturing cities in the East. At the period of my visit, there were eighteen flour mills in operation, grinding annually 2,500,000 bushels of wheat. The manufacturing interests are immense—ready-made clothing being the most extensive, and boots and shoes ranking next. Other leading manufactures are those of iron bridges, India-rubber goods, carriages, furniture, optical instruments, steam engines, glassware and agricultural machinery. Of flourishing industries may be mentioned breweries, tobacco factories, blast furnaces and fruit canning.

The largest nurseries in America are found here. Thousands of acres within a short distance of the city are devoted to the cultivation of fruit trees, and millions of these trees are annually shipped to other States and foreign countries. Over $2,000,000 is the annual product of these prolific nurseries.

The city is fast becoming a great distributing centre for coal, which is conveyed in vessels to all points on the Great Lakes. Rochester, being the business centre of the fertile Genesee Valley, shows a steady growth in business and wealth. It has a magnificent system of water-works, constructed at a cost of $3,250,000, the water being supplied from two sources—one from the river, which is used for extinguishing fires and running light machinery; the other from Hemlock Lake, twenty-nine miles from the centre of the city, and four hundred feet above it. This water is sent through sixty miles of mains, the pressure being such as to throw from the hydrants a stream one hundred and thirty feet perpendicularly. No city is more perfectly protected from fire.

At the corner of Main and State streets are the Powers' Buildings, a peculiar block of stores, built of stone, glass and iron, seven stories high. In the upper halls is a fine collection of paintings. A tower surmounts the building, from which a fine view of the city and its surroundings is obtained. "The Arcade" is roofed with glass and numerous fine stores line its sides. Opposite stands the County Court House, a handsome building of gray limestone, with a tower one hundred and seventy-five feet high. The handsomest building in the city is, I think, the Rochester Savings Bank, corner of Main and Fitzhugh streets. The First Baptist, the First Presbyterian and the Catholic Cathedral of St. Patrick are the finest church edifices.

There are twelve spacious parks here, and four elegant bridges cross the Genesee. The Rochester University, founded by the Baptist denomination in 1850, is located on a tract of twelve acres, a little to the east of the city. It has a valuable library and mineralogical cabinet. The State Reform School or Western House of Refuge for vicious boys is an imposing edifice, containing usually about four hundred inmates. Mount Hope, the site of the cemetery—before referred to—is a beautiful eminence overlooking the city.

At the time of my visit, Rochester supported thirty-four newspapers and periodicals, of which six were dailies. The population was about 90,000.

It seems that Fortune has favored the "Flour City," or at least that wise heads and generous hearts have planned for her greatest good. It is proper to look back into the beginnings for the keynote to success in our American towns, and in this case, we doubtless find it in the unselfish forethought of the first men added to its wonderful natural resources.

A simple little incident, told of Colonel Rochester, illustrates the principle, whose benefit others are reaping. He was working in his garden one day, setting out fruit trees, when a neighbor came along and stopped to chat. The Colonel said : "I do not know that I shall eat any fruit from the trees I am planting, but as I eat from trees somebody planted for me, I must set out trees for those who will come after me." It was this provision for those who were to "come after" that has done much towards making Rochester what she is to-day.

CHAPTER X.

ROCHESTER TO BUFFALO.

Thirty-fifth Day.

Sprague House,
CHURCHVILLE, NEW YORK,
June 12, 1876.

I FOUND as I mounted *Paul* at nine o'clock in front of the Osburn House that on this twelfth of June, 1876, my day's ride would be a trying one on account of the heat, but it was impossible to change the weather and impracticable to change my plans, so I accepted the inevitable. As usual through Central New York a number of Grand Army friends and others had assembled to see me off, and to wish me a safe journey to the "Golden Gate." This cordiality, shown me all along the route, took away the sense of strangeness natural to one travelling through comparatively unfamiliar places, and gave me an idea of the hospitality of our American people. The pleasant good-byes over, *Paul* and I started away in the direction of Chili, which we reached about noon. Here I had dinner and passed the remainder of the day, resorting again to the even-

THE DISTRICT SCHOOL HOUSE.

ing hours for resuming my journey; and I may add that in this instance I found "something in a name," for Chili was an admirable place to keep cool in.

At six o'clock I started on towards Churchville, coming in sight of its church spires a little after sunset, and lessening the distance to San Francisco by some fifteen miles.

Notwithstanding the stop over at Chili, I was glad when we came to the end of my journey, and must confess that as I rode into the village the sight of the Sprague House gratified me more than the view of the picturesque town as I saw it outlined against the evening sky.

Thirty-sixth Day.

Byron Centre Hotel,
BYRON CENTRE, NEW YORK,
June Thirteenth.

Soon after breakfast in Churchville, I threw myself into the saddle and started for Bergen Corners, reaching it by eleven o'clock. This distance of two miles was covered very leisurely, for there was no pressing engagement to fill, and I could "gang my own gait." When there was anything to attract the eye—a sightly field of grain, or change of scene, I usually stopped to notice it and add one more impression to the panorama which my overland journey continually spread before me. At the "Corners" I spent a few hours quietly, if I except the slight interruptions of the landlord of the Hooper House and his family. These interruptions for curiosity's sake were easily pardoned by me, for anything a little humorous and characteristic is always acceptable to one bent on see-

9

ing life in all its phases; and besides, the softening influence of home-made bread and other country luxuries, which were furnished me here, tended to make me look charitably upon everything.

In the afternoon I left for Byron Centre, reaching it at six o'clock and making eleven miles for the day. While at supper there, the guests of the Byron Centre House were greatly amused by two itinerant photographers who, after their day's work was done, made a practice of entertaining the public with fife and drum. Through this cunning advertising scheme it was my good fortune to see one of the most interesting crowds that rustic America could bring together. These enterprising "artist musicians" seemed to possess the magic powers of Orpheus, for the villagers attracted by their strains came flocking from every direction and unconsciously made up a group which would have been irresistible to a painter, and which was certainly interesting to the ordinary observer. The sight was an entirely novel one to me, for although I am a New Yorker, and have seen roving concerns of almost every description, this particular species had never come to my notice. Through the courtesy of Charles Leonard, the proprietor of the hotel here, I was introduced to several Byron Centre gentlemen, among them Rev. Edwin Allen, who called just before my departure. Mr. Allen was most cordial, and gave me a very clever idea of the place, and the country adjacent.

Throughout my journey I was often placed under obligations of this sort. They added to my pleasure and increased my facilities for becoming acquainted with the people and the country.

Thirty-seventh Day.

St. James Hotel,
BATAVIA, NEW YORK,
June Fourteenth.

A delightful shower of the previous evening cooled the air, and made my journey to Batavia exceedingly pleasant. During the day I passed some of the finest clover and wheat fields that I had seen since leaving Rochester. The rain may have brightened their color and made them look their best, but regardless of this, it is evident that the soil through this section of New York is under a very high state of cultivation, and signs of thrift are noticeable on every hand. I found, as is generally the case upon approaching a town, the farms more tastefully laid out, with their wide stretches of wheat, and their pretty conventional "kitchen gardens."

After these outskirting homes I came upon the more dignified buildings of Batavia proper, where push and enterprise have made some striking advances. It is quite a business town, having its share of manufactories, banks and newspapers, and, with its population of something over four thousand, possessing the benefits of a larger place. It is thirty-two miles west of Rochester and thirty-seven east of Buffalo. The State Institute for the Blind is situated here.

In the evening I lectured at Ellicott Hall, and was introduced by lawyer L. L. Crosby, a comrade of the Grand Army, who, during the late war, was an officer in the Fifth Michigan Cavalry. Among those who called upon me at the St. James before the lecture was Samuel A. Lester, a fellow-soldier of the Harris Light Cavalry, with whom I talked over many of our experiences in Company "E" of the "Old Regiment." Nothing has been so gratifying to me in the course of my journey, changes of scene, or new faces, as these meetings with old comrades, and the talks of camp and field. Separating at the close of the war, when the trying experiences we had equally shared had drawn us strangely together, it was natural that a glimpse of those we had known under such circumstances should be a delight after so many years. It gave a different phase to my journey, too, and made it not only a series of new and pleasant changes, but an extended visit which might delight any traveller.

Thirty-eighth Day.

Crossroads,
NEAR CROFT'S STATION, NEW YORK,
June Fifteenth.

I did not find it convenient to leave Batavia until eight o'clock in the evening, but as most of the six miles between the two places lay through a swampy region, I had a running fight with the mosquitoes, which encouraged me to make good time, so that I reached "Croft's" in an hour. On my arrival I found Babcock awaiting me with accommodation provided at a quiet little retreat situated at the Crossroads, which was hotel, grocery and farm-house in one. This odd grocery-tavern is about half a mile from the station; just far enough away to have peculiarities of its own. While its proprietor was throwing down

RURAL SCENE IN CENTRAL NEW YORK.

hay for *Paul* from his barn loft, he in some way lost his footing and fell through, but no serious damage was done.

This little incident simply added an extra attraction to the "horse that was going to California." In the course of the morning I went to the hotel sitting-room to make some observations and to post my journal. While quietly occupied in this way I noticed the arrival of several of the men and boys of the place, who came in, seated themselves on the wooden benches that were placed around the sides of the room, and began unceremoniously to "look me over." Phoebe, the proprietor's daughter, and the ruling spirit at the "Corners," a bright little maid, who filled the offices of cook, waitress, chambermaid and clerk, assumed one of her various roles and was standing behind the counter. Soon, one of her rustic knights sauntered up to her, pipe in mouth, and called out, "Pheeb, gimme a match!" Whereupon, her father, who was standing on one side of the room, country fashion, with trousers over his boot-tops, and in his shirt sleeves, stepped forward and said with admirable dignity, "Phebe, sir!" adding, as the nonplused offender made some bashful apology, "You's brought up well nuff, Jack, but you've forgot some on't."

This was an unexpected turn of affairs which I scarcely expected to witness at "Croft's," but it at least gave evidence of a certain sense of refinement which we Americans would hardly be credited with outside our cultivated circles. It afforded, too, food for reflection upon that assumption of equality which in this country so often tends to familiarity. We are prone to forget that "familiarity breeds contempt."

Thirty-ninth Day.

Crittenden House,
CRITTENDEN, NEW YORK,
June Sixteenth.

Started from "Croft's" at ten o'clock, stopping at the little post village of Corfu for dinner, where I was introduced to several people who had come together to greet me upon my arrival. Among them were Dr. Fuller, Dr. John McPherson and S. E. Dutton. Dinner over, I rested until five o'clock, resuming my journey at that hour and reaching Crittenden at six. As I rode up to the hotel at this place I found that a number of villagers had gathered to give me welcome, and to learn something of my journey and its objects. I talked to them for some time and then followed a strong inclination to walk into the country. There were no unusual attractions about this little village of a hundred souls excepting the cordiality of its people and the natural attraction that there always is about a small community in the midst of thriving acres. To one who has been "a country boy" himself, these things never lose their charm, and he will give them the preference, I think, to the finest sights in town.

They recall a certain old home somewhere, long since abandoned for the charms of Vanity Fair, or a quaint little "school house" where he first began to think about the great world beyond. They form, too, the resting-places in the ascent of the hill of life, from the vantage-ground of which we may review our progress since those early days.

Fortieth Day.

American House,
LANCASTER, NEW YORK,
June Seventeenth and Eighteenth.

My ride from Crittenden to this place, a distance of ten miles, was made in easy time owing to the oppressively warm weather; for my only aim was to reach my destination in season to meet my lecture appointment. Found the farmers along the route still working out their taxes on the public roads, which were greatly in need of attention. Speaking to them as I passed along I found that they looked rather curiously at the strange horse and rider, doubtless wondering whence we came and whither we were bound.

Addressed my Lancastrian audience in the Methodist Episcopal Church in· the evening, Captain G. S. Remington introducing.

Early in the morning I had found, upon going to the stable, that *Paul* was badly cut, and there was much speculation as to how and by whom the injury was done; but it was generally conjectured that he had had a battle with a horse belonging to the landlord, during the night. This horse, which was a large and powerful stallion, had recently been shod, so that in the matter of equipment he had a decided advantage over " *Paul Revere,*" who was possibly not averse to celebrating the anniversary of the Battle of Bunker Hill.

The day following my arrival at Lancaster being Sunday, Captain Remington called for me in the morning, and I accompanied him to the Presbyterian Church.

As we passed along on our way to church, I had a good opportunity to see this little town on Cayuga Creek, and the added advantage of a personal account of the place from one of its residents. Like all towns adjacent to a large city, Lancaster has a certain air of independence, and unmistakable signs of con- tact with greater forces; and besides its pretty homes, some of them the out-of-town retreats of Buffalo business men, it has its share of industrial enterprises.

Altogether, it is a pretty little neighbor of which any city might be proud, and which in its peace-loving way is very sensible in standing off at a distance from its busier sister. A few minutes by rail can take its thousand and a half inhabitants "to town," where they find the best that the great stores provide; and a ride of a few minutes more brings them out of the noise to their own quiet haven.

It is hard to realize a more delightful and thor- oughly restful existence than that found in suburban villages, where the influences of active forces are felt, but where they cannot disturb the even tranquillity. They seem to illustrate the "golden mean" which Horace recommends, and I find that it is always pleasant to reach such places and hard to leave them.

THE ROAD TO BUFFALO.

CHAPTER XI.

AN hour's ride from Lancaster, on the morning of the nineteenth, brought to view the motley array of chimneys and towers that overtop the "Queen City of the Lakes." While making my way towards them, and receiving first impressions, my attention was attracted by a brigade drill on the parade ground, which I halted to witness. This was the first instance during my journey in which I had encountered any considerable body of military men, with the exception of the Grand Army procession at Utica, on Memorial Day. The marching and manœuvres evinced close attention to tactics and excellent discipline, and the equipment of officers and men reflected much credit upon the Empire State, which has every reason to be proud of these her citizen-soldiers.

Drill over, I rode on into Buffalo, and, soon after registering at the Tift House, had the pleasure of meeting Major John M. Farquhar, who introduced me to my audience at St. James Hall in the evening.

Major Farquhar is a comrade, prominent in G. A. R. circles, and was then commander of the leading

187

post of the city. From him I learned something of the changes which had taken place since my last visit here, and which I was desirous to see as much of as circumstances would allow. Buffalo has a peculiarly rich history, and, like the old towns of the Mohawk Valley, the romantic view which Indian life and love have given.

Near here the arrogant Eries held their councils, and deliberated upon the downfall of their powerful neighbors of the Five Nations; who, in turn, ruined and almost exterminated them. The chronicles tell us that the Iroquois, coming by invitation to engage in friendly contest on the hunting-ground of the Eries, soon discovered the real intent of the wily "Cats," who were jealous of the renown of their red brothers. Failing in the games they had themselves proposed, and blind with rage, they saw their tolerant guests depart with the trophies of victory. No sooner were they out of sight than a council of war was held, and a decision to conquer them agreed upon. The war bonnets were donned, the dog sacrificed, and every preparation made for a raid into the enemy's country; but a Seneca woman who had been taken prisoner by the Eries some years before, apprised the great chiefs of her nation of the intended attack.

In this way the Eries were in turn surprised and defeated in their last game with their rivals. Only a few of their warriors were left to bear the hateful news to the women and old men who were waiting in the wigwams: and these with their allies, terribly punished as they had been in the encounter, were driven by their infuriated enemies beyond the Mississippi. The Senecas, who proudly called themselves the western gate-keepers of the " Long House," made a settlement near Buffalo, to which they gave the musical name of Te-you-seo-wa, the place of basswood, having found there huts covered with basswood bark, the remnants of some lately abandoned village. This settlement was not as near the lake-front as the city now is, but was cautiously laid out farther back from shore to prevent surprise. Here the young braves found a favorite hunting-ground, and were wont to conceal themselves near the salt springs that bubble up from the border of the creek, to await the buffaloes, which came there in herds. There has been some dispute as to the naming of the city, and the possibility of the American bison having frequented this part of the country, but it is generally believed that herds of these herbivorous animals did graze on Eastern soil, and that the attacks of carnivorous beasts and the constant warfare waged against them by the Indians drove them to the Western plains.

Nearly two centuries ago, when the site of the present city was still a wilderness through whose tangled labyrinths Indian eyes peered out over the gleaming waters of the lake, La Hontan penetrated these western wilds, and suggested to his sovereign the building of a fort here, as a safeguard against the Iroquois.

We see almost instinctively the scenes which he saw as we follow him through lake and stream—the great falls sparkling beneath an August sun, their wild surroundings unmarred and untrodden save by moccasined feet; the rapids and then the river, to whose current, farther up, he trusted his boat.

But it was not until long after this that the sound of the woodman's axe was heard in the forests at the foot of Lake Erie, when the pioneer had come to make his home, and to lay the foundation of a future city.

One after another crude cabins were raised, and in turn were replaced by more comfortable houses, so that in 1813 the settlement was large enough to make quite a bonfire for the British and their dusky allies. The events which took place at Buffalo, connected with this war, were singularly exciting; and, although there were brave hearts and stout arms ready to defend their country, we cannot but regret the peculiar circumstances which led to the general havoc here.

Historians have gleaned such glowing descriptions from those who were either witnesses or participants in these stirring scenes, that we cannot fail to be moved by them.

The night surprise, in the woods, near Black Rock, when the American troops were suddenly greeted by ambushed Britons: the rout which followed when the terrified horsemen dashed back in retreat through the ranks of the infantry, demoralizing them in turn, is so vividly drawn that it has the reality of later times. Afterwards when the alarmed people heard the cry that the British were coming, and we see them in confused masses trying to escape with their household goods, we sympathize with their terror as they saw in the distance the dreaded Indian jogging towards them with club and hatchet.

It was then that Job Hoysington, who was with one of the retreating parties, lingered behind his companions, saying that he would have " one more shot at the Red Skins." He evidently did have the coveted chance, and so did the enemy, for when the snow melted in the spring the brave fellow was found with his empty musket at his side, and a bullet through his brain. The work of vengeance had been completed with the scalping-knife. At the corner of Main and Niagara streets an old twelve-pounder stood. As the imposing column of British infantry were advancing upon the town, a patriotic citizen had the gun mounted and two shots fired into the ranks. He afterwards met the enemy with a flag of truce—a handkerchief tied to his cane—and requested a halt.

This was granted, and a parley begun, while the townspeople were escaping.

The firing of the houses and the plundering of them by the Indians followed. Buffalo rose, however, from her ashes full of new life and ambition, and much improved in appearance. Her firesides were again the scene of happy security, and her women, lately fugitives, fleeing in terror from fire and sword, were again the social inspirations of a thriving community. More than this, they were contributing to the enterprises of the city, for in 1821 between three and four thousand yards of cloth were woven in the homes of Buffalo!

The Erie Canal being completed in 1822, and commerce beginning in earnest, no doubt took away from the importance of the spinning-wheel and loom, for these busy little machines of the past have been stored away in the garrets long enough to make them well-seasoned relics. Housewifely attention at this time had to be turned to the management of larger establishments, for Buffalo had far outgrown her infancy, and was assuming certain new conceits in architecture, although she has never equalled the splendor of other large cities in her public buildings. The new City and County Hall approaches more nearly to the modern idea, and is very attractive within and without. It is built of Maine granite in the form of a double Roman cross, and is surmounted by a lofty tower bearing four symbolic figures. With the increase of canal and railroad traffic, the building of the immense grain elevators, which are a striking feature of Buffalo, was commenced.

Their number and size have been increased to such an extent that they almost make a town in themselves and are capable of accommodating eight million bushels of grain. The incessant work of storing and transferring is carried on about these wooden giants day after day, sometimes to the extent of more than three million bushels, while, at their feet, boats come and go in the great commercial game of "give and take." There is every facility for carrying on a trade of this kind, for Buffalo River is navigable for more than two miles from its mouth, which is protected by breakwaters which form an excellent harbor, while there is a water-front on the lake and the Niagara River five miles long. In 1869, the United States Government began the construction of an outside harbor, by building a breakwater 4000 feet long fronting the entrance of the Buffalo River.

Overlooking Buffalo River stand the office buildings whence come the calculating and controlling influences that keep in " clock work " order this mart where grain is " received, transferred, stored and forwarded with greater dispatch than in any other port of the country." Beyond these, in the heart of the city, are the retail and wholesale stores, where not only Buffalo finds her wants supplied, but numberless sister towns; and owing to her close proximity to the great coal region of Pennsylvania, she has very cheap fuel, which, no doubt, is a convenient item when a "cold wave" comes across the lake. Her iron works, reputed to be the largest in the country, add to her general good fortune by putting within easy access the necessary stoves.

Besides all this material comfort, the climate is extremely healthful, and the location of the city such as to make clean, wide streets a possibility.

There are several of these lined with handsome residences, and adorned with parks, which are wisely thought to be an indispensable luxury.

In the midst of the business hurry there are several quiet corners where one may quench his thirst for knowledge, and where master-thinkers lend their potent influence. One of these is the Grosvenor Library, the munificent gift of one of Buffalo's pioneers. It is admirably arranged for convenience and comfort, and has a pleasant outlook over a little park between Washington and Main streets. The Library of the Young Men's Association, although containing nearly twice as many volumes as the Grosvenor, is not so largely frequented, but is, nevertheless, a great resort for readers. There are also a number of smaller libraries, where eager minds may have their fill of books.

Here and there about the city one finds the familiar evidences of Christian thought and work in the beautiful tower-capped churches, each with its own

varied attractions. St. Paul's Cathedral—Episcopalian—a handsome structure of brownstone, ivy-grown
and picturesque, from whose walls in summer comes
the sound of birds, lies almost centrally among a hundred others, and not far away is the Roman Catholic
house of worship, the dignified bit of Gothic architecture which they have named St. Joseph's.

One of my favorite haunts here is the quiet, carpetless
" Historical Rooms," from whose walls the Indian warriors who helped make Buffalo's history look down in
unchanging stolidity. Not least among these is Red
Jacket, who forms such a striking figure in the city's
traditions. An amusing incident which his picture
recalls is that of Lafayette on his return from his Western tour in 1824. Among the preparations that were
being made for his reception was the guarding, by an
especial committee, of their "aboriginal lion," who
was a trifle too fond of his " firewater " and who was
to be the leading orator of the day. When the appointed time arrived, so the story goes, the sachem
was led upon the platform in all his conscious dignity.
A long conversation between him and the great
Frenchman followed, through an interpreter, whom
Red Jacket employed upon formal occasions; in the
course of which the Indian complimented the General
upon his youthful appearance. " Time has left you a
fresh countenance, and hair to cover your head," said
he, " while as for me—see ! " and he took off the scarf
that was wound about his own bald crown. This
provoked a laugh among the spectators who knew
that Lafayette wore a wig. When Red Jacket was
made aware of the fact, he added with ready wit that

he too might supply himself with a new head of hair by the aid of a scalping-knife!

Everything upon the walls and in the cases has been donated by private individuals, as the society has not yet been able to make valuable purchases, but there is enough already to make this treasure-house of the past interesting. Relics from pioneer times figure largely; among the rest, arrow-heads and tomahawks, pipes and belts of wampum, adding to the odd collection, and suggesting all manner of horrors to those who delight in Indian history.

"Forest Lawn," the place which Buffalo has selected for her dead, is a most lovely spot, the loveliest of its kind between Brooklyn's Greenwood and Chicago. Everything that art could do in the arrangement of shrub and flower has been added, and stands as a tribute to those who are "lying low" and as a witness to the faithful thought of the living. It is only one of the beautiful tokens of devotion which one sees, from the simple epitaph in a country grave-yard in the East to the solitary resting-place, high in some tree-top of the West, where our Red Brother "sleeps his last sleep."

Adjoining the Cemetery are a few acres of woodland that have been set aside for a kind of park. On warm summer days those seeking rest and pleasure, come to pay their respects to Dame Nature, who makes herself very attractive here. But this is only one, and a comparatively small one, of the various resorts where tired humanity may drop its burden, and roam at will. So Buffalo has her grave and her gay side, and her business side, which is neither grave nor gay, making their different impressions on the traveller's

10

eye, and combining, as a whole, in a very pleasing effect. She has made and will make some very striking changes, as all cities of consequence do; but changes worthy of the "Queen City of the Lakes," who, although she may have to relinquish her title to some outstripping sister, may always hold her head high with conscious importance. She is still the third city in the State of New York in point of population.

CHAPTER XII.

BUFFALO TO CLEVELAND.

𝔉𝔬𝔯𝔱𝔶-𝔣𝔬𝔲𝔯𝔱𝔥 𝔇𝔞𝔶.

North Evans Hotel,
NORTH EVANS, NEW YORK,
June 23, 1876.

IT had been my intention to leave the "Queen City" on the afternoon of the twenty-first, but I was delayed by my advance agents, who required more time to arrange the preliminaries of my lectures between Buffalo and Cleveland. Babcock went forward to Dunkirk, Farrington to Erie, while it was decided that my brother should accompany me as far as Angola. There were other reasons too, for a longer sojourn at Buffalo, as it was here I met my wife for the last time during my journey, and we had decided that it would be impracticable to meet again before my return from San Francisco. While I anticipated a pleasant and uninterrupted journey, she had some misgivings as to my ride across the Plains, and tried at the last to dissuade me, but I was sanguine of the outcome and thoroughly determined to continue, at any odds, a journey so delightfully begun. . At eight o'clock, therefore, on the morning of the twenty-second, I returned the parting salute of my wife and friends, and rode away. Turning into North Division street, I went out to Main, down Main to Ohio, and out Ohio to the Buffalo Road. Soon after passing the city limits, I saw Lake Erie, and leaving the highway rode down to the beach and into the water, giving *Paul* his first drink from the great inland sea, along whose shores we were to spend several days, and in which I and my faithful friend would doubtless quench our thirst many times. After this little diversion I pushed forward for thirteen miles and a half, which brought us to Lake View. After stopping here a few moments I rode on to North Evans. In this little village of something over a hundred inhabitants, my peace was in no wise disturbed and I was able to pass the day in comparative seclusion, thinking over the three days at Buffalo and anticipating the journey to Cleveland.

Forty-fifth Day.

Angola House,
ANGOLA, NEW YORK,
June Twenty-fourth.

The ride from North Evans to Angola was most delightful, carrying me as it did, along the shore of Lake Erie, which for the most part was plainly seen from the turnpike. The exhilarating breeze from over the water was in pleasing contrast to the intense heat which was felt in Central New York, and I found my appetite sharpening under its brisk influence. The eye had a continual feast of lake and field stretching off on either side, and as I rode along enjoying their diverse beauties, my only regret was that I had no companion at this time with whom I might share the pleasure.

To my right lay the shining lake, reflecting every change of cloud and sky; in front the Shore Road, and to my left as far as the eye could reach, rich green fields returning the salutation of sunny June. Easy travelling brought me into Angola in the early morning, as it is only six miles from North Evans. Here an unfortunate circumstance is identified with the name of the town, owing to a serious railroad disaster that occurred some years ago, in which many lives were lost; but one's attention is easily diverted from such thoughts upon entering the town. Several manufactories give it a wide-awake tone, and keep a good share of its five hundred inhabitants busy.

A small stream, known as Big Sister Creek, runs through the place and thence winds its way to the lake, three-quarters of a mile distant. This "Big Sister" adds a pretty touch to the matter-of-fact little village, while its pebbly bed is a charmed spot for young Angolans. Soon after my arrival here, J. S. Parker, formerly of Northern New York, called to see me, and I discovered that he knew many of my old acquaintances in St. Lawrence County. An hour was spent in pleasant conversation with him, during the course of which boyhood days at Gouverneur and along the Oswegatchie were discussed. I strolled about town in the afternoon, looking for "characteristics," and in the evening lectured in the Town Hall, the introduction being made by Leroy S. Oatman.

Forty-sixth and Forty-seventh Days.

Eastern Hotel,
DUNKIRK, NEW YORK,
June 25 & 26.

The road between Angola and Dunkirk led me
through one of the most picturesque and productive
counties of the State, which at this time promised well
for the haymakers who were busy in their ripened
fields. Hitherto the successive and varied scenes
along my route had in turn won my admiration, from
the pleasant ride across Massachusetts and over the
Berkshires to the Mohawk Valley and Western New
York, but these grain fields in their golden harvest-
time and the glimpses of the lake which the tortuous
course of the road now and then afforded, were certainly as lovely as anything I had seen thus far.
I had noticed that the haying season was well
advanced when I was passing through Central New
York, but owing to the retarding influence which a
large body of water always exerts over vegetation, it
had been delayed here. Fourteen miles through this
pretty section of Erie and Chautauqua counties
brought me to Dunkirk, where I lectured at Columbus
Hall in the evening, and was introduced to my
audience by Rev. J. A. Kummer. The following
day being Sunday, I had another opportunity of
meeting this gentleman, as he kindly accompanied me
in the morning to the Methodist Church, of which he
was pastor. During the services, in which I found
myself very much interested, there was an opportune
moment to study a character which I found to be a
thoroughly original one. Mr. Kummer was very

A JUVENILE PICNIC.

enthusiastic about the building of a new church which was much needed, and had been trying to fire his parishioners with the zeal which he himself felt. On this particular morning he made an appeal for co-operation and funds, and then asked for a generous offering. The good people of the congregation had hardly warmed to the subject, and their response was rather feeble. Another collection was made with somewhat better results, but still the amount was not raised by half. At last Mr. Kummer, who no doubt believed that the end justified the means, faced his people and said playfully, yet with evident determination, "Now I am going to order the doors bolted, that none may leave the house until this matter is settled!" In less than ten minutes the two thousand dollars necessary was obtained by donation or subscription, and the zealous clergyman looked down upon his people in happy approval. The scene was the most unusual one of the kind which I had ever witnessed, and I was tempted to applaud the generalship which won the situation. Dr. Kummer afterward gave me quite a lively description of his field, in which he had become much interested.

Lying on rising ground just within a little bay, at whose western extremity a lighthouse stands, Dunkirk forms a natural port of refuge in ·bad weather, and although in comparison with Buffalo its commercial importance seems rather insignificant, there is quite a brisk trade carried on by ship and by rail. Three lines centre here, connecting it with the East and West, and with the coal and oil regions of Pennsylvania, while the incoming and outgoing vessels are continually plying back and forth with their valuable cargoes.   In fact, as I soon discovered, my clerical friend was not too severe in demanding a sum for his new church which the people must have been well able to contribute.

Forty-eighth Day.

Minton House,
WESTFIELD, NEW YORK,
June Twenty-seventh.

Continued on the Shore Road from Dunkirk, having left that city at ten o'clock in the morning. While stopping a few minutes for dinner at Fredonia, a pretty little village three miles from Dunkirk, I saw for the first time during my journey quite extensive vineyards. The region is famous besides for its garden seeds, hence the people have their share of fruit and vegetables. Found the farmers of this entire section largely engaged in fruit culture, which seems to be a very successful enterprise. Apples and grapes are sent away to other points, and no doubt supply in a measure the breweries and distilleries of Dunkirk. In looking at the handsome vines already borne down by heavy burdens, the thought occurred to me of the currupt uses to which they would be put, and the havoc they would bring into human lives. The great bunches, not yet ripe, but promising a splendid harvest, looked tempting enough to one who had only seen them on fruit stands, or in market thrown together in unartistic confusion.

Reached Westfield in the evening, having made twenty-two miles for the day. Owing to my late

arrival, I saw very little of the place, but understand that it has quite large manufacturing interests,
a lively trade, two good schools for its young people:
and that unfailing sign of prosperity—a newspaper.
I recalled here, another Westfield, many miles away in
Massachuetts, which I passed early in May. The two
places appeared as unlike as possible, which was due,
no doubt, to one being in the "Bay," and the other
in the "Empire" State, which some travellers will
concede makes quite a difference.

Forty-ninth Day.

Haynes House,
NORTH-EAST, PENNSYLVANIA,
June Twenty-eighth.

Rode away from Westfield at ten in the morning,
halting just beyond the village at the pretty home of
W. N. Allen, where I passed a very pleasant half-
hour. While looking after the interests of a large
farm, Mr. Allen and his family were very much
interested in art matters, and showed me several valuable paintings which they had recently purchased.
I was delighted to find such refinement and taste, for
one is apt to believe that where people are not in
direct intercourse with congenial elements, they are
apt to lose their interest in the arts. As I looked
over their well-kept acres, and model buildings, I
thought of the influence such lives must exert over
the community in which they are passed. On my
way toward North East, I passed again through a fine
fruit region, stopping for dinner at a little hamlet
known as State Line.

OCEAN TO OCEAN ON HORSEBACK.

At first the prospects for the "inner man" looked rather doubtful, as I came up to the solitary State Line House, but a few moments' search brought me to the landlord, who was hoeing in a cornfield, and my wants were soon supplied. By five o'clock I was riding into the borough of North-East, where I found a number of people awaiting me. Upon dismounting, I learned that I was announced to lecture in the Town Hall that evening. This was a surprise, but I was ready to comply. The village band escorted me after supper to the hall, taking a position in front of the audience, and giving us "Hail Columbia" before, and "The Sword of Bunker Hill" after the lecture. The hall was so crowded that many were compelled to stand, and if hearty applause is an evidence of satisfaction, I may consider my effort to entertain the North-Easters a success. Captain Bronson Orton, a lawyer of the place, made the introduction, and I afterwards had a chat with him about experiences in Georgia, as he was with Sherman's army during its march from Atlanta to the Sea, and was quite familiar with many of its incidents. I too had followed the great strategist through that State, although in a very different capacity; it having been my lot to drop into the rear of his conquering legions during my escape from Southern prisons. The trying circumstances which I passed through, when I evaded the guard at Sylvania, the cautious tramps by day, and vigilance by night, in the friendly swamps, came back after the intervening twelve years, with all the vividness of yesterday. I related my experiences with the negroes and

A COTTAGE ON THE HILLSIDE.

meeting with good old March Dasher, who led me rejoicing into the Federal camp.

None of the events of those exciting days escaped my memory, and the chance of talking them over, with one of the men who had been with Sherman, was a rare pleasure. In the course of our conversation, we touched upon Captain Orton's present home, which is in a very pretty corner of the "Keystone" State, and which apparently has reached the golden mean between business and pleasure. Its residence portion suggests ideal comfort, while its office-buildings and stores are built upon a substantial and convenient plan.

Fiftieth Day.

Reed House,
ERIE, PENNSYLVANIA,
June Twenty-ninth.

Upon my arrival at Erie, I was pleasantly surprised to find a letter from Colonel F. H. Ellsworth, proposing to make me his guest at the Reed House during my stay in that city. I gladly availed myself of his kind invitation, and although my time there was necessarily short, I had, through the thoughtful interest of my host, every opportunity to see the city, and to hear something of its development.

Through Erie, Pennsylvania comes in contact with the great commercial interests of the Lakes, and although she only holds a small share of the valuable shore line, there is every advantage for reaping a large benefit. The harbor is most perfect, being protected by a strip of land known as "Presque Isle," and which, long before the persistent waves wore away its southern end, was connected with the mainland. Two lighthouses stand at its entrance, and guide the night traveller to one of the prettiest ports in this part of the country, while from the bluffs on which the town is built shine myriads of answering lights. The streets are wide and regular and lead to many handsome homes, which they say will bear comparison with the finest on the Lakes. Several parks relieve the monotony of brick and stone, and add to the sightliness of the place.

Besides her present importance as representative of her State on the great inland seas, Erie has had her share on the page of history since 1795; among her proudest annals being the departure from her port of Oliver Hazard Perry, who went in 1813 to meet the English in the splendid naval action which has made his name famous. There are many memorials of this engagement among the city's relics, which bring back the reality of those stirring times more forcibly perhaps than the volumes describing them.

Like Buffalo, Erie's leading enterprises are her iron works, where stoves, machinery and steam engines are made. Large quantities of coal and petroleum, the contributions from Pennsylvania, are sent here for shipment, and form a good share of the varied products which make their way through the large water channels to different parts of the United States. Her educational system is excellent and there are nearly half a hundred public schools, which offer quite good advantages to the children who help make her population of nearly twenty-five thousand. Erie undoubtedly has a bright future before her, which her rapid increase in population since 1870 predicts, and she may, in a measure, balance the power in the opposite corner of the State, where the "City of Brotherly Love" reigns supreme.   Having seen so much of the place as time would allow, and heard its story from those who knew it best, I ended the day by lecturing at the Academy of Music, Hon. C. B. Curtis introducing.

Fifty-first Day.

Farm House,
SWANVILLE, PENNSYLVANIA,
June Thirtieth.

Passed a very busy morning at Erie attending to business correspondence with advance agents, making notes, and with the assistance of Mr. Farrington brought my scrap-book up to date. I called also upon a few old acquaintances whom I had known in the East, and whose faces were a welcome surprise at this stage of my journey. The editor of the Erie *Dispatch* called after dinner and spent an hour with me in a general discussion of the incidents of my trip since leaving Boston, which had been, however, more pleasant than exciting. In this way the afternoon slipped by, and it was not until five o'clock that I found myself ready to leave Colonel Ellsworth's hospitable roof. Had I not been fully determined to make some headway before night, the cordial request of my host that I stay longer with him might have dissuaded me at the last from starting so late, but I resisted the inclination, and having bade good-bye to my newly-made friends put spurs to *Paul*, who soon carried me far beyond the city limits on the road to

Swanville. I had long since learned that in a case of this kind, the charms of hospitality, like those of Circe, were fatal to the interests of him who heeded. Made the eight and a half miles to Swanville in fair time, and was soon settled for the night at the home of John Joseph Swan, an old resident and pioneer, after whom the hamlet is named.

Fifty-second Day.

Farm House,
SWANVILLE, PENNSYLVANIA,
July First.

Was compelled to remain in this place two days on account of my lecture appointment for Girard, and was singularly fortunate in having cast my lot with the Swans, who were untiring in their efforts to make my stay agreeable. The head of the family was eighty-three years old and quite patriarchal in appearance. From him I learned something of their military record, which reaches over quite an extended period of our country's history, and which makes a noble background for the peace and comfort they now enjoy. Mr. Swan's father was a captain of militia in pioneer days, and his son Andrew was a lieutenant-colonel of cavalry during the late war. He was a participant himself in the war of 1812, and both he and his father were pensioners. In fact they have grown up with the country, having shared its trials and its triumphs. Mr. Swan was one of the earliest settlers in Erie County, and although more than half a century had passed since he had settled there, this veteran still remembered and vividly described the scenes and events of those stirring times. He saw the first steamer launched on the lake and said it was regarded as an evil omen by the Indians, who called it "The Devil's Canoe" and who ran frightened from the shore at its approach. His stories were most amusing, and their personal narration gave them a freshness which was untiring. While I was with these people, I had the pleasure of meeting Miss Eliza Swan, a talented daughter of the family, who had just returned from Paris, where she had been studying under Jules Le Fevre, the well-known painter. Among her better productions I was especially pleased with her portrait from life of an old man, for which she was awarded a medal by Peter Cooper.

Fifty-third Day.

Central House.
GIRARD, PENNSYLVANIA,
July Second.

Took a walk with Mr. Swan over his farm in the morning, looking at his stock and grain and quietly admiring the thrift and enterprise everywhere apparent. The comfort and refinement of these country homes had made a strong impression, and I became quite enthusiastic over the American farmer. My host took especial pleasure in showing me the changes which half a century had wrought upon his premises, and which certainly were surprising. It was difficult to realize that the fields which we were viewing had, within the memory of my companion, been transformed from a wilderness to cultivated acres. While strolling over the farm, the sky became clouded and by noon a torrent of rain deluged Swanville. Owing to this caprice of the elements, I was unable to leave until three o'clock in the afternoon. Made the six miles and a half between the two places in easy time. As I rode into town I was greeted by the Girard Brass Band, which, while it amused me, rather surprised *Paul*, who during our " triumphal procession " to the Central House did a little " dancing," greatly to the delight of the onlookers.

After lecturing at the Town Hall in the evening, where I was introduced by Jacob Bender, editor of the *Cosmopolite*, I was serenaded at my hotel by the indefatigable band, which certainly made me feel welcome. I was sorry that the limitations put upon my time by appointments ahead allowed me so small an opportunity to meet the people, and get a better idea of their occupations. I should have liked to visit the lumber and brick yards, which are the chief enterprise, but was obliged to content myself with only a " cursory glance," as our newspaper friends say. The soil of the region is almost entirely composed of clay, and is thus peculiarly adapted to the manufacture of brick.

Fifty-fourth Day.

Fisk House,
ASHTABULA, OHIO,
July Third.

A bright sun and clear blue sky gave promise of an exceedingly pleasant day, as I seated myself in the saddle at Girard at eight o'clock.

Before leaving I bade good-bye to Mr. Farrington, who had been with me from Boston, but who now found it necessary to return to his home at Elmira, New York, owing to business interests there. I regretted exceedingly his retirement, as he had rendered invaluable service in connection with my lectures, and had been a most genial and companionable fellow-traveller, whenever circumstances brought us together along the route.

I found the people everywhere engaged in preparations for the Centennial Fourth, which, as it was to be one of our greatest holidays, was to be celebrated with unusual enthusiasm. Owing to the excitement which prevailed, and to the fact that almost every man and woman was employed upon some active committee, I decided to waive my lecture at Ashtabula, and enter into the public demonstration. The Rev. Mr. Fisher, who had intended introducing me to my audience at this place, came to see me at the Fisk House soon after my arrival, and talked of the arrangements that were being made for the morrow. In the evening I called upon Rev. L. W. Day and had a chat with him about Ashtabula. The town is the capital of Ashtabula County, and lies at the mouth of a small river of the same name, in the midst of a good farming district. The principal products are wheat, maple sugar and those of the dairy. The chief interests of the town are its manufactures, which I understand are quite important.

As in all such towns, the population is varied. The combination of the farming and manufacturing elements gives a decidedly picturesque aspect.

Fifty-fifth Day.

Farm House,
NEAR PAINESVILLE, OHIO,
July Fourth.

This day has been indeed the greatest holiday in
the history of the United States. Such grand preparations and such lavish display have probably never
been witnessed before on this continent, and although
I chanced to be in a comparatively obscure corner of
the Republic, I found the prevailing sentiment as
deep as though I were in one of the great centres.
I doubt if there was sleep for anyone during the
preceding night, for the wildest excitement was manifested, and the dawn of the Centennial Fourth was
presaged by the booming of cannon, the blowing of
engine whistles, the ringing of bells and discharge of
firearms of every conceivable calibre and description.

The townspeople were stirring at an early hour, and
although I had found very little rest, I was in the
saddle by nine o'clock. A thunder-shower overtook
me about noon, thanks to the generous use of gun-
powder, and I took shelter under a tree, from whence I
was invited to dinner by Daniel Flower, a neighboring
farmer. With him and his family I passed a comfortable hour, and then moved forward in the direction of Painesville.

Toward evening I reined up in front of an invit-
ing-looking house—a feature which the traveller
soon learns to observe—and asked one of the farm
hands if Mr. Lee was at home. Before the man had
time to answer, a young girl came running down the

HAYING IN NORTHERN OHIO.

path toward the gate, saying, "Are you Captain Glazier?" I acknowledged that I was that humble person, whereupon Miss Lee asked me to dismount and "come right in," while Jack would take care of the horse. Her father and mother had gone to Cleveland in the morning, to celebrate the Fourth, and were expected back the same night. The little lady insisted upon my stopping overnight, and bustled about with all the importance of a housewife in preparing supper. I naturally felt some hesitation in accepting her invitation to remain all night, but she insisted that I be her guest, and made every effort to amuse me. After tea, I was ushered into the parlor, where my hostess soon joined me, saying that I was her "very first caller" and that she was going to entertain me "the best she knew how." Suiting the action to the word, she took her place at the piano, and began to play some national airs suitable to the occasion; but as the evening slipped away I began to feel the effects of the day's ride, and begged to be allowed to retire. This, however, the young lady seemed at first disinclined to do, asking me to wait for her father and mother, but finally I insisted as gently as possible; so she showed me to my room herself, wishing me a hearty good-night. Dawn was ushered in by the rattling of milk pans and the creaking of a pump under my window, so, knowing that further rest was out of the question, I dressed and went downstairs, where I met Mr. and Mrs. Lee. I found them very kindly people, and knew that their daughter had inherited from them her share of good nature. That odd little miss was up at the first cock-crow, and was waiting to bid me good-morning. As I was about to mount *Paul* after breakfast, she asked the privilege of a ride on him, and, bounding into the saddle, galloped down the road with the grace of an Indian. When she bade me goodbye at the gate, where her father and mother were standing to see me off, she asked me in her un-sophisticated way to remember her as my "Centennial girl," which I solemnly promised to do, and as I looked back from the road I could see her waving her handkerchief as a parting salute.

Fifty-sixth Day.

Farm House,
NEAR WICKLIFFE, OHIO,
July Fifth.

Starting rather late from Painesville, a town just beyond Mr. Lee's, and riding leisurely during the day, I found it necessary to keep to the road until dark, in order to place myself as near to Cleveland as possible, before halting. Reached Willoughby, the seat of a Methodist College, nineteen miles east of Cleveland, just before sundown, where I was tempted to stay over night, knowing that to ride farther would be gloomy and uninteresting, but in my eagerness to reach the "Forest City," towards which I had looked for several days, I pressed forward.

As there was no hotel at Wickliffe, I passed through the little hamlet of that name and secured lodgings at the farm house of Thomas Lloyd, an old settler of Lake County, and a very large land-owner. He told me the history of his pioneer life in this section of Ohio, and of his start in the pursuit of a fortune,

JUST OUT OF CLEVELAND.

221

which gave me a bit of the early history of Ohio from another standpoint. It may seem odd that during the "flying visits" which I sometimes paid to these small places, there was opportunity to hear anything about them, but country folk are accustomed to early rising, and as I learned the art, years ago, of waking with the birds, I very often joined my host, and had a chat with him before breakfast. The settlement near which I stayed overnight is six miles west of Willoughby, which brought me within thirteen miles of Cleveland. It boasts of nothing more than the necessary blacksmith shop and "store," and "looks up to" its big neighbor with due reverence. It lies in the fertile county of Lake, a northeastern corner of Ohio, measuring some two hundred and sixty square miles, of which a large portion is covered with forest, and whose surface is generally hilly or undulating.

CHAPTER XIII.

FIVE DAYS AT CLEVELAND.

FOUND a good night's rest at the quiet farmhouse of the Lloyds, on the night of the fifth, and after an early breakfast on the following morning called for my horse and started for Cleveland. On my way out, near Wickliffe, I overtook a troop of girls on their way to school. One of them, a bright-faced little maid, giving her name as Ettie Warren, and saying she was a granddaughter of Mr. Lloyd, asked me to accept a bouquet, which had no doubt been intended for her teacher. It was a mass of gay colors, which had been gathered from the home garden, and its huge proportions quite appalled me. However, I accepted it with mock gravity, and as she and her small companions kept beside me, I could overhear a whispered conversation of very secret import, which resolved itself into the question, "Do you like apples, mister?" I confessed my fondness for the fruit, and was soon the chagrined possessor of a pocketful of green ones, which this sunburned little daughter of Eve generously offered. Before riding into town I was obliged to consign these gifts to the roadside, but not without a certain guilty feeling, and sympathy for the cheated schoolma'am.

Passed through the village of Mentor, a pleasant little place six miles from Cleveland, the home of Hon· J. A. Garfield, then an Ohio Congressman.

Noting much excitement as I approached Euclid, I dismounted to learn the cause, and found it was due to a rumor that General Custer and his entire command had been massacred by Indians. The source of this information made it appear reliable, and yet comparatively few were disposed to believe it. My long association with the General during the War of the Rebellion led me to take the thought of his death very much to heart, although I was yet unwilling to credit what I had heard. At the Forest City House, whither I had been escorted by a delegation of G. A. R. friends, the truth of the report was discussed, and the deepest regret manifested, should such a fate have befallen the brave cavalryman.

In the evening I lectured at Garrett's Hall, where Major E. M. Hessler introduced me. Later, in behalf of a number of citizens, the Major proposed a banquet in my honor, but this I felt justified in declining, owing to imperative duties in connection with my journey. The rest of my time here was passed in looking about the city, and in talking with some of the " Forest City" people, who are pardonably proud of their home on Lake Erie. This part of the State was a great hunting-ground for the Indians in former days, who came to make war on the bear and beaver. They started eastward in the autumn and paddled down the lake, entire villages at a time, to the mouth of the Cuyahoga River, on whose banks they piled their birch canoes and then scattered through the neighboring forests. Returning in the spring to a small cabin which had been built near their landing-place by the Northwestern Fur Company, they disposed of their spoils, and when their business with their white brothers was over, re-embarked for their summer homes on the Maumee and Sandusky.

When General Moses Cleveland came with a surveying party in 1796 to lay out the site of the chief city of the "Reserve" for the Connecticut Land Company, the cabin of the fur-traders was still standing, but was in too dilapidated a condition to be of use. Two more cabins were therefore raised, one for the party, and the other for Job Stiles, and his wife Tabitha, who was housekeeper. When the plans were finished the woman of the settlement found herself the possessor of one city lot, one ten-acre lot, and one one hundred-acre lot, a donation from the directors and stockholders of the company, made no doubt in consideration of her services, and from the fact that she was the first white woman to take up her abode on the new ground. Two more gifts of the valuable land were made, one to Nathaniel Doane, the company's blacksmith, who had kept their pack-mules shod, and the other to James Kingsbury and his wife, the first who emigrated independently to the Reserve. Within eighty years the worth of this property had increased surprisingly, but the first owners had long since ceased to care for worldly goods, and the land had been resold many times. Buildings that would have astonished those early folk had replaced their simple cabins, and thousands of strange feet were treading in their old haunts.

For several years, in fact until the opening of the Ohio Canal in 1834, the population of Cleveland increased very slowly. A year after the survey, the homes "under the hill" along the right bank of the Cuyahoga had to be removed to the ridge, for even at that time fever and ague began to trouble the settlers. This disagreeable malady, wittily personified as "Ague-agueshakershake,"—the God of Lake Erie—was a continual bugbear and made yearly attacks upon the families. So widespread was the reputation it had gained that a stranger stopping at Buffalo, then a rival port, was told that if he went to Cleveland he "would not live over night." On the highlands the exposure was much less, and soon all the cabins were built there. Then they began to spread out along the ridge toward the east, in the direction of Euclid, following the line of the Euclid Road, which even then was a popular place on which to have a section and build. In 1801, the first well in Cleveland was dug on this thoroughfare, and was walled in with stones which the Indians had left from their wigwam fireplaces. Two years later Connecticut ceded her Western Reserve, which she had held under an old charter, to the General Government and the chief city transferred her allegiance to the new State of Ohio.

Gradually the settlement spread out into the surrounding country, where ambitious hamlets, having enjoyed their brief season of independence, ultimately cast their fortune with the larger city, and became a sharer in its triumphs. One of these, which had attained more importance than the rest, had started up on the opposite bank of the Cuyahoga, and assumed the bravado of a rival. Cleveland made several advances to her which were met with coolness, and at last both villages applied for charters; the one on the left bank receiving hers first and glorying in her new name of "Ohio City." Again Cleveland besought a conciliation and tried to persuade the independent little rival neighbor to change her name, and become one with her, but with ill success. As time wore on, however, population decreased on the left shore and increased on the right, and signs of union became apparent from the fact that "Ohio City" reached out to the southeast, while Cleveland met her half-way by extending toward the southwest. We are not sure how matters were arranged between the two rivals when the final step was taken, but at any rate it was a felicitous event, and now that the coveted neighbor has become the West Side, some Clevelanders find it difficult to determine which is the " better-half."

In those early days before the railroads reached her, this new Ohio town was obliged to look about for other means of transportation, and we hear of one of her pioneers establishing a boat yard in the woods a mile and a half from the lake. Here the engineer cut his timber and carried out his plan for the first boat built at Cleveland. The framework was raised in a clearing of the forest, from whence a rough road led to the water, and in this wild but convenient spot the schooner was finished, and ready to be introduced to the world as "The Pilot." The farmers of the surrounding country were invited to assist in the launching and accordingly came into town on the all-important day, with their oxen, to haul the craft down to the shore. The ceremony was greeted with resounding cheers, and Levi Johnson received his first congratulations from his fellow-townsmen. This was in 1814. He afterwards built a steamboat and gave it the name of one of his own characteristic traits, "Enterprise."

In 1816, although the itinerant preachers who had visited the place would scarcely have credited it, a church was organized and an Episcopalian form of worship established, which later grew into Trinity Church and Parish. Hitherto a bugle had called the people together when a clergyman appeared, and the most primitive services followed. On one of these occasions, well-known to those who lived in Cleveland when it was still a churchless community, Lorenzo Dow was announced to preach. He was an eccentric man and the place reputed to be a bad one. His congregation, who were waiting under a large oak, did not recognize the solitary figure approaching in his shirt sleeves, and, as he quietly sat upon the ground in their midst, and his head dropped upon his knees in silent prayer, one in the crowd enquired if he were Lorenzo Dow. Some one answered, "Yes," but another irreverently said in an undertone, "It's the devil." Dow overheard the remark, and rising, preached to his hearers such a sermon on Gehenna that they never forgot it, or him.

In 1821, the "Academy" became an institution, and began a course of instruction upon a very liberal basis, giving its pupils the full course for four dollars a term, and separate branches for much less.

In the year 1836 the city was incorporated, and with the new honor seems to have looked to the improvement of her appearance. The public square, which had previously been little more than a grazing-place for cows, was seriously considered as a possible ornament, and was graded and made more attractive, until now it bears little resemblance to the common on which the irrepressible Indian, "Omic," breathed his last. It has changed its name since then, and has become "Monumental Square," from the marble statue of Commodore Perry, which adorns its southeastern corner. A good view of the liveliest part of the city can be had from here, and from early morning until late at night there is a continuous stream of people passing through it.

Superior street, which forms its southern boundary, is lined with retail stores, and its fine buildings and neat pavements hardly suggest the indifferent houses and plank road of forty years ago. Ontario is another busy thoroughfare running north and south, and bisecting the square. Where it begins, at Lakeside Park, it is lined with private residences, but beyond the square it develops into a genuine work-a-day business street. In 1813 there was a small stockade on the lake shore just below it, for Cleveland was a depot for supplies, and was waiting to give a warm reception to the English. Most of the public buildings are on or near the square—the Post Office, Custom House, City Hall, and several of the churches. Not far away is the library of the Young Men's Literary Association, which has had a singularly favored career. Established in 1845 upon a very unpretentious basis in the Case Building, it was soon given a perpetual lease by the owner, and later received a large sum of money for its extension and support from a son of Mr. Case. The Public Library

ON THE SHORE OF LAKE ERIE.

is located in the old High School Building on Euclid avenue and has 26,000 volumes in circulation. The Board of Trade is another of the city's time-honored institutions, having been founded in 1848. It is now in the Atwater Building on Superior street.

Euclid avenue, which from its rustic popularity in pioneer days, came to bear the proud distinction of being one of the handsomest streets in the world, stretches off eastward from the square, for four and a half miles, until it reaches Wade Park, a beautiful spot, still shaded by the groves and forests which have been left from the wilderness. It was a gift from Mr. Wade, one of Cleveland's millionaires.

From this point the avenue continues for a mile and a half until it finds its terminus in Lake View Cemetery, a magnificent stretch of woodland overlooking the lake from a height of two hundred and fifty feet.

The avenue is in its entire length a feast of beauty. The homes that line it on either side are fine specimens of architecture, and the gardens surrounding them show a lavish devotion to the sweet goddess Flora. Thousands of people who are unable to leave town during the summer find a grateful change of scene here, and it so impressed Bayard Taylor that he bestowed upon it the splendid praise of calling it the most beautiful street in the world. Nor is its charm purchased at the expense of squalid surroundings, for the streets of Cleveland are well kept and almost all of its homes have their little gardens around them, while the tenement house is " conspicuous by its absence." In fact the people have chosen rather to sacrifice a trifle more to time and expense and less to space,

They have expanded and have built longer street-car lines in proportion.

The old eyesore of dilapidated huts and rubbish heaps along the river and lake shore was soon swept away after the railroads came, and a fine park substituted. The undertaking was a large one, but it proved to be well worth the labor and money expended upon it, and is now one of the city's chief adornments and one of her most delightful rendezvous.

The stranger, as he nears the "Forest City" wearied with his travels and sensitive to his surroundings, finds nothing to meet his curious gaze but a neat shore line on one side, and on the other the green slope of Lakeside Park, with its grottos and fountains, and an occasional suggestion of graveled walks. The top of the ridge is an excellent place whereon to take a morning stroll, and get a good breath of fresh air, and from this eminence the lines of the five railroads which centre here can be seen converging towards the Union Depot, where a large portion of the coal, petroleum and lumber is received that makes its way from distant points.

"The Flats" along the lake and river fronts are alive with business, and present a fascinating scene from some overlooking point. There are factories, ore docks and coal and lumber yards famous the country over, and water craft of every kind and size. One of the most important enterprises is that of the Cleveland Rolling Mill Company, whose buildings occupy thirty-two acres, and whose yearly pay-roll reaches more than $2,000,000. On the West Side is the Cuyahoga Steam Furnace Company, noted for having manufactured a patent horse-power cannon for the Government, and for having turned out the first locomotive in the West. The great Standard Oil Company, begun in the sixties and later developing into a stock company under its present name, is located here, and its cars, surmounted by the familiar white keg, are seen on almost all the railroads of the country.

Out from the river's mouth stretch two long piers, two hundred feet apart, which represent the final triumph of the engineer over the tides which have wrought such incessant mischief ever since a certain captain and his crew were delayed in the harbor of Cleveland sixty years ago by a sandbar. There is a lighthouse at the end of each pier, and one high up on the shore which was built by the Government in 1830 at a cost of $8,000.

Now, through this inviting gateway, large lake boats steam into port without hindrance, bringing with them the rich copper and iron ores of Lake Superior, the limestone of the Lake Erie Islands, and the miscellaneous products which they take up along their route. With these valuable cargoes, to which have been attributed much of her prosperity, Cleveland receives a large amount of coal from the mines of Ohio and Pennsylvania, having access to the latter through the Ohio Canal, which has been such an impetus to her growth.

On the other side of the river are her large Water Works, the incessant pumping of whose engines supplies this city of 140,000 inhabitants with water. The Reservoir lies upon the top of a cliff, and is a favorite resort in summer. From its crest a fine view of lake and river can be obtained, and if one were to allow his imagination a little freedom, this would be the most satisfactory place to get a retrospective view of Cleveland as it was to the pioneer. About here the Indians stayed unmolested long after they had sold their land to the white man, and across the river on the slope the first log cabin stood. The scene which takes its place is almost bewildering with its network of factories, lake and river craft and housetops. Here and there a dot of green rises above the buildings, betraying the presence of the elms and maples which have been jealously preserved and which are one of the characteristic beauties of the "Forest City."

During my stay here, nothing was more gratifying than a walk or ride through the broad streets in the shade of these trees. It made summer in the city something to stay for, and not something to run away from. There were many drives leading out beyond the limits daily frequented by pleasure-seekers, and inviting out-of-the-way places for those who were unable to go elsewhere. Beside these, the lake, though the shallowest in the chain and sometimes treacherous on that account, is a continual clarifier and beautiful to look upon. As for the old-time "God," and his attendant maladies, who tyrannized over the pioneer, they seem to have vanished, and now I venture to say there is no healthier city in the country than Cleveland and certainly none more attractive.

SUNDAY AT THE FARM.

CHAPTER XIV.

CLEVELAND TO TOLEDO.

Sixty-first Day.

Lampman House,
BLACK RIVER, OHIO,
July 11, 1876.

AT eight o'clock, my favorite hour for beginning a day's ride, I mounted *Paul* in front of the hotel at Cleveland, but before leaving the city I stopped at Major Hessler's office to hand him the proceeds of my lecture at Garrett's Hall, which were donated to the Soldiers' Monument Fund at Dayton. This brought me two very kind acknowledgments: one from General James Barnett, who forwarded the money, and the other from Rev. William Earnshaw, custodian of the Monument Fund. These letters, written in behalf of three thousand disabled veterans, amply satisfy me for any sacrifice I may have made, and are among my most prized possessions. General Barnett wrote as follows:

Headquarters
Post No. 1, *Department of Ohio, G. A. R.,*
CLEVELAND, *July* 12. 1876.

CAPTAIN WILLARD GLAZIER,

COMRADE: Through your unsolicited generosity I have the pleasure to acknowledge the receipt of the net proceeds of your lecture on

12

"Echoes from the Revolution," delivered in our city July 6, 1876, and by your direction have forwarded the amount to Chaplain William Earnshaw, President of the "Soldiers' Home Monument Fund," at Dayton, to assist in erecting a monument to the memory of the veterans who by the fortunes of war await the long roll at the National Military Home, and may your reward be no less than the love and gratitude of our unfortunate comrades.

By order of

GENERAL JAMES BARNETT, *Commanding.*

E. M. HESSLER, *Quartermaster.*

There are certain results following every undertaking which are looked upon either with gratification or dissatisfaction, and which, through side issues, very often assume the importance of those desired to be attained. The recollection of the splendid scenes through which I have passed, the people whom I have met, the cities I have visited, will be a lifelong satisfaction, but the opportunity to help perpetuate the memory of fellow-soldiers and to do others honor while they yet live, will be the most gratifying outcome of my journey. Knowing this, the following letter from Chaplain Earnshaw holds an important place among the papers of my correspondents.

National Soldiers' Home,
DAYTON, OHIO, *July* 27, 1876.

CAPTAIN WILLARD GLAZIER,

MY DEAR COMRADE: We have received, through Major E. M. Hessler, your generous donation to aid in erecting the Soldiers' Monument at the Home. You have the hearty thanks of three thousand disabled veterans now on our rolls; and a cordial invitation to visit us whenever it is your pleasure to do so. Again, we thank you.

Very respectfully,

WILLIAM EARNSHAW,
President Historical and Monumental Society

On leaving the city several gentlemen gave me the pleasure of their company for some distance, among

A COTTAGE IN THE WOODS.

them Alexander Wilsey, who before the war had been a scholar of mine back in Schodack, New York.

Meeting him was only one of many similar experiences, for here and there along my route I found old acquaintancès, whose faces I had never expected to see again.

After a ride of six hours, I rode into Black River and found it quite an enterprising village, but hardly suggesting its old position as the principal port in the county.

Sixty-second Day.

Huron House,
H U R O N , O H I O ,
July Twelfth.

Left the aspiring village of Black River or "Lorraine," as the inhabitants are disposed to call it, at nine o'clock, stopping at the Lake House, Vermillion, for dinner. The scenery is very attractive along the Lake Shore Road between Black River and Huron, and I followed it all day and for two or three hours after nightfall, covering a distance of twenty miles. My sense of the beautiful was somewhat dimmed, however, by the cloud of mosquitoes which beset my path, and which were hardly persuaded to part company at the hotel. There were nearly seven hundred people in Huron, and I must confess that upon entering the slumbering village I began to be generous in the hope that my attentive little tormentors would adopt the principle of equal distribution among the inhabitants. But for the rapacious mosquito the course of the traveller by night upon these highways is serene and uneventful, for, of all the hordes of wolves, wild-cats, buffaloes and panthers that made their homes about this part of the country in the times of the Indian, scarcely a vestige remains.

The race of the red man is becoming slowly exterminated, and his friends of the forest seem to be disappearing with him, while the white man and the mosquito fill their places. I am sure no one of average reason, especially our logicians of New Jersey, would deny that this is another proof of the survival of the fittest.

Although it was dark before I came into Huron, I could get a very good idea of its character, and had formed some notion of the place which was to shelter me. In 1848 it was spoken of as having been " formerly the greatest business place in the county," and this reputation, although it has not made it a Sandusky or a Cleveland, has left it a spark of the old energy.

Sixty-third Day.

West House,
SANDUSKY, OHIO,
July Thirteenth.

I was fortunate in having a comparatively short distance to travel between Huron and this city. It is only nine miles, and I did not start until two o'clock, allowing myself a two hour's easy gallop with the lake on my right all the way.

Along this shore more than a century ago, General Bradstreet, with three thousand men, sailed to the relief of Fort Junandat, while Pontiac, the great Ottawa warrior, was besieging Detroit. Reaching Fort Sandusky he burned the Indian villages there and destroyed the cornfields; passed on up to Detroit to scatter the threatening savages, and returning went into the Wyandot country through Sandusky Bay. To have attempted to ride alone on horseback in those days would have been a foolhardy, if not a fatal undertaking. Now the screech of an engine-whistle announced the approach of a train on the Lake Shore Road, the great wheels thundered by, and *Paul*, alert and trembling, was ready to dash away. How different it would have been in those old pioneer times! The horseman would have been the one to tremble then, his hand reach for his rifle, his eyes strained towards the thicket from whence the expected yell of the savage was to come.

Among the first proprietors of this section were the Eries. These were followed by the resistless Iroquois, and after them the Wyandots and Ottawas, who seem to have left the strongest impress upon the hills and valleys of Ohio. One of these tribes, the Wyandots, called the bay near which they built their wigwams Sæ-san-don-ske, meaning " Lake of the Cold Water," and from this the present name of the city comes. In the early days it was called Ogontz, after a big chief of that name who lived there before the year 1812. All about were rich hunting-grounds, which accounts for its having been chosen by the Indians in times of peace; and even now Sandusky is held to be one of the greatest fish-markets in America.

The place was bound to be attractive to the white man, and any one might have safely prophesied that a city would rise here. The ground slopes gradually down to the lake, the bay forms an ideal harbor, and looking off upon the boats and water, the eye rests upon a scene picturesque and striking.

My attention was called to Johnson's Island, which

was used for the confinement of Confederate officers during the late war. I learned that they were allowed the luxury of an occasional bath in the lake, under guard, of course, and in squads of a hundred men—a luxury which the boys in Libby and Charleston and Columbia would have thought "too good to be true."

Under the city are the limestone quarries, which furnish an inexhaustible supply of building material and which give an added distinction to this bright little city of the lakes.

On the evening of my arrival I spoke in Union Hall and was introduced by Captain Culver, who referred to my military record and the object of my lectures. Captain Culver is a comrade in the G. A. R. and was a fellow-prisoner at Libby and other prisons. He did much towards making my stay at Sandusky most agreeable.

Sixty-fourth Day.

Fountain House,
CASTALIA, OHIO,
July Fourteenth.

My Sandusky friend, Captain Culver, called at the West House for me soon after breakfast, and we spent the forenoon strolling about the city. I was shown the newly completed Court House, of which Sanduskians are very proud; met several of the officials and found much to admire. Left at five o'clock in the afternoon and by six had reached Castalia, five miles distant, which I soon found had something to boast of back of its classic name. As a stranger I

was of course immediately told of the wonders of the
" waters," which I learned form quite an attraction in
summer and keep the little place in a flutter of excitement.

Marshall Burton came in 1836 and laid out this
prairie town at the head of Coal Creek. Finding the
source of the stream in a cool, clear spring, now known
to be two hundred feet in diameter and sixty feet
deep, named the place "Castalia," from the famed
Greek fountain at the foot of Parnassus. The waters
of this spring are so pure that objects are plainly seen
through the sixty liquid feet, and they say that when
the sun reaches meridian, these objects reflect the
colors of the rainbow, which might suggest to Casta-
lians that the ancient sun-god, Apollo, favored the
western namesake of his Delphian fount. I met no
poets here, but possibly inspiration is not one of the
powers guaranteed. Indeed if it should treat devotees
of the Divine Art, as it does everything else that is
plunged into it, we should have petrified poets.

These petrifying qualities of the water, caused by the
combined action of lime, soda, magnesia and iron have
made the mill-wheels which turn in Coal Creek in-
capable of decay.

At a little distance from the town is a cave of quite
large dimensions, which was discovered accidentally
through a dog running into the opening in pursuit of
a rabbit. This cave I believe makes up the comple-
ment of natural attractions about the village. The
chief attraction, the social life of the people, cannot be
guessed at by the rapid glance of the traveller. But
even a short sojourn here is apt to be remembered
long and pleasantly. Ohioans are notably hospitable.

Sixty-fifth Day.

Ball House,
FREMONT, OHIO,
July Fifteenth.

I was awakened at twelve P. M. the previous night at Castalia by two villainous imps, who seemed determined to make an impression. Their evident object was " more rum," which to the credit of the landlord was not furnished them. Exasperated by this temperance measure, they attempted to enter the house, and finding the doors locked began a bombardment with fists and feet. This novel performance was kept up until the object of their wrath and his shot-gun appeared. Owing to this my ride of nineteen miles to Fremont was not as refreshing as it might have been.

As I approached the town I thought of President Hayes, who is so closely identified with it. Here he began the practice of law, and won such popularity, not only among his townsmen, but throughout the State, that in 1864, after a succession of honors, his friends were pushing him for Congress. In answer to a letter written from Cincinnati, suggesting that his presence there would secure his election, he said, " An officer fit for duty, who at this crisis would abandon his post to electioneer for Congress, ought to be scalped. You may feel perfectly sure that I shall do no such thing," and in a letter to his wife, written after he had heard of Lincoln's assassination, he expressed another sentiment quite as strong when he said : " Lincoln's success in his great office, his hold upon the confidence and affection of his countrymen, we shall all *say* are only second to Washington's. We shall probably *feel* and *think* that they are not second even to his."

Fremont of course is justly proud of the name and fame of Rutherford B. Hayes. Two years before he returned to his home, after refusing Grant's offer of an Assistant Secretaryship, but the people of Ohio were not satisfied with this. Their feelings were probably voiced by the words of a personal friend of Hayes, who said: "With your energies, talents, education, and address, you are green—verdant as grass—to stay in a country village." Soon afterwards, at the urgent and repeated requests of the people, he gave up his quiet life and once more entered the political arena, with results which the election of 1876 shows.

There were apparently many who were dissatisfied with the Nation's choice, but in Ohio, and especially where he was known personally, he was much beloved and admired. His uncle, Sardis Birchard, who died some years ago, leaving his property and fortune to his namesake, has given a park and a fine library to Fremont.

The town is on the Sandusky River, at the head of navigation, and has quite a brisk trade for a place claiming only a little over five thousand inhabitants.

Sixty-sixth Day.

Elmore House,
ELMORE, OHIO,
July Sixteenth.

My accommodations at the Ball House, Fremont, were quite in contrast with those placed at my dis-

posal at Castalia. I heard no stories of "mineral
springs" or wonderful freaks of Nature, but shall remember Fremont as the delightful little city where I
had two nights' sleep in one.

I began my day's journey at eight o'clock with
Elmore as the evening objective. Halted a few
moments at a hotel known in that locality as the Four-
Mile House. Took dinner at Hessville, where I remained until four o'clock in the afternoon and then
rode on to Elmore.

COUNTRY STORE AND POST OFFICE.

CHAPTER XV.

RDERED *Paul* and saddled him myself at Elmore, on the morning of July seventeenth. In fact it was my usual custom, while riding through the rural districts, to personally groom, feed and care for my horse, as I learned soon after leaving Boston that, unless I attended to his wants myself, he was most likely to be neglected by those in whose hands he was placed, and from a selfish standpoint, knowing also the importance of keeping him in the best possible condition, I never overlooked anything which was likely to add to his comfort.

On my way from Elmore, I stopped for lunch at a country grocery, hotel and saloon, four miles from this city. A small piece of bread, a bowl of milk, and a few crackers covered my refreshment at the " Jack of All Trades," as upon asking for a second piece of bread I was informed that I had just eaten the last in the house. There being no further appeal, I remounted and rode off in the direction of Toledo, where I lectured in the evening at Lyceum Hall, under the auspices of Forsyth Post, being introduced by Doctor

J. T. Woods, a surgeon of our Volunteer Army during the late war, and now an active comrade in the G. A. R.

Doctor Woods and I had a long and animated talk at the Boody House over old times, and especially of Custer, who was greatly admired by both of us, as he was by every one who knew anything of him. Doctor Woods had collected a number of articles referring to the General which he thought of especial interest, among others the following lines which seem to bear the very impress of Custer's martial spirit:

> "The neighing troop, the flashing blade,
>   The bugle's stirring blast.
> The charge, the dreadful cannonade,
>   The din and shout are past.
> No war's wild notes nor glory's peal
>   Shall thrill with fierce delight
> The breast that nevermore may feel
>   The raptures of the fight."

When our conversation turned upon Toledo, it became more cheerful. The city, after having survived many reverses of fortune, is now on the eve of rapid development, and can hardly be said to have a rival in Northern Ohio. The long and hard battle fought for the soil on which it now stands is almost forgotten, and instead of arousing the interest of the stranger with thrilling tales of massacre and war, the Toledoan now points to the emblems of peace.

Not so far away but that the patriotic citizen may become familiar with the place is the old battle-field of "Fallen Timbers," where "mad Anthony Wayne" brought the Indians to bay, and having conquered, pursued them for ten miles along the Maumee, until he reached Swan Creek, now in the centre of the town.

This battle is one of the most dramatic in the records of Indian warfare. It was at a time when the Wabash and Miami tribes had refused to accept any overtures from the Americans, and when they were determined to fight out their cause with the help of the British.

Knowing that pacific measures were then superfluous, and that the matter must be decided by war, Wayne at the head of a splendid support, marched to the Maumee, erected Fort Defiance at the junction of the Au Glaize, and then proceeded to a point where he knew the forces of the enemy were concentrated. The place was in every way favorable to the party in possession—the river on the left, heavy thickets on the right, and in front natural breastworks formed by fallen timbers, the result of a tornado. Into this trap it was necessary to march in order to meet the foe. Wayne's simple plan of attack was this: to rouse the savages from their lair with an irresistible bayonet charge, "and when up, to deliver a close and well-directed fire on their backs."

The result was a victory for the Americans. The Indians and their white allies, completely routed, made a precipitous retreat, leaving the battle-field covered with their dead. Hotly pursued, their cornfields and wigwams destroyed on the way, they were finally ready to acknowledge that peace was better than war. So ended the great battle of the Maumee, one of the most fatal in its effect upon the destiny of the red race.

It was after this, when actual contest was over, and

the Indians had been provided for west of the Mississippi, that the Cincinnati Company laid out a town on the present site and called it Port Lawrence, after the famous flag-ship in which Perry met the British on Lake Erie. Later, Major Stickney, a historic pioneer, whose sons, " One " and " Two " Stickney are equally immortal, laid out Vistula, which afterwards joined Port Lawrence, under a name destined to become a power in the State—Toledo.

The fortunes of the new town were fluctuating as April weather, and the faith of property-holders must have grown weak through wavering. Most of these hard times were due to malaria, which was bred in the neighboring swamps and forests, and which was an ever-present menace; yet when the cloud of contention lowered over the tract of land lying between the territory of Michigan and the State of Ohio, Toledo, the very centre of the trouble, being claimed by both, was animated enough, although her neighbor, Monroe, was wont to vex her with such taunts as this:

"The potatoes they grow small, on Maumee,
And they eat them, tops and all, on Maumee."

Potato-tops must have possessed singular virtue, for there was no want of spirit when the test came " On Maumee."

The " Toledo War," much talked of and laughed over in its day, is passing slowly into oblivion, and now only an occasional grey-beard brings its scenes back with amusing reminiscence. The cause of the trouble lay in a mistake of Congress, which established an impossible boundary line between Michigan and Ohio, so that the " bone of contention " was a tract of land eight miles wide at the western end, and five at the eastern, which both claimed. The people living in this tract were therefore between two fires, some preferring to be governed by the laws of the territory, and the others giving their allegiance to Ohio. The respective governors were the principals in the quarrel, and showed a strong disposition to fight, while the chief executive at Washington, being unable to interfere, was obliged to assume the role of a spectator, advising, however, that the interested parties defer action until the convening of Congress.

The advantages were pretty evenly divided, except that Michigan, as a territory, in attempting to prevent the State from enforcing her supposed right, aroused a strong State pride among the "Buckeyes." The militia was called out on both sides and Michigan threatened with arrest those who should attempt to re-mark the boundary line—the compliment being generously returned by Ohio.

In the midst of these hostilities the Legislature of Ohio created a new county, calling it Lucas, after the Governor, which included a portion of the contested territory, and had for its seat the town of Toledo. To hold court at this county-seat without the intervention of the authorities of Michigan would virtually decide the case in Ohio's favor, but how this bold *coup d'etat* was to be accomplished, and on the date appointed— the seventh of September—was a question that puzzled the Governor himself. General Brown, in charge of the Michigan militia, was reported to be in Toledo at the time, with a force twelve hundred strong; while Colonel Vanfleet, the Ohio warrior, was to rely upon the stout hearts of a hundred men, who were to act as *posse* for the protection of the court.

When the judges, sheriff and attendants met at Miami to perfect their plans, on Sunday the sixth of September, they were somewhat fearful of the issue, and finally left the decision of the matter in the hands of Colonel Vanfleet. This intrepid Leonidas immediately assumed the championship of his State with admirable skill, and, walking up and down, sword in hand, in front of his hundred followers, for a moment's meditation, turned at last to the judges with these impressive words:

"If you are women, go home; if you are men, do your duty as judges of the court. I will do mine. If you leave this matter entirely with me, I will be responsible for your safety and insure the accomplishment of our object; but if otherwise, I can give you no assurance!"

In the light of present knowledge, the reader of these words, while he respects and admires the spirit in which they were uttered, and the man who spoke them, cannot avoid a mild sense of amusement. But this is not to the point. Matters proceeded seriously on that sixth of September, 1835. Vanfleet called for twenty volunteers, and these having quickly responded to the call, the Colonel then informed his protégés, probably not to their surprise, that the seventh of September would begin immediately after midnight; that the law did not specify any time for the opening of court, and that if they would rely upon his protection, they could accomplish their purpose in the face of the foe.

"Governor Lucas wants the court held," he added,

"so that by its record he may show to the world that he has executed the laws of Ohio over the disputed territory in spite of the vaporing threats of Governor Mason. Be prepared to mount your horses to start for Toledo at precisely one o'clock in the morning. I will be ready with my escort."

The appointment was met, and Toledo was reached at three o'clock. The party proceeded directly to a school-house, and there court was held in due form of law, its proceedings written out on bits of paper being deposited in the tall crown of the clerk's hat. When business was over, the entire party went to a tavern near by for refreshments. Just as the men were about to indulge in a second cup of cheer, some one called out that General Brown, with a strong force, was on his way to arrest them. Glasses were dropped, the little matter of indebtedness to the saloon-keeper was waived without ceremony, and a moment later not a sign of the Ohio dignitaries remained.

When they had placed a sufficient amount of the contested soil between themselves and General Brown, they halted upon a hill to fire a salute, but at that time it was learned that the clerk's hat, containing the all-important papers, had been knocked off his head by the limb of a tree during the retreat. To return might mean capture and the failure of their plan. To abandon the recovery of the missing hat would be equally deplorable. Vanfleet accordingly sent back a small detachment to search the road ; "the lost was found," and, at last triumphant, a loud salute was fired. To say that the men did not then let the grass grow under their feet is but a mild assertion. It has been said by good authorities, that if the retreating party had charged General Brown's regi-

13

259

ment with half the force they employed in getting
away, they could have routed a force twice its size.
When Congress convened, however, they had the satisfaction of having a favorable verdict pronounced upon
their "unlawful act, lawfully committed," although
Jackson had previously expressed himself in sympathy
with the cause of Michigan. The defeated party, to
even up matters, was given the northern peninsula
between Superior and Huron, now her richest section.

During the course of the "war" Toledo was full
of Michigan troops, who left many anecdotes behind
them and whose generally harmless behavior raised
many a laugh among the townspeople. As one of
these stories goes, Major Stickney, walking out into
his garden one morning, noticed something that
looked like a human figure in his potato vines. He
called out to the mysterious object and asked what
was going on there? The call brought to his full
length a soldier in uniform, who stretched up and replied:

"Drafting potato-tops to make the bottoms volunteer, sir!"

And so, half in jest, and half in earnest, the affair
continued and ended.

When the forests were cleared away and the
swamps drained, the dread malaria partnership was
dissolved; good health brought good cheer, and prosperity followed. Very soon after the trouble with
Michigan, the Miami and Erie Canal was built, which
has been one of the important factors in making the
"Corn City" so strong commercially Besides this
great inland waterway, eight railways bring into her

AN OHIO FARM.

marts the products of the rich farms of Illinois, Indiana, Michigan and Ohio.

From her ports enormous quantities of grain are yearly shipped to England either direct, or *via* Montreal, and her people say, without expecting to be contradicted, that no city in the United States can point to such a wonderful development of commercial resources. This scarcely suggests the time when Toledo was little more than the dead carcass of speculation, the prey of the tax-gatherer, waiting the resurrection that followed the War of the Rebellion, when men remained her citizens simply because they had no money with which to get away.

Commerce takes the lead here, but there is one enterprise of which Toledoans seem to be even prouder, and to see which they take the visitor "whom they wish to impress with their greatness." This is the thriving and truly imposing Milbourn Wagon Works, put into operation in 1875 and already become famous. The brick buildings are unusually fine and, architecturally, would leave the uninformed stranger under the impression that they might belong to some institution of learning.

I was enabled to see more of the city than I had expected, owing to an unforeseen circumstance. A little friend who lived in Detroit, and who was dying with consumption, had expressed a wish to come to Toledo to see me and my horse before it was too late. I therefore remained longer than I intended, that her friends might bring her down by boat, although they hardly hoped that she would survive the journey. She was given the pleasure of a quiet trip to Put-in-Bay, the well-known resort, and with this and the gratification of seeing *Paul,* in whom she was deeply interested, her visit ended.

Of all the strangers who come to this bright and busy city, active with the impetus given it by fifty thousand souls, I doubt if any take more keen delight in looking upon its business enterprises and individuality than did this bright-minded girl, just about to relinquish her hold upon earth. She knew nothing of the dark pages in its history, and only guessed at the wealth and strength back of the thronged harbor. To her it was a happy place—the temporary home of friends.

CHAPTER XVI.

TOLEDO TO DETROIT.

Seventy~second Day.

Erie Hotel,
ERIE, MICHIGAN,
July 22, 1876.

MY Toledo friends were ready at the Boody House to give me good-bye when I mounted at nine o'clock, and I received a right hearty send-off. Upon leaving the city, instead of continuing westward as usual toward the " Golden Gate," I had determined for various reasons to swing off from the direct course, and ride northward to Detroit, moving thence to Chicago. This new route would take me through Monroe, a town with which the life of General Custer was more closely associated than any other, and knowing that I would find much there that would give me a more intimate knowledge of the man, I looked forward to this part of my journey with eager anticipation.

The ride to Erie being at some distance from the lake, and over a flat region, was rather monotonous. Erie itself is a small unimportant hamlet at the western end of the lake, and a modest landmark in my journey from Toledo to Detroit. *Paul*, probably impressed with the air of peace that enveloped the place, made up his mind upon his arrival to give the good people a display of his mettle, and accordingly tore through the village streets in the wildest fashion. Having thus introduced himself, he pranced after I had dismounted until he had had enough; then returning to his master, his eyes seeming to flash mischief, he looked as though he would have said, had he been given the power of speech: "I have been having a fine time, haven't I? and would you like to mount me and enjoy the fun too? but I dare you!"

When his superabundant spirits had found vent, I had him led away and myself attended to his wants. Beyond this animated exhibition of my horse the day passed uneventfully, and at night I enjoyed to its fullest extent the quietude of a country inn.

Seventy-third Day.

Erie Hotel,
ERIE, MICHIGAN,
July Twenty-third.

Weather cool and pleasant; went to church in the morning and listened to a sermon by Rev. E. P. Willard, on the text, "Remember the Sabbath Day to keep it holy." Doubtless the preacher had his reasons for bringing to the minds of the Erieans this particular command, but judging from appearances they needed a very mild admonition. It looked as though every day were Sunday here.

A letter reached me at this point from my wife,

full of concern as to my welfare if the journey were to be continued across the Plains; and as she was in very indifferent health at the time, I was about to abandon my purpose and return. The news of Custer's tragic death had reached the East, and my intended route running as it did across the Indian country, filled my friends with apprehension. Closely following this letter, however, came another, informing me that my wife was improving, and, with this assurance, I decided not to turn back. By this time, the freedom and charm of this mode of travel had aroused my enthusiasm; the imaginary line, losing itself in the Pacific, promised a rich experience, and the opportunity was golden. The good news from home was therefore joyfully received.

Seventy-fourth Day.

Strong's Hotel,
MONROE, MICHIGAN,
July Twenty-fourth.

I was detained at Erie until after dinner, spending part of the forenoon in a blacksmith shop, where *Paul* was being shod. By two o'clock I was on the road again, riding briskly toward Monroe, for the weather was so much cooler than it had been during the previous week, that I could move comfortably at a good pace. *Paul* seemed very proud of his new shoes, and, although I halted two or three times, covered something over ten miles by five o'clock.

As I reached the outskirts of Monroe, I was considerably surprised to find a large number of people assembled on the picnic grounds. They were accompanied by a band, and greeted me with several national air, including "Hail Columbia" and the "Star-Spangled Banner." The Custer Monument Association received me at the City Hall, where I had been announced to lecture in the evening, as it was my intention to speak in the interest of the Fund ; but the date was changed to the Thursday following my arrival, with a view to giving its members an opportunity to co-operate with my advance agents.

Great enthusiam was everywhere apparent, and the people of Monroe needed no urging to lend their patronage, when the movement was likely to reflect honor upon their illustrious dead.

My emotions upon entering this town, long the dearest place in all the world to Custer, can better be imagined than described. That it was a favorite with him is not strange, for aside from the tender associations which it held for him, its pretty homes and broad streets, deeply shaded by maples, make it a most lovely spot and the very type of peace.

Seventy-fifth Day.

Strong's Hotel,
MONROE, MICHIGAN,
July Twenty-fifth.

Wrote to my mother in the morning, and after dinner took a stroll about town. Beyond its associations with Custer, Monroe is interesting through its connection with one of the most romantic and sanguinary scenes connected with the war between Great Britain and the United States ; for on the banks of the River Raisin, which runs through it to the lake, occurred the famous Indian massacre of 1812. Relics of the bloody encounter are still found on the field.

It was at a time when the British were making successful inroads upon Michigan, and General Winchester, at the head of eight hundred Kentuckians, had been ordered to Frenchtown, the old name for Monroe, the same point toward which General Miller had previously moved on a mission equally fatal.

Winchester was warned of the advance of the enemy, but thought there was no cause for immediate alarm, and on the night before the engagement, he crossed to the side of the river opposite his men, leaving the camp open to attack. The result was, that he awoke the next morning to find Proctor's troops putting his men to rout, at the point of the bayonet, while their Indian allies were adding to the confusion by their deadly assault.

Although a part of the Americans escaped on the ice of the river, the field was covered with their dead and wounded, General Winchester being among the former. When the engagement was over, Proctor rode away, leaving a detachment to guard the prisoners and wounded, with instructions that no violence was to be committed; but some of the savages who followed him having become intoxicated, returned and fell upon the prisoners with unrestrained frenzy. Most of the latter had been placed in two small cabins. These were fired, and the victims perished in the flames, the Indians pushing them back when they attempted to escape through the small windows. The remainder were massacred and their bodies left a prey to the wolves. It was this horrible affair that aroused the Americans and particularly the Kentuckians to revenge; and when Tecumseh, the Shawnee warrior, who was the chief instigator of these atrocities, urged the British to hazard an engagement at the Thames, after their defeat by Perry, they prepared to return with full interest the blow given their comrades on the Raisin. The battle of the Thames is well known. Tecumseh, with the war cry on his lips, met his reward through a Kentucky bullet early enough in the fight to be spared the shame of defeat. With him fell a powerful foe, but one whom we must admire even in his death.

> " Like monumental bronze, unchanged his look,
>   As one whom pity touched, but never shook;
> Train'd from his tree-rocked cradle to his bier
>   The fierce extremes of good and ill to brook.
> Unchanging, fearing but the shame of fear,
> A stoic of the woods, a man without a tear."

Seventy-sixth Day.

Strong's Hotel,
MONROE, MICHIGAN,
July Twenty-sixth.

Received a large forwarded mail from my advance agents and others, which I attended to in the afternoon. I was also favored with Detroit papers referring to my proposed lecture in that city, and the following notice from the Monroe *Monitor*, which, together with letters from the Fund Association, I kept as souvenirs of my stay at this place:

" The lecture announced to be given for the benefit of the Custer Monument Fund, on Monday evening, at the City Hall, was post-poned for various reasons until Thursday evening, at the same place. On Monday evening several members of the association met

Captain Willard Glazier, and were most favorably impressed with him. They are convinced that he is thoroughly in earnest, and that his proposition is a most liberal one. He offers to give the entire pro·ceeds of his lecture to the association; and not only in this city, but throughout the State, he generously offers to do the same thing. This is certainly deserving of the warm recognition of our own people, at least, and we hope on Thursday evening to see the City Hall filled. Captain Glazier comes with the strongest endorsements from well-known gentlemen in the East, both as to his character as a gentleman and a soldier, and his ability as a speaker and writer. The Captain served under the late General Custer in the cavalry, and has something to say regarding his personal knowledge of the dead hero."

When I started from Boston in May, I little dreamed that before my journey was finished the troubles in the West with the Sioux would bring such a result as *this!* It is true, affairs in Montana and Wyoming territories had assumed a threatening aspect, but no one doubted the efficacy of "Custer's luck," and those who followed the campaign looked upon it as a dramatic and striking incident, rather than a tragic one.

News was slow in reaching points east of the Mississippi and was then often unreliable, so that if I may judge from personal observation, the people were wholly unprepared for the final result which was flashed across the country on the fifth of July.

Seventy-seventh Day.

Strong's Hotel,
MONROE, MICHIGAN,
July Twenty-seventh.

Rose at an early hour in the morning, and was very busily occupied during the day with correspondence and preparations for my lecture. The people of

Monroe had asked that I would tell them something of my experience with Custer during the late war before beginning the lecture, as everything relating to him was at that time of the most thrilling interest to them. It was not difficult to comply with this request. The old scenes of 1863 were as fresh in memory as though they had been witnessed but yesterday.

My first meeting with Custer was at the third battle of Brandy Station on the twelfth of September, 1863, as the Cavalry Corps then acting as the advance of the Army of the Potomac was moving toward Culpeper in pursuit of Lee's retreating columns. Custer had but recently been commissioned brigadier-general and this was the first time he went into action at the head of his brigade. His appearance was very conspicuous. A mere boy in years, gorgeously equipped, in short, bearing upon his person all the gold lace and other paraphernalia allowed his rank, he formed a striking figure—such a one as is seldom seen on the battle-field. His arrival at Brandy Station was at a critical juncture, and while we were momentarily expecting a conflict with Stuart's cavalry, then directly in our front, all had a curiosity to see how the gayly dressed brigadier would acquit himself. It seemed to be the general impression that he would not have the nerve to "face the music" with his bandbox equipment, but he soon proved himself equal to the occasion. Being ordered to charge the enemy, he snatched his cap from his head, handed it to his orderly, drew his sword and dashed to the front of his brigade, then formed in column of squadrons. The command "Forward!" was instantly given. A moment later "Trot!" was sounded; then "Gallop!" and "Charge!" and before

the Confederates had time to realize that we really intended an attack, they were swept from the field, and a
section of a battery with which they had been opposing
our advance was in the possession of the young
general and his gallant cavalrymen.

No soldier who saw him on that day at Brandy
Station ever questioned his right to a star, or all
the gold lace he felt inclined to wear. He at once became a favorite in the Army of the Potomac and his
fame was soon heralded throughout the country.
After this engagement I saw Custer at Culpeper and
Cedar Mountain, and in the skirmishes along the
Rapidan during Lee's retreat from Gettysburg; later,
when Lee again advanced through Northern Virginia,
at Sulphur Springs, Newmarket, Bristoe and in the action of October 19, 1863, near New Baltimore, where
I was taken prisoner.

The incidents which I recalled were those of war,
but Custer's friends here gave me the incidents of
peace. Mr. J. M. Bulkley, who is perhaps more intimately acquainted with the General's early life than
any other man in Monroe, was his old school-chum
and seat-mate at Stebbin's Academy.

When this institution was broken up, and its
property sold, Mr. Bulkley bought the old desk at
which he and Custer had sat, and on which as school-
boys they had cut their initials. It stands in his store,
and in it are kept all the papers relating to the Monument Fund.

Custer's next experience was in the Monroe Seminary, and it was while he was a student there that
the pretty little face of his future wife flashed into his
life. The story of this meeting is laughable and odd.

Custer, then a rough, flaxen-haired lad, coming home one afternoon, his books under his arm, was passing Judge Bacon's residence, when a little brown-eyed girl swinging on the gate called out to him, " Hello, you Custer boy!" then, half-frightened by the blue eyes that glanced toward her, ran into the house. The little girl was Libbie Bacon, daughter of the Judge. It was love at first sight for Custer, and although they did not meet again for several years, he was determined to win the owner of those brown eyes.

Having finished a preliminary course of study and wishing to enter West Point, he urged his father to apply to John Bingham, then a member of Congress for the district in which Monroe was situated, for an appointment. This his father hesitated to do as Mr. Bingham's politics were opposed to his. The young man was therefore obliged to rely upon his own efforts. He called upon the dignitary himself. Mr. Bingham was pleased with the applicant, promised to lend his influence, and the result was that George Armstrong Custer ultimately received a formal notification from Washington, bearing the signature of Jefferson Davis, to the effect that the recipient was expected to report immediately to the commanding officer at West Point. His course there was about finished upon the breaking out of the late war. He went at once to Washington, and through General Scott was launched upon his military career. What sort of a soldier he was the world knows. What his character was the following incident may partially suggest. It occurred early in the war when Custer was beginning to feel somewhat discouraged over his affairs. He had already done much that was worthy of promotion and, having

OUTSKIRTS OF A CITY.

a boy's pride and ambition. Fate seemed to be against·
him. The clouds vanished one day, however, when
the Army of the Potomac was encamped on the north
bank of the Chickahominy near Richmond.

General Barnard, of the Engineers, starting out to
discover if the river was fordable at a certain point,
called upon Custer to accompany him. Arrived at the
bank of the stream, he ordered the young officer to·
"jump in." He was instantly obeyed, although the
·pickets of the enemy were known to be on the opposite side, and dangerously near. Nor did Custer return, after having found that there was firm bottom.
until he had made a thorough reconnoissance of the
Confederate outposts.

Upon their return, Barnard rode up to McClellan,
who was about to visit with his staff his own outposts, and began reporting the recently acquired information, while his late aide, wearied with the undertaking, and covered with Chickahominy mud, had
fallen to the rear. Gradually it came out that Custer,
and not Custer's superior officer, had performed the
important duty. He was immediately called for, and
to his great embarrassment, for his appearance was far
from presentable, was asked by McClellan to make a
report of the situation himself. At the end of the re-
cital he was asked by his commander, to his amaze-
ment, how he would like to join his staff. McClellan
had, by a rare power peculiar to him, in that short
interview, won Custer's unfailing loyalty and affection,
and when Custer was asked afterwards how he felt at.
the time, his eyes filled with tears, and he said ↑
"*I felt I could have died for him.*"

This promotion marked the beginning of his future

success. In recalling his career, these simple lines, written by a poet unknown to me, and with which Frederick Whittaker, in his admirable life of Custer, brings his biography to a close, involuntarily suggest themselves:

"Who early thus upon the field of glory
    Like thee doth fall, needs for his fame
Naught but the simple telling of his story,
    The naming of his name."

Seventy-eighth Day.

Varney House,
ROCKWOOD, MICHIGAN,
July Twenty-eighth.

Before ordering *Paul* in the morning, I called again at the home of the Custers. The General's father seemed greatly interested in my journey, and asked many questions concerning my plans for crossing the Plains. I was shown the rich and interesting collection of relics from the Indian country which Custer had accumulated, and which adds a picturesqueness to every corner of the house, and with these, some very striking photographs of the General taken in every variety of position and costume. After a pleasant chat, in the course of which Mr. Custer assured me of his kind solicitude, he walked back to the hotel with me to see me off.

While riding out of town, I met Mr. Bulkley, and was introduced to several gentlemen of his acquaintance, many of whom were schoolmates of Custer during his boyhood. Mr. Bulkley, speaking for the Monument Association, assured me that everything would be done that could further my wishes in Michigan.

The lecture last evening was well attended and proved a financial success. It was therefore gratifying to give the entire proceeds to the treasurer, Judge T. E. Wing, although he generously offered to divide, Parting with Mr. Bulkley, I continued on my route, my mind filled with the events of the three preceding days. Just beyond the town I halted to look back, and then, determined to prevent any sombre thoughts, which might follow, put spurs to *Paul*, who very soon covered the thirteen miles between Monroe and this place. As we neared the village, I caught sight of Huron River, the *Wrockumiteogoe* of the Indians, meaning, " clear water." On its banks are found those mysterious legacies of the Mound Builders—whether dwellings or tombs, remains for the antiquarian to determine.

Seventy-ninth Day.

Farmers' Hotel,
ECORSE, MICHIGAN,
July Twenty-ninth.

Moved from Rockwood at ten A. M., halting for a few minutes at Trenton, a small village seven miles north of Rockwood ; and from there, riding on to Wyandotte, which I reached about one o'clock, and stopped only a moment at the Biddle House, finding that dinner was awaiting me at a private residence. I was ready to answer the hospitable summons promptly. Between two and five o'clock, I occupied part of the time in looking about the village, which is chiefly noted for its iron industries. Farm implements, iron ships, iron rails, and in fact everything that can be made out of iron, is produced here. After dinner I rode on to Ecorse, which is three miles beyond, and there found letters and papers telling me that I was expected at the Russell House, Detroit, on the evening of the coming Monday. Once within my hotel, I found the heat almost unbearable, but following a certain method which I had found by experience to be a successful one, I was enabled in a measure to improve my surroundings. To those who might think my *modus operandi* somewhat unbecoming, I would only suggest that they try my mode of travel through the same region of country, and at the same season of the year. Personal experience might change their opinion.

Having been shown to my apartment by the land-lord or one of his assistants, I quietly entered and secured the door, betraying no surprise upon seeing the inevitable "feather bed." Taking off my coat, I began by removing the layers of mattresses. which had in them a wonderful reserve force of July heat. I then took my lamp and held it so that its lambent flame could warm the cockles of every mosquito's heart clinging to the ceiling. The mosquitoes, quite averse to the intense heat, quietly dropped into the little purgatory which I had prepared for them, and troubled me no more.

So did I secure my repose at the Farmers' Hotel, and in the morning was in the humor to give the good-natured proprietor, Louis Cicotte—a typical French Canadian—a very hearty greeting, and an assurance of my refreshment.

Eighteth Day.

Farmers' Hotel,
ECORSE, MICHIGAN,
July Thirtieth.

The weather was oppressively warm again on this day, and business in Ecorse was apparently not "booming." I found the place quite in keeping with the majority of French villages along the Detroit River—unambitious and lifeless.

Two acknowledgments came from Monroe soon after I left, referring to the aid which I had the pleasure of giving to those interested in the Custer Monument. One was a brief and courteous bearer of thanks, and is as follows:

Headquarters,
Custer National Monument Association;
MONROE, MICHIGAN,
July 28, 1876.

This is to certify that the proceeds of the lecture by Captain Willard Glazier, in this city on Thursday evening, July 27, 1876, have been paid into the treasury of this association, for which the members hereby tender him their sincere thanks.

T. E. WING,
Treasurer.

The other was a letter of introduction and explains itself:

Headquarters,
Custer National Monument Association;
MONROE, MICHIGAN,
July 28, 1876.

TO AUXILIARY SOCIETIES AND ASSOCIATIONS OF THE CUSTER MONUMENT ASSOCIATION:

Captain Willard Glazier, having kindly and generously volunteered to devote the proceeds of his lectures through Michigan to the fund being raised by this Association, for the erection of a monument to the memory of the late General George A. Custer, has made arrangements to remit to our treasurer here the money derived from such lectures, and we bespeak for him your earnest endeavor in aid of our common, glorious cause.   Respectfully,

J. M. BULKLEY,
Secretary.

Our second day at Ecorse ended pleasantly.   In the afternoon my brother and I went for a row on the river, and in the evening took a walk into the country. We did not meet with any game, although natural history proclaims this section the haunt of many varieties of bird and beast.   The first settlers even remember having a casual acquaintance with the deer, bear, wolf, wild cat, and a variety of smaller game, including that interesting little quadruped, the wolverine, whose name has become the nickname of Michigan.

CHAPTER XVII.

FOUR DAYS AT DETROIT.

FTER a much-needed rest of a day and two nights at Ecorse, I left that quiet retreat on the afternoon of July thirty-first, with Detroit as my evening objective. At Fort Wayne, I was met by Babcock, who brought me the sad intelligence of the death of my little Detroit friend, Kitty Murphy, who had failed very rapidly after her brief visit to Toledo. We rode forward together, reaching the Russell House at five o'clock, and there I was met by General William A. Throop and others, who were appointed as a committee to receive me. In the evening I lectured at St. Andrew's Hall, being introduced by General L. S. Trowbridge and was accompained on the platform by several Grand Army comrades.

Immediately after the lecture, I hurried to the home of my bereaved friends, where I found the mother and sisters of the dead girl completely prostrated with grief. The one who had gone was their favorite, for whom they had the highest hopes, and it was hard to be reconciled to the passing away of a life so full of promise and noble purposes. I was proud to know that one universally loved and admired had thought of me in her last moments and had left a token of her friendship.

On the morning of August first, I arranged my affairs so as to be able to attend the funeral services of my young friend the following day.

The proceeds of my lecture were handed to the Monument Fund committee with a letter from me to be forwarded to Monroe, and its representatives here acknowledged this in the following note:

> *City Hall,*
> DETROIT, MICHIGAN,
> *August* 1, 1876.
>
> Received of Captain Willard Glazier, forty dollars, for the benefit of the Custer Monument Association, as the proceeds of his lecture, at Detroit, on the evening of July 31, 1876, in aid of such association.
>
> [*Signed*]   L. S. TROWBRIDGE,
> WILLIAM A. THROOP,
> *Committee.*

On the afternoon of August second, I went to Kitty's grave with her family and friends, where we arranged on the little mound our gifts of flowers. I placed my own offering—a crown—at her head. It was the last tribute, the " farewell " which we hoped might one day be lost in " welcome."

During my stay here, many friends extended invitations to visit them, but I was able to accept very few. Among those whom I met was my old comrade, Captain Charles G. Hampton, who was at the Russell House to greet me when I arrived. No one could have been more welcome. Captain Hampton and I began our somewhat peculiar acquaintance as classmates in the State Normal College at Albany, New York, in the spring of 1861, where we joined a military organization known later as the "Normal Company" of the "Ellsworth Avengers"—Forty-fourth New York Infantry—whose members were put through a course of drills in anticipation of future necessity, our voluntary drill masters being Professors Rodney G. Kimball and Albert N. Husted.

It was argued by the principal and by the faculty generally, that while young men were learning how to teach the schools of the State, it would be well also for them to be prepared to defend the flag of the State. We had just closed our term when President Lincoln issued his call for seventy-five thousand volunteers, and as it was not at this time the apparent intent of the Normal Company to enter the service as a body, we decided to enlist in some other organization.

Hampton went to Rochester where he joined the Eighth New York Cavalry, while I enlisted in the Second New York-Harris Light Cavalry, at Troy. We did not meet again until November, 1863—when, by the fortune of war, we both became inmates of Libby Prison. The circumstances that brought us there were, on his side, wounds and capture in an action with guerrillas under Mosby; on mine, capture in a cavalry battle near New Baltimore, Virginia, during Lee's retreat from the field of Gettysburg.

During our imprisonment at Richmond, Danville, Macon, Savannah, and Charleston, Captain Hampton and I belonged to separate messes, so that, while we met daily, we had very little intimate intercourse. At Columbia, however, it was different. We arrived there in the midst of a violent thunder-storm, and were marched to our "quarters," in an open yard where the water was running in streams. Hampton had managed to get possession of a board about twelve feet long when he met me, and immediately asked if I had anything to stand or lie on. Upon receiving a negative answer he said: "Come on, let us share this plank together." From this time we were messmates, being joined later by Lieutenant Arthur Richardson of Albany. When I escaped from Columbia I intrusted to Captain Hampton a small box in which I had kept some manuscripts and sketches, that I intended to use in future work. This he managed to keep until his exchange, when he expressed it to my home in Northern New York. We did not meet again until after the close of the war. The possession of the contents of this box was of inestimable value to me in getting out my first book, "Capture, Prison-Pen and Escape." Being embarrassed for funds before the first edition of it was published, I wrote to Captain Hampton, and by the next mail received a generous sum sufficient to carry me through that critical period. Since then he has been a most loyal friend and comrade, and during my stay here, did much to make enjoyable my visit to the city which he had chosen for his home.

One needs no friends though, to make Detroit attractive, for its past history and present beauty give it an unfailing interest. As to the latter, it can never be justly drawn, however vivid the description, nor truly understood, however careful the reader. It must be *seen*. As to its history, that is general and belongs to the country, and I know of no great American city which has a more romantic past.

In the days of the early explorers the present site was looked upon as favorable for a settlement, commanding as it does a rich tract of country and lying at the very entrance to the Upper Lakes. The Iroquois were then in possession and their village was known as Teusha Grondi. Both the English and French coveted this point, but the latter were more enterprising, and anticipated their rivals by making an appointment with the Iroquois for a great council at Montreal, in which the Governor-General of Canada and others were to have a voice. The wary Frenchmen presented their claims very plausibly, but failed to win the approbation of the equally wary Indians. They were told that their brothers, the Englishmen, had been refused, and that it was not well to show partiality; but this excuse had very little weight with the subjects of the Grande Monarque, who had been accustomed to make themselves at home generally. The Governor-General in an impressive speech replied that neither the Iroquois nor the English had any right to the land which belonged to the King of France, and that an expedition had been already sent out to establish a fort on the Detroit River!

This was indeed the case. La Motte Cadillac, with a Jesuit missionary and one hundred men, was on his way, while his countrymen, with the consistency which has ever marked the dealings between the red and white races, were asking permission of the Indians. The French fleet, composed of twenty-five birch canoes bearing the colors of France, reached the Detroit River in July, 1701. There was a telling significance in the floating of that flag over the boats decorated with Indian symbols and, if the savages had discerned it, the French commander and his followers would never have reached their destination. As it was, they came quietly as friends, and were allowed to establish themselves without interference.

On the first rise of ground overlooking the river, the palisades were raised and the guns set, and by the close of August, Fort Ponchartrain became a reality. The Miamis and Pottawattomies were soon induced to make a settlement near by, and afterwards a few Huron and Ottawa bands collected on the opposite shore of the river near the site of Windsor. The point quickly attracted the fur trader, being in a direct line from Michilimackinac to Montreal and Quebec. For sixty-two years the French held possession of Detroit, profiting by her superior location, and the friendship of the Indians, but their day ended when the sharp eyes of Wolfe discovered the steep ascent to the " Plains of Abraham," in Canada, and pointed a way for British supremacy. .

The Treaty of Paris, which was the outcome of the French and Indian War, called for the surrender of all the forts held by the French, but news travelled so slowly that when Captain Rodgers with his two hundred rangers came to take possession of Fort Ponchartrain, he found still floating over it the flag of France. While on his way to execute this mission, he was met by Pontiac, the Ottawa chief, who was angered by the transfer of claimants to his land, and who demanded of Rodgers " what right he had in entering the dominion of the great Indian King without permission." The answer he received was far from satisfactory, but he bided his time to make his dissatisfaction felt. The same feeling was manifested everywhere by the Indian allies of the French, but their wrath was concentrated upon Detroit, on account of its being the great stronghold of the West.

In 1763, Pontiac had arranged his famous scheme for either annihilating the obnoxious newcomers or driving them east of the Alleghenies. They did not treat him so considerately as the old claimants, and he was far-seeing enough to realize the result. Aflame with hatred and determined to save his people from the fate that awaited them, he visited the great tribes that were friendly, and sought their co-operation. In a speech at the great council held at Ecorse on the twenty-seventh of April, 1762, he said, " As for these English—these dogs dressed in red who have come to rob you of your hunting-grounds and to drive away the game—you must lift the hatchet against them and wipe them from the face of the earth." The plan was worthy of a Napoleon. The confederated tribes were to attack simultaneously all the Western forts, while his particular band was to be brought against Detroit. This point he had expected to take by stratagem and would no doubt have succeeded but for the betrayal of the plot by an Ojibway maiden who was in love with the British commandant. The day before its execution this Indian girl brought Major Gladwyn a pair of moccasins which he had asked her to make for him, and on her way home with the re- mainder of the deer-skin, which he had furnished for the same purpose, she lingered about the gate so as to attract the attention of the sentinel. He saw that she seemed to be troubled about something, and asked her to return. Wavering between love and duty to her race, she hesitated; but finally the im- pulse of her heart prevailed, and returning to the room of the commandant, she told him the terrible secret.

Pontiac was to come to the fort on the morrow ostensibly to hold peaceful negotiations with his white brothers, but really to massacre them. His warriors, who had cunningly shortened their rifles by sawing off a part of the barrels, so that they might carry them concealed beneath their blankets, were to fall upon Gladwyn and his men at a given signal. This news was lightly received although the statements of the Indian girl seemed to be verified by a slight thread of evidence which had from time to time been brought to Gladwyn's notice. He laughed at the thought of danger at such a time, when the peace which had lasted for two years appeared so likely to continue; but while he doubted Pontiac's real intentions, he decided to be prepared for any issue. The guards were doubled, sentinels were stationed on the ramparts, and when the great chief came in the guise of friendship, he was completely nonplussed by the show of discipline in the garrison. Entering the north gate with his sixty blanketed conspirators, he found himself confronted by a double line of red-coated soldiers, their muskets held at " present arms." At the corners of the streets were groups of fur traders, and at regular intervals the silence was broken by the beating of drums.

Surprised at every turn, and fearing that his plot had been discovered, Pontiac walked on sullenly endeavoring to conceal his annoyance. When he reached the council-house he said to Gladwyn, " Why do I see so many of my father's young men standing in the streets with their guns?" The commandant lightly replied that he had just been drilling them to preserve discipline and that it was moreover a custom with the English to thus honor their guests. These suavely spoken words failed to reassure the chief, who sat down for a few moments without speaking; but having recovered his self-possession and assuming with it an habitual expression of stoical defiance, he arose and began his harangue. Gladwyn, he noticed, instead of listening to what was being said, kept his eyes steadfastly upon the movements of the other Indians, and when the belt of wampum was taken up and the chief began to reverse it in his hands—the signal for attack—Gladwyn made a quick motion and in an instant the dusky semicircle was startled by the grounding of arms and the beating of drums.

Thus interrupted and foiled, Pontiac took his seat in silence. Gladwyn then arose, and began his speech as though nothing unusual had occurred; but after a few moments he changed his tone, accused Pontiac of treachery, and stepping quickly to the nearest Indian threw open his blanket and disclosed the hidden weapon. He then told Pontiac to leave the fort at once, assuring him that he would be allowed to go in safety. The unfortunate result of this act of clemency was very soon felt, for as soon as the Indians were outside of the gates, they turned and fired upon the garrison, thus beginning the terrible siege which was to last fifteen months.

Autumn approached, and, as the crops were poor, several of the tribes withdrew for the winter, but Pontiac, untiring in his efforts to harass his enemies, remained, sending messages in the meantime to several of the French posts, asking their help. In November he received word from the commandant of Fort Chartres on the Mississippi telling him that it was impossible for the French to give any help as they had signed a treaty with the English; and later similar messages reached him from other points. Still he did not give up. His allies had captured eight forts, and if he could take Detroit success would undoubtedly follow.

In the spring the tribes returned to renew the attack upon the wellnigh exhausted garrison, keeping up their fiendish tortures, capturing vessels sent with supplies and reinforcements, and bringing the handful of brave men within the palisades to the verge of despair. As summer advanced the anxious watchers, hearing the sunset gun thunder out across the water, thought that each night might be their last; but off in the East, General Bradstreet and his large force were starting to the rescue, and by midsummer they had crushed the hopes, if not the proud spirit of Pontiac. Sending one of his officers to this chief with terms of peace, his advances were received with the coldest disdain. Captain Morris, who was the ambassador, was met beyond the Indian camp by Pontiac himself, but the chief refused to extend his hand, and bending his glittering eyes upon the officer said, with a voice full of bitterness and hatred, "The English are liars!"

All attempts at conciliation were made in vain. Pontiac, taking with him four hundred warriors, went away, revisiting all the tribes, sending the wampum belt and hatchet stained with vermilion far and wide, and exhorting the Indians to unite in the common cause, threatening, if they refused, to consume them

"as the fire consumes the dry grass of the prairie."
He failed to rouse them, however, and was forced at
last to return to Detroit and accept peace.

The feelings that surged in his savage heart, when
he found himself thus defeated, can only be guessed.
Chagrined and disappointed, he retired to Illinois,
and there perished by the hand of an assassin. No
stone marks his burial-place, "and the race whom he
hated with such burning rancor trample with unceasing footsteps over his forgotten grave."

The early history of Detroit is full of tragedy, and
although the beautiful river and its islands, the splendid forests and sunny fields that encompass it, seem to
have been intended for peace and the play of romance,
they were instead the scenes of treachery and carnage.
During the war of the Revolution, Detroit and Macki-
naw, far from the field of action, nevertheless had
their share in it.   From their magazines Indians were
furnished with arms and ammunition and were sent
out with these to harass and destroy the frontier settlements of New York, Pennsylvania, Virginia and
Kentucky, receiving a price upon their return for the
scalps which they brought!   Besides these Indian expeditions, the local militia went out, at one time under
Captain Byrd, and again under Henry Hamilton.
The latter, in an attempt to protect the British interests
on the Wabash, was cleverly captured at Vincennes
by General George Clarke, who advanced upon this
post with his men supported by a formidable but
harmless device in the form of a cannon cut out of a
tree.   Hamilton, dreading the artillery, surrendered,
and the people of Detroit, believing that the victor
would march against them, erected a new fort near the

present corner of Fort and Shelby streets, which they named Lenault. During the war of 1812, this name was changed and the post became known as Fort Shelby.

After the treaty of 1783 the western posts did not at once acknowledge American jurisdiction, and among these Detroit seemed to be the most defiant, but when Wayne effectually weakened the strength of the Indians, there was a general surrender, although the United States forces did not take actual possession until July eleventh, 1796. With childish spite, the British, upon leaving this fort, broke the windows of the barracks, filled the wells with stones and did all they could to annoy those who were to succeed them, and when General Hull came there as governor of the territory, it is possible that the ruin which he found was occassioned by the same spirit of revenge.

During the succeeding years, Detroit was again one of the points towards which an unpropitious fate pointed a finger. The Indians, still believing that the Americans were driving them from their land, were making preparations to attack the settlements, led on by the powerful influence of the two chiefs, Tecumseh and the Prophet.

At a grand council the assembled tribes were told, according to the policy of these chiefs, that the Great Spirit had appeared to chief Tront and had told him that He was the father of the English, French, Spaniards and Indians, but that the Americans were the sons of the Evil One! Under such influence the uprising which resulted in the war between Great Britain and the United States began.

When General Brock, seconded by Tecumseh,

marched on Detroit, he requested of the Chief, in case the place was taken, that the inhabitants should be spared massacre, to which the haughty savage replied, " that he despised them too much to have anything to do with them." The result of this attack, and the inexplicable conduct of General Hull, had aroused a strong feeling of disgust, and universal sympathy was felt for those brave men, who, upon hearing that their superior officer was surrendering without an attempt at resistance, " dashed their muskets upon the ground in an agony of mingled shame and indignation."

Victories elsewhere finally obliged the British to evacuate, and on the eighteenth of October, General Harrison and Commodore Perry issued a proclamation from this fort, which once more assured the people of Michigan of protection.

Passing through the test of fire and sword, Detroit has gradually progressed in all those ways which go to make up a great and prosperous city. Fulfilling her natural destiny she has become one of the most important commercial centres in the United States, and as a port of entry can boast with reason of her strength. The narrow lanes which were enclosed within the pickets of Fort Ponchartrain, and trodden by men in the French uniform, in English red coats and in the skins of the deer and beaver, have reached out over many miles, and have become an intricate maze of streets and avenues, lined with homes and business houses which bear no trace of the old time block house and trader's cabin.

Here and there, where history is preserved, one finds a few relics of the " dead past " embalmed in paint or print or labelled within the glass case of a museum;

but the present Detroit is interesting enough without these. In every direction it is brightened by parks and adorned by fountains; and the broad avenues lined by generous borders of grass and shaded by cool lines of trees, are something for Americans to be proud of, especially when they recall the fact that "Johnny Cra-peau" once asserted that this particular corner of the new world belonged to the Grande Monarque; and "John Bull" in turn claimed it for his own.

One of the prettiest parts of the city, and perhaps within the possibility of description, is the Campus Martius. On it stands the suggestive if somewhat unusual monument designed by Randolph Rogers and erected by the city at a cost of sixty thousand dollars. The surmounting figure is that of an Indian maiden representing the State, and on the tablet beneath, the inscription tells us that it was placed there "in honor of the martyrs who fell and the heroes who fought in defence of Liberty and Union." Everywhere are evidences of a high appreciation of beauty and comfort, and if the people of Detroit are sometimes tempted to seek a change and rest on some of the little island resorts of the river, or on Lake St. Clair, it is not because their own homes are unattrac-tive. Some one has said, "if places could speak, they would describe people far better than people can describe places," and this is especially true of this great city. It is impossible by words to do it justice. The public buildings, the thronged streets, the busy harbor, the shady avenues, must be seen to be appreciated, and there are very few places which will justify praise and repay expectation more liberally than this splendid City of the Strait.

CHAPTER XVIII.

DETROIT TO CHICAGO.

Eighty-fifth Day.

Inkster House,
INKSTER, MICHIGAN,
August 4, 1876.

HAVING before me a lecture appointment at Ypsilanti, which, considering the object I had in view through Michigan, I felt must be met, I rode out of Detroit at three o'clock in the afternoon, somewhat reluctantly perhaps, but within a very short time the love of travel was again upon me, and I found myself easily reconciled.

Paul being in the most delightful spirits, after four days of unbroken rest, displayed quite a little animation as I mounted him in front of the residence of friends on Cass Avenue, and when we had reached the open country, I gave him the rein and allowed him to trot or gallop, as he felt inclined. The edge of his impatience having worn off, he resumed his habitual easy canter which made the saddle so enjoyable, and at this pace we covered fourteen miles, reaching our destination a few minutes after six o'clock. There was an agreeable if not decided contrast be-

tween the last stopping-place and the present one. A
hundred towers announced the approach to a great
city, as we neared Detroit; but here a solitary spire rose
against the sky, and while the Detroit River teems,
throughout its entire length with water-craft of all
sorts, the almost unknown little river that winds along
between Detroit and Inkster, is at this point as quiet
as one of the untravelled streams of the North. The
Michigan Central Railway follows its shore for many
miles, and as I kept to the highway in the same direction, I could see it shining occasionally through an
opening in the trees. The waters of this river are no
doubt full of fish, as are all the streams of Michigan,
and they have besides a fine characteristic—a sparkling
clearness.

Eighty-sixth Day.

Hawkins House,
YPSILANTI, MICHIGAN,
August Fifth.

A forbidding sky hung over Inkster as I took my
seat in the saddle at ten o'clock, but "Forward" was
the watchword, and there was moreover a charm in
variety, for sunny skies had become rather monotonous
and, under the circumstances, uncomfortable. The
dust was well laid when we had gone only a short
distance, but it rose again in a new form as *Paul*
quickened his pace, so that we did not present a very
dashing appearance to the Ypsilantians, after sixteen
miles of such travel.

Several times I was obliged to turn from the road,
once taking shelter under a tree and again in a woodshed. There were in town, however, those who could

A SUMMER AFTERNOON.

excuse the appearance of a bespattered traveller—brave men who had gone from Ypsilanti in the early days of the Rebellion, and who had learned from long campaigning to look upon their comrades without criticism. The brave Fourteenth Infantry started out from here under Colonel Robert Sinclair, and joining Sherman in Georgia took a lively part in all the movements of his army, until the fall of Atlanta; numbering among their proudest achievements the repulse of the enemy at Bentonville, North Carolina, where the hurriedly constructed works of the Federals were charged and taken and then regained at the point of the bayonet; and their part in the battle of Jonesboro, Georgia, in 1864, which was the last of Sherman's brilliant operations around Atlanta. Many of these brave fellows perished on the field of battle, but enough remain to keep fresh the memory of those stirring days and to add the influence of their patriotism to the young Ypsilanti.

Eighty-seventh Day.

Hawkins House,
YPSILANTI, MICHIGAN,
August Sixth.

On the previous evening I met a large number of men of the town, who gave me a hearty welcome, and as many of them were old soldiers, they expressed their satisfaction with the purpose of my lecture, favoring me with considerable enthusiasm in Union Hall.

The patriots of Michigan have many proud deeds to tell of, and are distinguished for their gallant service.

Their military leaders were invariably zealous, and their civil leaders unceasing in their encouragement. "We cannot consent to have one star obliterated from our flag" was the sentiment, and with the saving of the Union at heart, the men went into battle.

During Wheeler's repulse at Strawberry Plains in August, 1864, eight Michigan men were left to guard McMillan's Ford on the Halston. One of these, knowing the danger of his position, deserted, leaving his seven companions to "hold the fort." This handful kept back a brigade under the Confederate general almost four hours, but the Rebels crossed above and below the ford and captured the guard. One of their number, a farrier, was wounded, and Wheeler coming up to him began a conversation. Finally Wheeler said, "Are all the Tenth Michigan like you fellows?" "Oh, no," said the other, "we are mostly horse farriers and blacksmiths and not much accustomed to fighting." "Well," said Wheeler, "if I had three hundred such men as you, I could march straight through h—l!"

Eighty-eighth Day.

McKune House,
CHELSEA, MICHIGAN,
August Seventh.

Left Ypsilanti bright and early in order to save time, for although nearly the middle of August, I still felt the intense heat, and the dry dusty roads often made my daily journeys far from agreeable. For several days the mercury ranged between 85° and 90°, and as the route was at this time due west, the sun nearly stared me out of countenance in the afternoon.

Ann Arbor was reached about ten o'clock, but I did not take more than a passing glance at the University, noticing, however, that women as well as men were among the students—a recent and wise change in the law of the institution. The people were raising a flag over one of the buildings as I rode through, and on it in conspicuous letters were the names of Tilden and Hendricks.

Delhi, with no signs of a Lalla Rookh, and Scio, modest under the dignity of its suggestive Latin name, were quaint landmarks along my way, but I rode on a mile beyond to have dinner at Dexter. The Huron River has its source near here, in one of a cluster of lakelets, bordering on Livingstone and Washtenaw counties. All Michigan is covered with these small bodies of water, which, with the streams, lie upon its green surface like pearls in a network of silver.

Leaving Dexter, I had company all the way to Chelsea. Large flocks of sparrows flew along, lighting upon the telegraph wires, and as I approached they would fly away and settle again farther along, keeping up a kind of race, which was evidently fun for them, and which greatly amused me. It seemed as though they were tireless, and when I and my horse reached our destination fatigued, after twenty-six miles of travel in the sun, these strong-winged fellows were ready for another flight. I do not doubt that they easily accomplished the return journey, for we cannot compute the distance they can cover in a day. They are hardy little fellows and, despite the objections urged against them, have many admirable qualities, not the least among which is their tenacity of purpose.

Eighty-ninth Day.

Hurd House,
JACKSON, MICHIGAN,
August Eighth.

A few minutes after seven in the morning found me
in the saddle at Chelsea. I stopped on my way at the
Herald office and then struck off towards the main
road, along which I cantered to Grass Lake, where I
had dinner and remained until three o'clock. This
rest was thoroughly enjoyed, the more so perhaps, as I
learned before leaving Chelsea that if my advance
agents had not made arrangements for me elsewhere,
the people would have asked me to lecture here. In
that event I should not have been so familiar with
the quiet charms of Grass Lake.

Probably there are those who, if they had been in
my place, would have denied themselves these halts
along the way, but they would have been deprived of
a double gratification. In the first place they would
miss much of the character of the country through
which they passed, the real difference in the manners
and customs of the people; and they would miss the
opportunity of assuring the credulous that they were
not making a test ride across the continent within a
certain time and for a certain reward.

News often travels incredibly fast when there are no
evident means of communication, and I was often
amused by the curiosity which my advent excited
and the reasons which were whispered about in the
villages through which I passed, as to the object of
my journey. Indeed many Michiganders, from quiet

haunts in their native wilds, made short pilgrimages "to town" in order to look at one whom they fancied might hold a proud place for having crossed the continent in so many days, hours and seconds. My horse even was looked upon with awe, as "the charger upon which General Washington rode during the war of the Revolution!" But this anachronism belongs to New York.

Leaving Grass Lake late in the afternoon, it was necessary to make better time in order to cover the remainder of the twenty three miles lying between Chelsea and Jackson. The pace quickened. I came into the latter city at six o'clock, and rode directly to the hotel.

Ninetieth Day.

Hurd House,
JACKSON, MICHIGAN,
August Ninth.

I clipped the following notice from the *Citizen* of this date, as a memento of my stay at Jackson. It chronicled the fact that:

"Captain Willard Glazier lectured last evening in the interest of the Custer Monument Fund. His lecture was a good historical review delivered with graceful rhetoric and at times real eloquence. The Captain is still in the city giving his horse a rest; a noble Kentucky Black Hawk, whom he has ridden all the way from Boston, and whom he expects to carry him to San Francisco. He starts to-morrow morning for Battle Creek, where he lectures on Saturday evening."

My advance agent, Babcock, went on to Battle Creek in the morning, where arrangements were made with local committees for my lecture on the twelfth. After he had gone I made a leisurely inspection of the city. It was impossible to do more on account of the extreme heat.

This may no doubt be considered the center of the closely populated southern end of Michigan, a region dear, in times past, to the heart of the Indian, but which knows him no more. A Chippewa chief standing upon this soil, once said: "These lakes, these woods, these mountains were left to us by our ancestors; they are our inheritance, and we will part with them to no one." He knew not the strength of the pale faces who listened; for within a few years they were ready to claim, on the same grounds, those hills, and lakes, and mountains for their own.

Compared to the peninsula, whose mineral-laden shores are washed by Superior, Michigan and Huron, there is the greatest contrast; and La Hontan, making a little exploratory trip up there before anyone else, called it "the fag end of the world." These words might still be applied to some of the wildest northern points, but here is the very heart of civilization.

Jackson lies in the coal fields that reach down through several of the southern counties. This deposit is not rich, owing to the amount of sulphur in it, and the demand is chiefly local. The Grand River divides the town and, with the bridge that spans it, adds much to the picturesque effect.

Ninety-first Day.

Cooley House,
PARMA, MICHIGAN,
August Tenth.

Spent the forenoon in my room at the Hurd House, Jackson, writing letters to my wife, Major Hastings and others. In the afternoon there was a street parade of Howe's London Circus which was a very fantastic affair, but which seemed to be hugely enjoyed by everybody. Later in the day the great tent was upset by a gust of wind, accompanied by a thunder-shower, and a droll scene followed, which caused considerable excitement. The people were left exposed with the rain coming down upon them in torrents. So far I have seen nothing more amusing than the country boys and girls rushing up town drenched, and for once at least indifferent to the charms of the " big show."

The storm having passed, I ordered *Paul* after supper, rode down to the office of the *Patriot and Citizen,* and after a few minutes' conversation with the editor, hurried on toward Parma, which was reached late in the evening. The ride in the dark was cool, but somewhat lonely.

It was probably on such nights as this that young Dean, the enterprising settler of years ago, played his nocturnal tricks upon his neighbors. He came out to Michigan when it was a wilderness, to make his fortune by clearing land at ten dollars an acre, and while he was drudging he expected to have a little fun. It was his habit to work away all day chopping trees within an inch of the falling point, and then about ten o'clock, when the settlers were well asleep, to go out and give a blow to the end tree, so that it would fall against the others and send them crashing like a row of ninepins. How the old forests must have rung with their thundering and how that plotter Dean must have relished his mischief!

As I approached Parma, in the darkness I could see nothing about the village to suggest that other Parma,

far away under an Italian sky, but there is a resemblance, for the European duchy and its modest
American namesake both lie in a rich agricultural
region; and if I mistake not the dull white freestone
that is quarried here in such large quantities, finds a
prototype over the sea.

Ninety-second Day.

Witt House,
MARSHALL, MICHIGAN,
August Eleventh.

As there was a heavy rainfall in the morning, I
waited in Parma until nearly ten o'clock, and even
then was obliged to start in a thunder-shower in
order to keep my appointment for the following
evening at Battle Creek. This required no sacrifice,
for, excepting the discomfort of wet clothes, the change
was agreeable. I reached Albion in time for dinner,
and immediately made myself comfortable at the hotel.
Rest and refreshment having the desired effect, I afterward took a short stroll through the town, which I
found very wide awake, although the Methodist
college, the life of the place, was still closed for the
summer vacation. In the meantime the men of the
village had met, and before I remounted, came to me
and persuaded me to return by rail and deliver the
Custer lecture on the fifteenth. Glad to do all I
could for the "Benefit Fund," I readily consented and
started away with the good wishes of the impromptu
committee. Marshall, being only twelve miles beyond,
was reached early in the evening, so that before dark I
had time to get a mental picture of the place. Calhoun

THE COUNTRY PEDDLER.

County has its capitol here, and in 1853 it was looked upon as one of the most flourishing towns in Michigan. It has not reached the predicted pinnacle of importance, but it has a pleasant situation, some flourishing flour mills, and is altogether a credit to the " Wolverines."

Ninety-third Day.

Potter House,
BATTLE CREEK, MICHIGAN,
August Twelfth.

As soon as *Paul* was led out in front of the Witt House at Marshall, a large crowd gathered about us; and when I had taken my seat in the saddle, one of the number stepped forward in behalf of the towns-people to invite me to return at a time which had previously been agreed upon and lecture on the heroes of the Revolution. Giving them the best promise I could, I hurried away as I had a good six hours' ride before me.

Since the day before there had been a decided change in the weather. The sun blazed down with almost tropical heat, drying up the roads and making my way a veritable fiery furnace. I had a rare opportunity for watching "Old Sol" on these solitary rides, as he appeared unfailingly in the morning, swung through the heavens, and vanished in the west at night. It was now harvest time, and since that early day in May on which I started westward, I had kept my eye on him like a true worshipper, half understanding the pagan with his devotion to Apollo, and half in sympathy with the Indian who greets the Sun-god and weaves the splendid symbol into pouch and canoe and mocassin. Between the hours of ten and four particularly the heat was intense, but in other respects the day was uneventful.

Ninety-fourth Day.

Private House,
BATTLE CREEK, MICHIGAN,
August Thirteenth.

On the preceding evening a full house greeted me at Stuart's Hall, where I was introduced by a comrade of the G. A. R., Lieutenant Eugene T. Freeman. After the lecture I met several of the leading men of the town and later was invited to a private residence, where I was made at home during the remainder of my stay. The Lieutenant called for me on Sunday morning, and I accompanied him to church, meeting the pastor, Rev. L. D. Palmer, who spoke with animation and warmth and made the service an effective one. I enjoyed it all the more perhaps as I realized that before many Sundays I would be on the Great Plains beyond the Mississippi, where churches are known to be very rare. Continuing his courtesies, my comrade friend drove me out to the favorite resort, Lake Goguac, in the afternoon and there I had several fine views of the surrounding country. This little incident suggests an interesting theory concerning one of the pre-historic races who are supposed to have occupied this section of the country. It seems that in the ancient symbolic manuscripts of the Aztecs frequent mention is made of a land which they called Aztelan, compounded of the symbols A. T. S. and signifying " Lake Country," from which also their own name is derived, making it to mean " the people of the lake country." They refer to their former home as a country lying towards the north and giving further details which might be descriptive of the Peninsular State—so the theorist thinks. As a coincident, but advanced nevertheless as a strong argument, the learned gentleman states that the Wyandots have a tradition to the effect that hundreds of years ago, the builders of the mounds were driven southward by invaders from the northeast; and pursuing the magic thread, he suggests that the Aztecs were usurpers in Mexico according to their own traditions and the corroboration of Spanish history. If this is the case, my comrade and myself, in visiting this pretty little lake, may have trodden upon the same soil which had been pressed by the feet of the mysterious builders of the mounds. I am personally a trifle sceptical on this point, and believe that the key to this part of ancient history is yet to be found.

Ninety-fifth Day.

Kalamazoo House,
KALAMAZOO, MICHIGAN,
August Fourteenth.

On this day I passed a fine wheat-growing section in the valley of the Kalamazoo, whose richest part is probably near the Big Village—its namesake. This river, which drains Hillsdale, Kalamazoo, Calhoun and Allegan counties, and is navigable for forty miles above its mouth, has, I believe, more traffic than any one of the rivers of Michigan. Throughout its length of two hundred miles it flows through pine and oak forests, through the richest section of a State famed for its agricultural products, and like the Nile, if I may so compare the relics of a great people with those of one comparatively unknown, is looked down upon by the silent monuments of the past. To me the comparison is not unreasonable, for I consider the tumuli of those mound-builders scattered over the hills and valleys of America, worthy of as much interest and respect as the more splendid remnants of a higher civilization.

At this point the stream is still broad and picturesque. As to its name I am undecided. According to some it is a corruption of Ke-Kenemazoo, meaning "the boiling pot," and according to others of Kik-alamazoo, "the mirage river," because to the fanciful Indian the stones that jutted, dark and wet, out of the river-bed looked like otters. The village on its banks was settled in 1829, and after being known for two years by the name of its first settler, Bronson, became, in 1836, Kalamazoo. It is thoroughly alive, has a population of about 18,000, and its position as the half-way place between Detroit and Chicago adds considerably to its importance. I lectured here to a full house, being introduced by Major R. F. Judson, formerly of General Custer's staff, and bearing a high reputation as a soldier. Intercourse with one who had known the General so well, and who held him in such loyal regard, gave me a new insight into the life of

"That mighty man of war,
A lion in battle, and a child by the fireside."

Ninety-sixth Day.

Albion House,
ALBION, MICHIGAN,
August Fifteenth.

I came back to this place from Kalamazoo on the afternoon train and was met at the station by R. A. Daniels, who went with me to the hotel. The introduction at the Opera House where I lectured in the evening was made by Captain Rienzi Loud. When I concluded, I found that the good old custom of " passing round the hat " had not yet lost favor, for two gentlemen, having furnished the " hat," assumed the rôle of collectors and the " Fund " was within a very short time substantially increased. When this ceremony was over a man in the audience rose and said : " Captain Glazier ! I came in after the hat was passed, but I want to give something toward the ' Monument ;' " and suiting the action to the word he made his contribution. The whole ceremony was so suggestive of a certain little church up in St. Lawrence County, New York, where the same custom prevails on Sundays, that I came very near fancying myself the parson, and if some of my comrades had not come up immediately and given me a hearty greeting, I might have been guilty of pronouncing a benediction !

As it was quite late when I reached this point, having made twenty-five miles since ten o'clock, there was very little time for sightseeing, but I learned that here was the seat of Ames College, a thriving Methodist institution admitting both men and women, and proudly referred to by the people of Albion.

Ninety-seventh Day.

72 West Main Street,
BATTLE CREEK, MICHIGAN,
August Sixteenth.

Called at Captain Loud's law office at Albion in the morning, and had a delightful chat over old times, our topic an inexhaustible one—the battles and incidents of the late war. As this town was only a short distance away, I was tempted to prolong the chat into a visit, finding the Captain a cordial comrade.

According to previous agreement I lectured in the evening at Wayne Hall, Marshall, having an introduction by Colonel Charles W. Dickie.

My horse was now in Michigan City, being treated for the sore on his back by an old comrade, who since the war had attained quite a reputation as a veterinary surgeon. The delay was somewhat annoying as I anticipated trouble in crossing the Rockies, if I did not reach them before the season was too far advanced; but there was a possibility of disabling the animal if his affliction were neglected, and my sympathies were with him. As the delay could not be avoided I availed myself of the "Iron Horse" and on it made brief tours to the neighboring towns.

At this time it was very easy to agree with the theory of the fatalist that "whatever is, is right," for by an accident I was enabled to meet more agreeable people, to enjoy their hospitality, and to see more, which was my chief purpose in crossing the continent.

A philosopher never worries about little hindrances, for he soon learns that a delay often proves to be an advantage. Such was my case.

A MILL IN THE FOREST.

Ninety-eighth Day.

72 West Main Street,
BATTLE CREEK, MICHIGAN,
August Seventeenth.

Soon after breakfast I left Marshall for Battle Creek on a freight train, as there were no passenger coaches over the road until the afternoon. This mode of travel, if not the most luxurious, was at least novel, and we made very good time. Between the two places the face of the country hardly changed in appearance. There were the same fields of wheat and corn, and at Battle Creek evidently as much business in the flour mills as at Marshall.

The creek, uniting here with the Kalamazoo, after a serpentine course of forty miles, supplies the water-power and gives the necessary impetus to trade.

I have heard that the tributary won its bellicose name through a little difficulty between the first surveyors of public land who came to mark this section and some Indians. The quarrel ended seriously, and, as the tradition goes, two of the Indians were killed.

It may have been that the latter were making an attempt to hold the ground, and that it was but one of the many similar occurrences which were to convince the red man that he was superfluous. Calhoun County was certainly worth making a stand for. Its soil was rich, providing abundantly for the simple wants of the savage, and in the clear waters of the St. Joseph and the Kalamazoo tributaries many a paddle had descended with a deft stroke, upon the gleaming back of pike and pickerel.

Ninety-ninth Day.

32 Portage Street,
KALAMAZOO, MICHIGAN,
August Eighteenth.

At nine o'clock I was once more on *Paul's* back possessed of a stronger sense of satisfaction than had been mine for many days. The truth is, I had missed my four-legged companion sorely. Reached Augusta at noon. I had a good old-fashioned dinner, and the horse something that was quite satisfactory, and at four o'clock we started on again for Kalamazoo. Soon after I left the village a thunder-shower came up, but there was a convenient tree at hand and we were not slow in reaching it. Thinking that all was well I again put spur to *Paul* and we started forward, this time coming in sight of the little village of Comstock, three miles east of Kalamazoo, before our progress was interrupted. Off in the distance the warning whistle of an approaching train broke in upon the stillness; the familiar rumble of wheels followed, and in a moment more, as it was rushing by, *Paul* made a leap of forty feet over the embankment. He was good enough to leave me and the saddle behind. It was a narrow escape and I was severely stunned, but was soon up again getting my bearings. I found my horse standing in the stream stripped of everything except the bridle, and, with the exception of a slight trace of nervousness in him, looking as though nothing unusual had occurred. We reached Kalamazoo a little later, and there I wrote to Mr. Bulkley as follows:

Kalamazoo House,
KALAMAZOO, MICHIGAN,
August 18, 1876.

J. M. BULKLEY, ESQ.,
   Secretary Custer Monument Association,
      Monroe, Michigan.

DEAR SIR:—I have the pleasure of transmitting to Judge Wing, through Major R. F. Judson, the net proceeds of my lecture, delivered in this place on the evening of the sixteenth instant. I desire to accompany my gift with an acknowledgment of many courtesies extended by the press and band of this patriotic village. I resume my journey this afternoon and shall speak at Niles, South Bend, and Laporte before the close of the present week. Hoping that your brightest anticipations for the "Monument" may be most fully realized, I remain

   Very sincerely yours,   WILLARD GLAZIER.

This letter I preserved, as I wished to have all the correspondence upon the subject of the "Monument" for future reference.

One Hundredth Day.

Dyckman House,
PAW PAW, MICHIGAN,
August Nineteenth.

Had an early breakfast at Kalamazoo. Ordered *Paul,* and mounting him rode through the Big Village to take a last look. Before leaving I called upon Major Judson and Colonel F. W. Curtenius. The latter of whom has had a brilliant career. Graduating from Hamilton College in 1823, he studied law and later went to South America, enlisting in the cause of the Brazilians. He served through the war with Mexico, was appointed adjutant-general of Michigan in 1855, holding this office until 1861, having received the high title of Senator in 1853 and being re-elected to the office in 1867. The Colonel's father was a general in the war of 1812, and was for many years a member of the New York Legislature. I am only familiar with Major Judson's military record, but his services as a citizen are no doubt as honorable as was his career as a soldier.

With these gentlemen I entrusted the proceeds of my lecture and the letter to Mr. Bulkley, with the request that they be transmitted to the Monument Association at Monroe. They expressed their appreciation of my gift in warm terms and handed me the following acknowledgments:

KALAMAZOO, MICHIGAN,
August 19, 1876.

Received of Captain Willard Glazier the net proceeds of his lecture at this place, which sum is to be applied to the fund for the erection of a Monument to the memory of the late General Custer at Monroe City, Michigan. We take great pleasure in speaking of Captain Glazier in the highest terms, not only on account of the self-devotion he has manifested in a noble cause, but of his indomitable perseverance and energy. We trust he will, wherever he goes, receive the unanimous support of the citizens whom he addresses.

F. W. CURTENIUS,
Late Colonel U. S. Volunteers.

I take great pleasure in fully endorsing the above, and recommending to public confidence and support Captain Willard Glazier, in his efforts in behalf of the Custer Monument Association,

R. F. JUDSON,
Late Aide to General Custer.

With an exchange of salutations and good wishes from the friends whose courtesies I considered it an honor to receive, I left Kalamazoo for Paw Paw. The ride between these towns was unusually trying. *Paul's* back was still tender, the heat was intense, and under these circumstances it was necessary to cover fourteen miles before any refreshment could be had.

One Hundred and First Day.

Dyckman House,
PAW PAW, MICHIGAN,
August Twentieth.

This Sunday was a perfect day for rest, and I indulged in a generous amount. Had breakfast at eight o'clock, after which I strolled through the streets of the Van Buren County capital, finding them generally like all other village streets, but with enough individuality about them to make them interesting. The High School stood, with the usual dignity of educational institutions, prominent among the neat cottages, and in the business portion two or three newspaper offices gave unfailing proof of local alertness.

The east and west branches of the Paw Paw River meet here and hurry on to pay their tribute to the Kalamazoo, offering their united strength to the business concerns which man has erected on their shores. The outlying farms thus naturally irrigated are very rich, and give, with the extensive lumbering interests, a very flourishing and prosperous appearance to this section of country and a certain briskness to the trade at Paw Paw.

On returning to my room I copied the testimonials given me by Colonel Curtenius and Major Judson of Kalamazoo, wrote several letters, attended to some neglected dates in my journal, and made my plans for the next few days. It was my intention to go to South Bend by rail the following morning, to lecture there in the evening and then proceed to Grand Rapids, where I was announced for Tuesday. My horse was in the meantime undergoing new and vigorous treatment which I hoped would permanently cure him.

One Hundred and Second Day.

Grand Central Hotel,
SOUTH BEND, INDIANA,
August Twenty-first.

At ten o'clock I left Paw Paw, reached Decatur at noon, registered at the Duncombe House and then continued my journey by rail. I hardly realized that I was out of Michigan in this town on the St. Joseph, for the river belongs to the "Wolverines" with the exception of the capricious South Bend, and the streets have the breadth and abundance of shade that have won so much admiration for the cities of Michigan. It has, besides, the Hoosier enterprise, and began to be an important manufacturing place fifteen years ago. The first settlement began in 1831 with a handful of houses and a population of a hundred souls. It has now reached over 10,000. Prominent among the resources to which its growth may be attributed is its proximity to the hard-wood forests of Northern Indiana and Michigan.

These woods have proven a bonanza to South Bend. Enterprising manufacturers have drawn from their unfailing source; prominent among them being the Studebaker Brothers, who have had an enviable career. These enterprising men started in 1852 with a cash capital of sixty-eight dollars, and a knowledge of blacksmithing which they had acquired at their father's forge on the Ohio. Thus equipped they went to work, turning out two wagons the first year. The present output makes that humble beginning seem almost incredible. Studebaker's wagons are famous and the firm controls capital stock amounting to a million of dollars. The other notable enterprise is the Oliver Chilled Plow Works, founded in 1853 by James Oliver, a Scotchman, who came to Indiana to follow the vocation of an iron master, and who ultimately had the satisfaction of exporting his manufactures to his native country.

The most distinguished citizen of South Bend at the time of my visit, and the most prominent man in Indiana, was Hon. Schuyler Colfax, whose career as a statesman was a singularly brilliant one. For over a quarter of a century he had been eminent in state and national politics. Beginning life as an editor he founded in 1845 the *St. Joseph Valley Register*, an organ of considerable popularity and which at the time had a strong influence in local Whig circles. His subsequent duties as Speaker of the House of Representatives and the friend and adviser of Lincoln, kept him out of editorial work, and later he was entirely engrossed with affairs of state. In 1868 he was elected to the office of Vice-President under General Grant as chief executive.

One Hundred and Third Day.

Sweet's Hotel,
GRAND RAPIDS, MICHIGAN.
August Twenty-second.

My birthday. Went by rail from South Bend to Kalamazoo in the morning ; had dinner at the latter

place, and then caught an early train for Grand
Rapids, where, finding that George had made unusually good arrangements, I spoke in Luce's Hall to
one of the largest audiences which greeted me in
Michigan, General W. P. Innes, well known in
Grand Army circles and a mason of high rank, introducing me. A large and strongly executed painting
of the Battle of Lookout Mountain, stretching across
the rear of the platform, made a striking effect and
gave zest to my reference to the War for the Union.

My reception at this place was so hearty that I
should have enjoyed a longer visit; but plans already
laid prevented. I knew the town itself well, for I
had previously been there. It is full of interest both
on account of its past history and its present activity.
The city lies on both sides of the Grand River and
seems to be hedged in by the great bluffs that reach
along at the water edge of the valley two miles apart.
Below is a stratum of limestone rock, forming the bed
of the river, for about a mile and a half with a descent
of eighteen feet causing the rapids and supplying
the water-power. Gypsum is quarried here in large
quantities, and this industry supplemented by manufactures and fruit culture gives it its commercial importance. Perhaps its most striking peculiarity is to
be found in the large proportion of Hollanders who
swell the population. Their churches, their newspapers and their general thrift give them a high
standing in the community, and what they have ever
been accorded—a reputation for being loyal and enterprising citizens.

In 1760 there was a very different state of things
here. The Ottawa Indians had a large village below

the rapids, and there Pontiac's voice was heard, calling upon the chiefs to aid him in his projected siege of Detroit. Here the fur traders had their grand depot, and the missionaries labored in the cause of Christianity; and when in 1834 the Indian settlement began its metamorphosis, some bold prophet declared that it would soon be " the brightest star in the constellation of western villages." This prophecy has been more than fulfilled, for Grand Rapids is the acknowledged metropolis of Western Michigan. In the mail that awaited me was a copy of the South Bend *Herald,* containing a pleasant notice which chronicled in true newspaper diction the fact that

" Captain Glazier delivered his lecture ' Echoes from the Revolution' at the Academy of Music last evening. Promptly at eight o'clock the lecturer, with Mr. J. F. Creed, appeared on the platform. Mr. Creed in introducing the lecturer stated the object of the lecture to be in aid of the Custer Monument Association of Monroe, Michigan. He also read several letters introducing Captain Glazier to the public, from well-known citizens of Michigan, and acknowledging receipts of the proceeds of the lectures delivered in Detroit and Kalamazoo. The theme of the lecturer afforded a fine field for the display of his talents as a speaker. Possessing a fine imagination, good descriptive powers and the real qualities of an orator, he could not fail to please the really intelligent audience which greeted him last evening. Probably one hour and a half were consumed in its delivery; but the interest and attention did not flag nor tire, and when the speaker took leave of his audience he was greeted with several rounds of applause."

One Hundred and Fourth Day.

Duncombe House,
DECATUR, MICHIGAN,
August Twenty-third.

Came down from Grand Rapids in the morning intending to stop on the way at Lawton, but was carried

by through the carelessness of a brakeman who neglected to announce the stations. The town is quite an
important point on the road for its size owing to the
extensive fruit orchards of the surrounding farms.
This common industry which has sprung up in all
parts of the State, but especially in the southern portion, and which attracts more attention than anything
else, is a contradiction to the statements of those who
examined the country while it was yet a wilderness.

In 1815 the surveyor-general of Ohio made a
journey through the State and soberly reported that
not more than one acre in a thousand in Southern
Michigan would in any case admit of cultivation,
yet notwithstanding that worthy's opinion, six hundred thousand peach trees flourished in South-
western Michigan in 1872! Surely that is a fact to
be proud of. On my arrival at Decatur I found the
Eagle of Grand Rapids, containing mention of my
lecture at that place as follows:

"A very large audience gathered at Luce's Hall last night to hear
Captain Willard Glazier. The speaker was earnest and impassioned,
his lecture was delivered with a force and eloquence that pleased his
hearers, and all who were in the hall went away glad that they had
been there, and ready to add to the praises that have been bestowed
on Captain Glazier as soldier, author and orator."

Such notices were gratifying—not for the leaven of
flattery which they contained, but because they helped
along the cause which was to raise a shaft to the
deserving dead. For this reason I appreciated the
comments of the press and owed much to its co-operation. It is a pleasure to me to acknowledge my
indebtedness to this most powerful agent of modern
times.

One Hundred and Fifth Day

Dyckman House,
PAW PAW, MICHIGAN,
August Twenty-fourth.

Took the Michigan Central to Lawton, and changing cars there continued my journey to this place by the Paw Paw Road. Thinking that it might facilitate matters, I had my saddle padded here, and had a talk with the saddler besides, as the delay was becoming serious. At this crisis, if man and horse could have set up a partnership, like the fabled Centaurs, how we could have flown before the wind—or even outstripped the Michigan Central—as we galloped across country towards the setting sun! That old myth was an inspiration. Was it invented by some fanciful traveller-horseman hindered on his way to Rome or Athens, by a saddler or a veterinary surgeon?

During my forced visit, the people of Paw Paw were very kind, making the time pass agreeably and giving me a pleasant recollection to take away. These small social influences carried great weight with them, and helped to bear out the universally acknowledged fact that associations are all powerful.

It is not strange that people, rather than their abode or works, strongly impress themselves, nor that, realizing this, they should be cordial in their hospitality. If, then, I praise the beauty or enterprise of these American towns, I bear witness at the same time, to the kindness and courtesy of their inhabitants. Whether East or West, these qualities were everywhere apparent, proving the universality of generous feeling.

One Hundred and Sixth Day.

Private House,
NILES, MICHIGAN,
August Twenty-fifth.

Leaving Paw Paw after breakfast I went down to Lawton by rail, where I changed cars, taking the Michigan Central to Niles, this for the purpose of making use of the extra time that now hung heavily upon my hands. A good proportion of the six thousand inhabitants came to Kellogg Hall in the evening to manifest their interest in the Custer Monument and the old Revolutionary heroes, Mr. J. T. Head giving the introduction.

Reaching Niles before noon I had ample time to look about, and to hear from old residents something of Berrien County and their home here on the St. Joseph.

For those who delight in searching out events from the doubtful past, there is suggestion enough here to keep them occupied for at least a week. Even this small town possesses records that date back to 1669, when Pere Allouez came along down the river on a voyage of discovery and who may have encamped on the very site of Niles, for all that the people who live there now know. But putting this aside, it is certain that in 1700 the Jesuits had a mission a short distance south of the present city, and that there were forts built here and there in the vicinity as a protection against the Indians. Later, when matters were settled and the English and French had long since withdrawn, the Reverend Isaac McCoy came out into the wilder-

NO ROOMS TO LET.

ness with his family and established Cary Mission, probably in sight of where the old Jesuit Mission stood. This was in 1820. Six years afterwards a handful of cabins made their appearance, and out of this nucleus the town of Niles was evolved. This is a mere outline without the adornment of those pleasant little fictions that cling about the sober history of every inhabited place on earth, and which delight the ear of most travellers, for there may be those who follow me who echo the sentiment of the Michigan pioneer, "From legend and romance, good Lord, deliver us!"

One Hundred and Seventh Day.

Private House,
LA PORTE, INDIANA,
August Twenty-sixth.

Was compelled to avail myself of livery accommodations in order to meet my evening engagement at La Porte. Rode in a hack to South Bend, and finally reached my destination by way of the Michigan Central and Southern Indiana roads. My advance agent, Babcock, met me at the station, and I accompanied him to the home of a Mr. Munday, who I discovered was the father of an old fellow-prisoner at "Libby."

I was delighted with the situation and appearance of the town. It rises on the border of a beautiful and fruitful prairie, its northern end bounded by a chain of seven lakes which make an ideal resort in summer, and is at a sufficient distance from the great body of water which dips down into that corner of the State, to enjoy a comparatively mild climate. Its population is about 8,000, of which a good share is employed in the foundries, machine shops and mills that make up its business activity. The younger element is provided for in good schools, and that luxury of modern communities—the public library—is zealously supported. On a line with it, as a free and instructive institution, the Natural History Association, founded in 1863, holds an honored place, and unlike most societies of a similar character has succeeded in making its researches of interest. In fact for its size the city has made great progress in literary and educational directions.

One Hundred and Eighth Day.

Jewell House,
MICHIGAN CITY, INDIANA,
August Twenty-seventh.

After my lecture of the previous evening at La Porte, I took the first train to this city—emphatically the City of Sand. Time and winds have raised great hills of sand on every side, and from their crests one can look off for miles over the lake, getting perhaps a deeper impression of its vastness than from a less monotonous lookout.

These sand dunes are supposed by some to be caused by a peculiar meteorological phenomena of currents and counter-currents acting vertically, instead of horizontally. Whatever the cause, they have made Indiana's only port of entry a place of such striking peculiarity, that, once seen, I doubt if it would ever be forgotten.

In the forenoon I went out on the lake in a small

yacht; but finding the little craft unequal to the heavy waves which were rushing in from the north, I soon turned back, having gained by the venture a better idea of the dunes and of their extent as they stretch along the western shore.

The fact that they are "building upon the sand" gives the people of Michigan City very little concern, probably because they know there is *terra firma* somewhere beneath their foundations.

Ames College occupies a site here, and the Car Shops are important and extensive.

One Hundred and Ninth Day.

Duncombe House,
DECATUR, MICHIGAN,
August Twenty-eighth.

Taking an early train, I returned to this place in the morning, where I had decided to remain for a few days in order to allow more time for the treatment of my horse, and to give my brother and Babcock an opportunity to insure a full house at Farwell Hall, Chicago, where I was announced to lecture on the eleventh of September.

I had begun to fear that the irritation on *Paul's* back would develop into that most disgusting and painful disease of horses known as fistula; and although he never showed any impatience, I had not the heart to ride him while in this condition.

My quarters were quite comfortable at the only hotel in town, and I thanked my stars that I was not stranded in some little backwoods place with the choice of "the softest boards on the floor for a bed," and other accommodations to match—a state of affairs which a waylaid journeyman once had to face, who, with the soul of a Stoic, left on his window-pane the comforting couplet:

> "Learn hence, young man, and teach it to your sons:
> The easiest way's to take it as it comes."

In fact I was doubly fortunate. No sooner had I reached Decatur than I lost the consciousness of being "a stranger within the gates," having been so cordially made to feel that I was among friends, and that the cause which I had taken up in Michigan met with their hearty sympathy.

One Hundred and Tenth Day.

Duncombe House,
DECATUR, MICHIGAN,
August Twenty-ninth.

Met George L. Darby, an old comrade of the "Harris Light," in the afternoon. He had noticed my signature on the hotel register, and came at once to my room, where after the heartiest of greetings we sat down for a long talk. Thirteen years had slipped away since the time of our capture at New Baltimore, Virginia, which led him to Belle Isle and me to Libby Prison, and yet as we discussed it all, the reality of those events seemed undiminished. Kilpatrick, Stuart, Fitzhugh Lee—their clever manœuvring, and our own unfortunate experiences on that day, kept us as enthusiastically occupied as though it were not an old story: but soldiers may be pardoned for recurring to

RURAL SCENE IN MICHIGAN.

those events which, while they impressed themselves
upon witnesses with indelible distinctness, may yet have
lost their bitterness, when it is remembered that before
many years they and their stories will have passed
away.   To those who indulge in the absurd belief that
such topics are discussed with malicious intent, no
justification need be made.

Led on from one thing to another, I found Darby
finally plying me with questions of kindly interest
about my peaceful march from Ocean to Ocean, and
anxiously asking about my horse, which I had previously left in his care.   He offered to do all he could
for the animal and with this comforting assurance took
his leave.

One Hundred and Eleventh Day.

Duncombe House,
DECATUR, MICHIGAN,
August Thirtieth.

Early in the afternoon Darby called with fishing
tackle and proposed that we go out to Lake of the
Woods and try our luck with hook and line.   The
expedition was not successful as far as fish was con-
·cerned, but we had a delightful boat ride and plenty
of talk.

The lake, a pretty little dot lying, as its name
implies, in the heart of the woods, is an ideal spot for
rest and enjoyment, and its miniature dimensions bear
no resemblance to its famed namesake of Minnesota.
As we had such poor success with our tackle I took no
note of the kind of fish that make their home within
its sleepy borders, and my companion gave me very

little information. The truth is, we were more interested in our concerns and the serious affairs outside the sport which so fascinated Izak Walton.

One Hundred and Twelfth Day.

Duncombe House,
DECATUR, MICHIGAN,
August Thirty-first.

Albert W. Rogers, to whom I had been previously introduced, called late in the afternoon, and invited me to drive with him, determined, he told me, that I should see something of Decatur's surroundings. The time was favorable for agreeable impressions. It had been a typical summer day, with blue sky, a slight breeze and the mercury at 70°; in short, just such weather as I had encountered in this section of Michigan throughout the month of August, and as evening approached, I was prepared to enjoy to the utmost the pleasure which my new acquaintance had provided.

On the outskirts of the town one gets a view of gently rolling country under a splendid state of cultivation, the yellow of the grain fields predominating, and dotted here and there with farmhouses. Dark outlines against the horizon suggested the forests of oak, ash, maple, birch and elm, which stretch over such large tracts of Van Buren County, and which have made a little paradise for lumbermen. Wheat, maize and hay appeared to be flourishing; but I believe that agricultural products do their best in the rich bottom-lands bordering the rivers. I have dwelt so enthusiastically upon this fertile country that to say more would seem extravagant, so I will bring

SPINNING YARNS BY A TAVERN FIRE.

my note, the chronicle of a most delightful day, to a close.

One Hundred and Thirteenth Day.

Duncombe House,
DECATUR, MICHIGAN,
September First.

Received and answered a large mail after breakfast, and in the afternoon took a walk through the village. One is, of course, reminded of the gallant Commodore whose name, once among the greatest in America, now honors this modest Western town, and whose deeds, once upon every lip in the young republic, are well-nigh forgotten. The question even suggests itself as to how many of those who live here, where his name is perpetuated, are familiar with his life and character.

His capture of the frigate *Philadelphia,* which had been seized and held in the harbor of Tripoli in 1801, during the pacha's seizure of our merchantmen, was said by Admiral Nelson to be " the most daring act of the age," and his diplomacy at Algiers and Tunis and Tripoli, where in 1812 his demands were acceded to, received the applause of all Christendom, especially because those demands included the release of the Christian captives at Algiers and of the Danish and Neapolitan prisoners at Tripoli, and ended, forever, the pretensions of the Barbary powers.

After the trial of Commodore Barron for cowardice, Decatur made some remarks which the former thought should not be allowed to pass unnoticed, and accordingly called upon his accuser to retract them. This Decatur refused to do, but attempted to bring about a reconciliation. Barron refused this and threw down the gauntlet, and when shortly afterwards the two met to settle the difficulty "with honor," both fell at the word "Fire!"—Decatur mortally wounded. The affair was universally deplored, for his loyal services had endeared Decatur to his country, and when his remains were taken to the grave, they were followed by the largest concourse of people that had ever assembled in Washington.

One Hundred and Fourteenth Day.

Duncombe House,
DECATUR, MICHIGAN,
September Second.

This was a great day for Decatur. With the morning came the completion of arrangements for a Republican mass-meeting, and a rustic band from an adjacent village arrived at nine o'clock in a farm wagon. The "Stars and Stripes" floated majestically over the heads of the patriotic musicians, and the people were drawn from every quarter to the stirring call of fife and drum, eager to see their leaders and to listen to their views upon the vital questions of the day. The "Silver Cornet Band" of Dowagiac co-operated with the "Decatur Fife and Drum Corps," in rousing the dormant element of the place, and, as its imposing appellation would imply, did so with dignified and classical selections.

The political campaign which had been slumbering since the nomination of Hayes and Tilden reached an interesting stage of its progress at this time, and the friends and champions of the rival candidates were

fully alive to the issues of their respective plat-
forms.

By nightfall the place was the scene of great activity, and to an onlooker produced a singular effect.
Men were collected in groups engaged in excited conversation, torches flared in every direction, while at
brief intervals all voices were drowned in some lively
tune from the silver cornets or the fife and drum.

At an appointed hour the speakers of the evening
appeared, and I noticed among them Hon. Ransom
H. Nutting and Hon. Thomas W. Keightly—the
latter a candidate for Congress from this district. The
meeting closed at a late hour, after a succession of
heated addresses, and yet the politicians of Van Buren
County seemed not at all averse to continuing their
talking until sunrise.

One Hundred and Fifteenth Day.

Duncombe House,
DECATUR, MICHIGAN,
September Third.

Accepting an invitation from Albert Rogers, I accompanied him to the Presbyterian Church in the
morning, where Rev. Mr. Hoyt, a young clergyman,
conducted the services and preached a very good sermon. I was pleased by the courtesy extended me
when he said, in the course of his announcements. " I
take pleasure in calling attention to Captain Glazier's
lecture at Union Hall to-morrow night. I shall be
present myself, and recommend all who wish to listen
to an instructive and patriotic lecture to be at the hall
before eight o'clock." When the service was over Mr.

Rogers and I waited to have a few words with Mr. Hoyt, who was evidently very much interested in my journey across country and who intended to lend his influence in behalf of the "Monument Fund." We then returned to the hotel where I passed the remainder of the day quietly in my room.

One Hundred and Sixteenth Day.

Duncombe House,
DECATUR, MICHIGAN,
September Fourth.

Lectured to a full house at Union Hall in the evening. My sojourn of a week at this place and the interest felt in the effort to perpetuate the memory of Custer, brought about the most gratifying results. Among those who were with me on the platform were Hon. Ransom Nutting, Rev. Mr. Hoyt, Prof. Samuel G. Burked and Albert W. Rogers. I was presented by Mr. Nutting, after which testimonials from the Monument Association were read by Prof. Burked, and later the following pleasant acknowledgment from these gentlemen was handed me :

DECATUR, MICHIGAN,
September 4, 1876.

- CAPTAIN WILLARD GLAZIER,

MY DEAR SIR : We take this means of expressing to you our appreciation of the highly instructive and very entertaining lecture delivered by you at Union Hall this evening. Truly we admire your plan and your generosity in giving the entire proceeds to the Custer Monument Fund. Our endorsement is the expression of our village people generally. You have made many friends here.

May success attend you throughout your journey.

Very respectfully,

S. GORDON BURKED,
RANSOM NUTTING,
ALBERT W. ROGERS.

Such greeting as this, extended to me all along my way, gives substantial proof of the universal kindness with which I was received, and of the spontaneous hospitality of the American citizen.

One Hundred and Seventeenth Day.

Seymour House,
DOWAGIAC, MICHIGAN,
September Fifth.

There was a large gathering in front of the Duncombe House in the morning when I mounted *Paul* and faced westward, turning my back upon the hospitable little village in which I had spent so many pleasant days, and where I felt that I had indeed made many friends. Mr. Rogers and a young man of the place, whose name I am sorry to have forgotten, escorted me out of town intending to ride with me to Dowagiac, but an approaching rain-storm obliged them to turn back. As I came in sight of the village I noticed unmistakable signs of a stream which I discovered was the Dowagiac River, a tributary of the St. Joseph, entering it near Niles. It has been put to good account by the millers, who have established themselves here, and in its small way adds to the blessings of the Michigan husbandmen on its shores.

One Hundred and Eighteenth Day.

Private House,
NILES, MICHIGAN,
September Sixth.

The threatening storm which led my Decatur friends to turn back on the previous afternoon, set in soon

after my arrival at Dowagiac, and I considered myself very fortunate, as it was accompanied by the most
violent thunder and lightning that I had yet encountered. Notwithstanding this disturbed condition of
the elements, I was greeted by a full house at Young
Men's Hall, where I was introduced by Dr. Thomas
Rix.

I found a few familiar faces at Niles which I had
seen during my previous visit, and several new places
of interest about the town. Navigation on the St.
Joseph ends at this point, and the narrowed stream is
spanned by a railroad bridge; and the water-power increased by a dam. There is a brisk business carried
on at the water's edge.

The mills are well supplied with grain from outlying fields, and boats are continually plying back and
forth laden with lumber, grain, flour and fruit, which
are shipped from here in large quantities. In fact, for
its size—it claims I believe, a population of something
over 4,000—Niles is full of energy and ambition. I
found myself on this second visit very much interested
in the place and pleased that circumstances had made
necessary a second halt.

One Hundred and Nineteenth Day.

Kennard House,
BUCHANAN, MICHIGAN,
September Seventh.

Resumed my journey at two o'clock in the afternoon at a small way place between Niles and Buchanan, where I rested at noon. The heavy rains of
the preceding days had left the roads in a most

wretched condition, and the distance was considerably lengthened as it was necessary to avoid pools and wash-outs, so that it took two hours of slow riding to reach my destination. Darby, who had gone forward with my advance agents, was the first to greet me at this place and to inform me of the arrangements made for my lecture in the evening.

As my day's journey had been undertaken leisurely, I started out on a tour of inspection, after having first made comfortable provision for *Paul.* I found a flourishing village, having a population of something over 2,000, and prettily situated on the St. Joseph River. As I walked in and out through its streets and looked for the last time upon the stream, which for its romantic history and natural charm had forced itself upon my notice so often, I could not avoid a certain feeling of regret that this was to be my last halt in the great State through which I had made such a pleasant and profitable journey. Pictures of orchard and meadow, of wheat field and river, passed in review once more, and with them the recollection of the splendid part the patriots of Michigan bore in the War for the Union, than whom was none more loyal than the heroic Custer, for whose memory I had spoken and received such warm response.

One Hundred and Twentieth Day.

Private House,
ROLLING PRAIRIE, INDIANA,
September Eighth.

Called for my horse at Buchanan at nine o'clock in the morning, intending to stop at New Buffalo, but once on the road, I decided instead to make this village my evening objective. A heavy rain-storm, setting in early in the forenoon, compelled me to take refuge at a farm house for about an hour, where I was initiated into the home life of the Northern Indiana "Hoosier." I am sorry to say that during this day's ride I encountered the worst roads and the dullest people of my journey. Many who have resided in this part of Indiana for thirty and even forty years are not only exceedingly illiterate, but know much less of the topography of the country than the average Indian—and absolutely nothing of the adjacent towns. As a consequence I was obliged to trust to chance, which brought me to Galion, a tiny hamlet on the outskirts of a swamp, where I had dinner. My ride thither was made under circumstances which suggested the ride of the belated Tam O' Shanter, and while my tortures could not compare with his, they were none the less acute while they lasted. I was met on the edge of the swamp by a swarm of mosquitoes—known in France as *petite diables*—who forced their attention upon me without cessation, in spite of the fact that I urged my horse forward at breakneck speed, *Paul's* steaming flanks and mire-covered legs attesting to the struggle, when we drew up in front of · Galion Inn.

One Hundred and Twenty-first Day.

Jewell House,
MICHIGAN CITY, INDIANA,
September Ninth.

I considered myself fortunate, during my ride from Rolling Prairie to Michigan City—a distance of six-

A HOOSIER CABIN.

teen miles—in having a sandy road and no rain from the time of setting out in the morning until my arrival here in the evening, but I was less favored than usual in obtaining information.

The Presidential campaign was now at white heat and very little outside of politics was discussed. I found, however, that the ideas of many of the farmers were confused upon the issues. The three candidates in the field made the canvass unusually exciting. Hayes and Tilden were, of course, the central figures, but Peter Cooper of New York had many staunch supporters and a few enthusiasts rallied around Blaine, Conkling and Morton. The proprietor of the Jewell House—a Cooper man—was at this time much more interested in the success of his favorite than in the receipts of his hotel, and his halls and parlors were the rendezvous for men of all parties.

One Hundred and Twenty-second Day.

Jewell House,
MICHIGAN CITY, INDIANA,
September Tenth.

As it was Sunday and I had a desire to visit the most imposing institution connected with Michigan City—the Northern State Penitentiary, I decided to make the two miles on foot, and be there for divine service. I found everything admirably conducted, and although such a place is not the most cheerful in the world to be shown through, I was well satisfied that I had gone, and was strongly impressed with the effect of the stern hand of the law. In the afternoon a heavy rain and wind storm came up, and I stayed in my room, the greater part of the time, writing up my journal, and arranging for my lecture tour across Illinois and Iowa, thereby accomplishing certain duties which fair weather might have tempted me to neglect.

It was my intention to go by rail to Chicago on the following morning, where I was announced to lecture at Farwell Hall.

Darby, to whom I have previously referred in connection with Decatur, and who was acting as advance agent in the small towns and villages that lay along my route, was with me during my stay at the Jewell House, and we had frequent talks over our adventures in the "Harris Light"—Second New York Cavalry— in which most of our active service was passed.

A CIRCUS IN TOWN.

CHAPTER XIX.

THREE DAYS AT CHICAGO.

ON the eleventh of September, I took the 7.50 morning train at Michigan City for Chicago, instead of going forward on horseback, as I had discovered by a study of the map of Illinois, that I could save *Paul* some thirty miles, in my journey across the State, by riding directly from Michigan City to Joliet, and I saw no good reason why I should ride him up here, especially at a time when he was greatly in need of rest.

When I had registered at the "Grand Pacific," I went to the Fidelity Safe Deposit Company to attend to some business matters and then over to the Express and Post offices, concluding my rounds by a call upon friends on West Washington street.

Lectured to a full house at Farwell Hall in the evening, the introduction being given by Major E. S. Weedon, editor of the *Army and Navy Gazette*. The Major alluded in eloquent and touching terms to the record of the gallant Custer and immediately put my audience in sympathy with me. My brother-in-law, Madison H. Buck, of Lake Mills, Wisconsin, called

357

upon me in the evening and was with me on the platform. The lecture closed before ten o'clock, and I hurried over to McVicker's Theatre, to see the last acts of "Mulberry Sellers," in which John T. Raymond was playing his favorite rôle. The play was having quite a run, and one heard at every turn the expression that had caught the popular fancy—Mulberry's inimitable assurance, "There's millions in it!"

On the morning of the twelfth, I settled with George and Babcock. The former went forward to Ottawa, and the latter to Joliet. It was my intention at the time to push on to Omaha and Cheyenne as rapidly as possible in the hope of passing Sherman, at the summit of the mountains, before the snow was too deep to interrupt my journey. Eight general halts had been decided upon between Boston and San Francisco, and these were Albany, Buffalo, Toledo, Chicago, Omaha, Cheyenne, Ogden, and Sacramento. I had now reached my fourth objective and felt the importance of more haste and less leisure and sightseeing. My time, therefore, in this great city was necessarily cut short.

The Exposition had just opened at the time I reached Chicago, and this enabled me to see more in a few hours than I could have possibly seen in any other way, and gave me quite an idea of the industries carried on in Cook County.

I had never seen a finer local affair of the kind and was confident that its object—the encouragement of agriculture and industry—would be successfully accomplished. Anyone who sees the way in which Chicagoans throw themselves into an undertaking of this sort, and in fact into everything that has to do with the enterprise or prosperity of their city, cannot but be struck with admiration.

Their irrepressible hopefulness, which effected such marvelous results after the great conflagration of 1871, is a case in point, and those who have been fortunate enough to see the transformation, are forced to admit that the calamity was, after all, not so much to be deplored. Out of the great waste in which the business portion was laid, handsome buildings have sprung up with almost magic rapidity and auguring well for the future of the "Windy City." Especially is this feature striking in the vicinity of the City Hall, where finer edifices rose upon the old ruins.

The very name of Chicago carries us back to the barbaric scenes of more than two hundred years ago. Where the beautiful city now stands, those days of long since past knew only a morass, an oozy, desolate stretch of water-soaked swamp. There was a stream in this desolate region, the banks of which, tradition tells us, were parched and cracked and blackened by the frequent, ravages of lightning. The early explorers found on its banks an old stone mound, supposed to have been erected for the sacrifice of human victims to propitiate the wrath of the Indian deity Chekagua, the Thunder God.

On the oldest map of this region now extant, one published in 1684, the little river itself bears the name Chekagua, and it may be, that our fair Western metropolis of to-day was also a namesake of that same weird divinity.

Others, claiming a more propitious christening, assert that Chicago was a derivative from Chacaqua, the Indian term for the Divine River.

Or perhaps the city was named from the successive titles of the proud, old Tamawas Chiefs.

"Not a monarch in all that proud Old World beyond the deep" bore more haughtily his inherited title of Herod or Cæsar than did one of these Tamawas rulers exult in the ancient title of Chacaqua. If this theory of the origin of Chicago's cognomen be accepted, then indeed can the "Windy City" claim a royal title from the first.

In 1673, certain Catholic missionaries became interested in exploring the Western Wilds. They were especially enthusiastic in regard to the waterways of darkest America. The Mississippi they had heard of. Was it possible that it ever could be made to join hands with the Great Lakes, of which they had some knowledge?

So questioning, Fathers Marquette and Joliet took two canoes and five men from the upper lake regions, and started to explore the charming Valley of the Mississippi.

On their return they reached the mouth of the Illinois, where they were informed of a new way of reaching Lake Michigan.

"Taking the Des Plaines branch, they were able to reach the water shed, but eight feet higher than canoeable waters, crossing which they launched into the stream which conducted them into the lake."

In so doing they made perhaps the greatest discovery of their time—namely, a discovery of that supremely important portage which insures Chicago's supremacy so long as American civilization exists.

In October, 1674, Marquette returned to this spot and erected the first white man's dwelling which was ordained to be the beginning of the great metropolis of the West. His little hut was both a home and a sanctuary. Here he wintered, shooting turkey, deer and buffalo from his door. Here in the spring, from toil and exposure, he died, mourned by the savages whom he had taught.

Thus was Chicago begun in embryo.

There in that lagoon, filled with ooze, with its impassable fens, and drifting sands, civilization and religion had their representative who laid the foundation of the great Coming City bravely with teachings of "The love of God, and the brotherhood of man."

We have good maps of 1688 which show us that a little later this lake end of the water communication with Louisiana was made a military post, called Fort Chicagon.

This place became at one time a favorite settlement for French missionaries. However the spot is supposed to have been abandoned about 1763, after which date for about one hundred years white men avoided it.

In 1774 the site of Chicago, with all the surrounding country, became a part of Virginia, being conquered by a military expedition from that State.

In 1778 the region became known as County of Illinois, State of Virginia.

After the close of the Revolutionary war, Virginia "divided herself by the Ohio River," ceding all the territory beyond that boundary to the United States for the "common benefit of all the people."

In 1795 the Indians also ceded to the general government any rights which their tribes possessed to "one piece of land six miles square, at the mouth of

Chekajo River, emptying into the southwest end of Lake Michigan, where a fort formerly stood." This extinguishment of the Indian title in 1795, being in the nature of a quit-claim deed for lands, is sometimes called the earliest real estate transaction in Chicago.

Thus, she who was to become the "Queen City" of the West, made her *debut* into the Union, where, possibly, she may yet,

"The fairest of her daughters,"

rule supreme.

In the midst of all the down-town rush, at a point where noise and confusion scarcely cease, one notices upon a decidedly modern building a white stone tablet which informs the stranger that it was upon this spot Fort Dearborn stood—the oldest landmark that remained to tell the tale of the wilderness. In 1804 two block-houses were built here and a subterranean passage made from the parade to the river, the whole surrounded by a picket and furnished with three pieces of light artillery, the object being "to supply the Indian wants and control the Indian policy." The tribes of Pottawatomies overran the country round about and with the little group of French and Canadian settlers made the life of the isolated post. In 1809 Tecumseh marked it out as one of his objects of vengeance, but fortunately other schemes occupied his attention, and it remained in comparative security until the war of 1812. Then, when all the country was disturbed and the Indians were making mischief everywhere, the commander of Fort Dearborn was betrayed by the Pottawatomies and every vestige of a settlement destroyed.

It was not until 1818, after Fort Dearborn was again demolished, that the pale face was courageous enough to establish his home at this point. Nor was courage alone required, for the unfavorable position—on a morass where vehicles invariably floundered in its black loam, and where the air was necessarily unhealthy—was well known ; but these first men whose rude homes constituted the embryo city must have possessed to a great degree that indomitable spirit which has become the very foundation of Chicago.

Nine years from this time a most unfavorable report of the place was sent to the Government and from this report the picture is called up of a wretched, unclean and disreputable community. But this state of affairs was not to last long. An event of importance took place here in 1833, when the United States commissioners and chiefs of the Pottawatomie, Chippewa and Ottawa tribes met, that the former might persuade the latter to give up more of their valuable land in Illinois and Michigan and ultimately to relinquish it altogether. The exact amount stipulated for was twenty millions of acres. Then population increased, for one of the points agreed upon, along with the land, was that the Indians should move west of the Mississippi. As a result, Chicago became the centre of much speculating. Eastern capitalists were interested, invested and lost heavily, but after the depression which inevitably followed, the people went to work in earnest and brought the town out of her trouble.

The one point of advantage that Chicago possessed—her possibilities as a commercial post—was put to the test, and so rapidly did she advance, that in 1842, after several remarkable advances, she sent out

600,000 bushels of wheat. She was already becoming a big cattle market, ranchmen further west driving their stock here and helping to increase the importance of the place as a centre of trade. At this time a canal was in process of construction, to connect the Illinois and Chicago rivers, thus making Chicago the centre for commerce between the Southwest and East, and giving her the opportunity to extend her business from the Gulf of Mexico to the Atlantic Ocean.

This was a splendid opening, and, with the co-operation of the railroads which soon afterwards were extended to this point, the future prosperity of the place was secured. It then only remained for Chicago to improve her appearance and sanitary condition. This she did by having the streets drained, filled up and graded. Local pride was manifesting itself in various improvements and in private and public buildings, so that by 1871 there was plenty of fuel for the great fire which laid so much of the city waste.

The well-known origin of the conflagration was in a barn where "Mrs. Scully's cow" innocently turned over a lighted lantern on some dry hay. Soon the barn was in flames and the fire quickly spread to the lumber yards along the river and from thence, the dry timber and wind favoring, leaped along and licked up the homes on the North Side and the business houses on the South Side.

The first stroke of the alarm sounded about nine o'clock in the evening of October 8, 1871. "By eleven o'clock 100,000 people were hurrying through the streets of the doomed city," spreading terror as they went. "All over the city it was as light as day, and, in the remotest suburb fine print was read by the glare of the conflagration three or four miles away. By midnight nearly every vehicle in the city had been pressed into service, and the frightened animals attached to them, in many cases beyond control, went flying through the streets in all directions, making a racket and a rumble which, coupled with the hoarse shouts of men, the moaning of the gale, the roar of the conflagration and the crash of falling buildings made a conglomeration of sight and sound so appalling that none who saw it, or were of it, are ever likely to forget. Few in the city took any notice of the break of day or the rising of the sun. These occurrences seemed to make little difference in the quantity of light. It was only now and then that Old Sol was visible through the almost impenetrable smoke clouds. Nothing could be seen but smoke, smoke, smoke, here and there interspersed by dark rolling masses of flames. It was chaos come again. The earth was seemingly resolved into its original elements."

At the end of three days, 300,000 people were destitute, 100,000 were absolutely homeless, 200,000 were without water. The food supply was doubtful for all. Robbers and incendiaries were at work. The gas was gone—blown sky high. Churches, newspapers, police, telegraph offices and public institutions were gone, while nineteen-twentieths of all the mercantile stock in the city was consumed.

The tract destroyed was about a mile in breadth, and the losses were roughly estimated at $200,000,000. Still, so alive was public sentiment and hope, that at the time of my horseback journey, five years later, scarcely a trace remained to tell the tale of this disaster and that of 1874, except the records of history.

The story of just how Chicago proved herself a veritable Phœnix is a very interesting one.

On the evening of October ninth, only twenty-four hours after the commencement of the conflagration, a car-load of provisions arrived from Milwaukee. By the next morning fifty car-loads had come to the afflicted city. Donations of food and clothing kept pouring in until Chicago was fairly sated. By October eleventh every person had food enough and each one's pressing physical necessities were attended to. On the eleventh, also, the Board of Trade met and resolved to require the honoring of all contracts. On the twelfth the bankers met and resolved to pay all depositors in full. The State sent an instalment of $3,000,000 with which it then voted to re-imburse the city for its expenditures for the canal enlargement, thus placing the city in the possession of much-needed funds. From all over the civilized world came contributions in money for the resurrected city. The amount so received within three months after the conflagration being about $4,200,000.

The Relief Society alone built four thousand houses within five weeks of those dreadful days when all seemed lost.

In two years after the fire, sixty-nine million, four hundred and sixty-two thousand dollars were expended in erecting buildings of brick, iron, and stone, while miles of humble frame houses were built, each costing from $500 to $10,000.

Now, in place of the original city of wood, there stands by the Great Lake, a city of stone and iron, able to vie with any other city in growth, enterprise and wealth, bearing the distinction of being the greatest grain and lumber market in the world, and boasting a population, at the time of my journey, of about five hundred thousand. From the Atlantic to the Pacific I rode into no city that made such an impression of grandeur, business power and wealth as this youthful "Queen of the Lakes."

Chicago's baptism of fire seemed but to prove an inspiration, goading the city to more activity, to greater success.

The aggregate amount of business done in the city the year after the fire—entirely excepting the building trades—greatly exceeds that done the previous year, as the following figures will show. During this one year the wholesale merchandise trade increased fifteen per cent. Receipts of grain increased 8,425,885 bushels ; receipts of live-stock by 872,866 head. Deposits in the city banks increased $1,910,000.

So much for the splendid pluck of Chicago.

The Pacific coast has Chicago for her smelting furnace, four large silver mills being located here.

From the Pacific coast also, she has a considerable trade in the productions of the Orient. In the first half of 1873, Chicago received assignments of three-million pounds of tea, two million pounds of coffee, eight hundred thousand pounds of foreign wool, and three hundred and nine thousand, seven hundred and twenty four pounds of foreign silk. Cotton came to her from the Pacific Isles, and nuts from South America.

Some idea of the commercial importance of Chicago's trade may be reached by the amount of some of her exports by rail during 1872: namely, two hundred and thirty-four million pounds of meat; eighty million, two hundred and fifty thousand pounds of lard; one million, nine hundred and sixty-five thousand whole swine; four hundred and eighty-four thousand head of cattle, and one hundred and sixty-two thousand head of sheep.

I found Chicago justly proud of her public schools. It was roughly estimated that in the city about fifty thousand children between six and twelve years of age received daily instruction.

The graded system employed in these schools is so advanced, and has proved so successful, that it has become a general model for all the schools of the great Northwest.

More than that, it has been adopted, in part, by the Minister of Education in France, and at the late Vienna Exposition a reward for progress, in the shape of a beautiful medal, was awarded to the school system of Chicago. Chicago claims for herself absolute superiority in two particulars over all the public schools in the United States, the "Hub" institutions of Boston not excepted. *First:* Perfect discipline is said to be attained without the use of corporal punishment. *Second:* The musical culture of the school children is said to far excel anything attained before on this Continent.

I found that the city contained a number of colleges, theological seminaries and universities. The University of Chicago occupies one of the most elegant and commodious buildings in the West.

The Dearborn Observatory, which is a part of this University, contains the famous Clark Telescope, one of the most magnificent instruments of its kind in existence.

The Chicago Theological Seminary is noted for the beauty of its chapel and lecture rooms, and the extent and quality of its library. The Academy of Science was incorporated in 1865. It has a vast building, well stocked with natural curiosities.

The Historical Society organized in 1856 possesses a rare collection of public and private documents, as well as a library of nearly one hundred thousand volumes.

There are two hundred and thirty-eight houses of public worship in Chicago; all of the great religious denominations, and perhaps some new ones, being well represented. Differing as they do, they are, as some one says: "Agreed on one point, namely, an uncommon sense of mutual toleration and mutual love for each other, and a feeling of

Peace and sweet good will to all mankind."

There is a good deal of fine pulpit oratory to be heard every Sabbath in Chicago; and the people of the surrounding country know it. It is no uncommon thing for the Saturday night incoming trains to be crowded with young men, some of them from homes one hundred miles away, who are yet regular attendants at the religious services of the city. Having enjoyed these to the full, the Sunday evening sleeping cars are again crowded with the same youthful army, very sleepy, but very happy, making the return trip.

Chicago is justly proud of her streets. About eighty feet wide, and meeting at right angles, they present a beautiful object lesson to some of her elder Eastern sisters.

The city is said to contain thirteen million dollars'

worth of hotel property. Perhaps no structure for which any part of this immense sum has been expended is more beautiful and remarkable than the Palmer House. This building is said to contain more bricks than any two hotels on the Continent, and more iron than most of them put together. The flooring contains ninety thousand square feet of marble tiling laid in massive beds of cement. The beams are laid in beds of cement also.

The immense carriage court is entered by three *porte cochères*. There are said to be one hundred miles of electric bell wires in the building. The magnificent office is twenty-four feet in height. It is wainscoted with Italian marble, studded with panels of remarkably rich rose brocatelle marble, and with many natural mosaics of rare and curious beauty. The wainscoting of the counter is made of the same exquisite material. The grand staircase is made of the same.

Mr. C. M. Palmer travelled extensively for some time, before building, throughout Europe, making an especial study of continental hotels, with a determination to surpass the excellences of them all in his beloved Chicago.

Mr. Palmer's spirit seems to be characteristic of all true Chicagoans. To have their city excel, to have it something more extensive, more impressive, more famous, grander, nobler than any other place which the sun shines on, this is their hearts' desire. Some one said to a great man :

"What paramount word of advice would you give to young men?"

The answer came,

" Aspire."

" What would your next advice be ? "

" Aspire."

" But what then ? "

" Aspire."

Chicago believes in that advice.   She has always believed in it.   Nay. more, she has lived it.

CHAPTER XX.

CHICAGO TO DAVENPORT.

One Hundred and Twenty-sixth Day.

Jewell House,
MICHIGAN CITY, INDIANA,
September 14, 1876.

IN the morning I settled with Darby, and in the afternoon he returned to Decatur.

At nightfall here, the excitement which had been rising during the day reached its climax when the Michigan City Democrats repaired to the New Albany depot to hold a mass meeting.

. Notwithstanding my own sentiments, I went too, and was highly entertained by the speakers, among whom were Hon. Daniel W. Voorhees of Terre Haute, Hon. James Williams —better known in the Hoosier State as "Blue Jeans" Williams—and Hon. Morgan Weir, of La Porte.

When Voorhees arrived his enthusiastic partisans had him driven in state from the station in a carriage drawn by four white horses. He was no doubt the lion of the occasion and his energetic language drew forth frequent applause. The strong features, straight brows and broad forehead of this politician would pro-claim him a man of force anywhere.

A large crowd had gathered at the appointed place and business began at eight o'clock. As time passed the excitement grew more intense, and towards the close of the meeting an amusing incident was noted, when the honorable senator took issue with his opponents. I then became aware that there were others present of a different faith, besides myself, for no sooner were Voorhees' anti-Republican sentiments voiced than a vehement champion of the Republican party jumped to his feet denouncing as false the statements made, winding up his remarks by thumping his cane on the benches and saying that all that had been spoken was a "pack of lies!" Off in another part of the building an excited Irishman also jumped up cry-ing out: "Mr. Voorhees is a perfect gintleman, sor!" A compliment which the Hoosiers quickly took up and the depot rang with: "Mr. Voorhees is a perfect gintleman, sor!"

My co-partisan was silenced, if not convinced. The other speakers scored several points for their cause and the meeting closed with three cheers and a tiger for the Democratic candidates.

One Hundred and Twenty-seventh Day.

Jewell House,
MICHIGAN CITY, INDIANA,
September Fifteenth.

Being detained on account of the condition of my horse, and as the weather now was most delightful, I made the best of the situation by looking about the

place, since I had seen comparatively little of it up to
this time. Possibly no city or town along my route
labors under greater disadvantages from a geographical
or commercial point of view than this "city of sand,"
situated as it is at the extreme southern end of Lake
Michigan, with the water splashing against it on one
side and the wind and sand storms beating against it
on the other.

However, it has overcome these obstacles to a certain degree and is hardly lacking in enterprise, as the
mass meeting of the preceding day testified. Here,
perhaps, more than at any other of the towns and
cities lying around Lake Michigan, one is impressed
with the resistless force of this splendid inland sea,
and so unique an impression did the place make upon
me that my detention did not become irksome, although all the fascinations of the Great West lay beyond.

One Hundred and Twenty-eighth Day.

Hobart House,
HOBART, INDIANA,
September Sixteenth.

Did not get on the road until nearly eleven o'clock.
The rest and treatment which *Paul* had received at
Michigan City put him in excellent spirits for a rapid
journey and he stepped off nimbly when I gave him
the reins in front of the Jewell House. I was greatly
encouraged by the condition of my horse and now that
the word was once more "onward," all the fascination
of the ride came back.

Although the scenes I passed through were very

like others, there being nothing of marked interest to the traveller in this section of Indiana, I still found much pleasure in looking over the farms as I passed them and noticing the variety of methods and effects.

A good stimulating breeze came inland from the lake and by noon it had added zest to my appetite. I stopped for dinner at the village of Chesterton and then pushed on to this place which was reached in the evening by seven o'clock—twenty-eight miles having been covered during the day.

The only accommodation to be found was nothing more nor less than a beer-saloon with sleeping rooms attached, a characteristic, I regret to say, which I ob- served in many of the small towns through this sec- tion of the country. As immediate environment has an influence in making impressions, my opinion of this halting-place on the borders of " Hoosierdom " was not the most exalted.

One Hundred and Twenty-ninth Day.

Rohmer House,
RICHTON, ILLINOIS,
September Seventeenth.

Owing to the late hour of my arrival at Hobart the previous evening I was unable to observe my usual practice of looking through the place and making a note of its striking points in my journal, and for this reason I was not in the saddle until ten o'clock A. M., although the time was spent more in seeing than in chronicling what was seen.

Paul was still in the happiest of spirits and I rode away from Hobart at a gallop, stirring the dust of this sleepy little village as it had possibly not been stirred for many moons. The cheerful fact was made clear to me before leaving that I was as far from Joliet at Hobart as I had supposed myself to be at Michigan City.

In the course of the day, in which twenty-eight miles were again covered, Centralia, Sherryville and Dyer were passed, these towns being on Grand Prairie, across which I rode from morning till night. At four o'clock I reached the boundary between Indiana and Illinois, realizing that at this point six States had added their rich scenes and splendid enterprises to my memory.

As I was moving along on the prairie just before dark my ears caught the sound of a peculiar barking and soon a pack of what I supposed to be dogs were following me. I noticed that *Paul's* manner changed and he appeared disturbed, but attributed this to the barking and the persistent keeping at his heels of the little animals. To a man whom I met later, I explained that I had been followed for some hours by a pack of dogs, when he promptly informed me that they were doubtless prairie wolves. Of course to an Easterner this news gave an added interest to Grand Prairie.

One Hundred and Thirtieth Day.

Robertson House,
JOLIET, ILLINOIS,
September Eighteenth.

Had *Paul* brought out at eight o'clock. As soon as he was saddled at Richton the man who attended to him threw the rein over the neck of the horse, and a

COUNTRY ROAD IN ILLINOIS.

moment later he made his appearance unaccompanied in front of the Rohmer House. This being an undoubted sign of his anxiety to be off, I mounted at once and we were soon lessening the distance to Joliet, our evening destination, twenty-one miles away.

Was all day again on Grand Prairie, which may give some idea of this the greatest and truly the grandest prairie yet passed on my route. Its proximity to Chicago is doubtless one of the chief causes of the high winds for which the " Windy City " is noted ; and if Chicago could, she would gladly change her inconvenient environment.

At Lenox I halted for dinner, reaching Joliet at four P. M. In riding through Jefferson street, I was met by Babcock who seemed much surprised at my early arrival. Notwithstanding the fact that "Rip Van Winkle " was being played at the opera house, Robert McWade, a young actor of some prominence, taking the leading *rôle*, I found a fair audience awaiting me at Werner Hall in the evening, which proved that interest was still felt in the Custer Monument movement.

One Hundred and Thirty-first Day.

Hopkins House,
MORRIS, ILLINOIS,
September Nineteenth.

On calling for my bill at the Robertson House, Joliet, in the morning, Mr. Conklin the proprietor, declined to accept any pay for my accommodations, and when I insisted, said he wished the pleasure of making me his guest during my stay. I did not get a very early start, as a family by the name of Horner, upon hearing of my arrival, called at the hotel and at their solicitation I made them a short visit. They knew of my journey and interest in the Custer Association, and being patriotic made this their reason for wishing to meet me. Their friendliness was but another proof of the hospitality of the people of Joliet, among whom I had come the day before as a comparative stranger, but whom I left with the kindliest of feeling.

Before leaving, Mr. Conklin suggested that I ride along the tow-path of the Michigan Canal from Joliet to Chanahon, and I followed his advice, having dinner at the latter place. It happened that the inn-keeper was well supplied with sweet cider and I helped him to dispose of it by drinking the contents of six well-filled glasses. Beyond Chanahon, on the Illinois River, I borrowed a hook and line of a farmer who was fishing and caught twenty-three perch in half an hour.

At four o'clock I reached the summit of a hill on the border of a prairie from which I could look off for fifteen or twenty miles over a fertile country through which two silver streams wound to unite just below—the Kankakee here paying tribute to the Illinois. The atmosphere was perfect—clear and pure; the trees were tinged red and yellow with the first frosts, and to all this was added the glory of the sunset which I lingered to admire before turning away from so charming a scene.

Such a view leaves a deep impress on the memory, and stirs recollections of more youthful days. Emotions like these have a purifying effect upon all men.

AN ILLINOIS HOME.

One Hundred and Thirty-second Day.

Clifton House,
OTTAWA, ILLINOIS,
September Twentieth.

I rode out of Morris in the morning just as the public school bells were ringing nine o'clock. My journey now lay along the north bank of the Illinois River, and took me through some of the finest cornfields I had ever seen. Acres and acres, miles and miles stretched in all directions as far as the eye could reach whenever the elevation of the road was high enough above this waving sea of grain to permit of my looking about. Otherwise I passed through it completely shut in, except as I could look ahead and behind and see the avenue of giant stalks. My horse, sixteen hands high, did not elevate me sufficiently to enable me, sitting in the saddle, to look over the corn tops, and they still towered above my head like so many small trees.

Those who are privileged to see this agricultural wonder must, however, associate it with that other source of pride among Illinois farmers—the " hogs "—for most of this splendid harvest is fed to these animals and they, well-fattened thereby, are driven to market. Thus the enterprising farmer is saved the expense of hauling his corn to Chicago or other points, as the pork, into which it has been transformed, is able to carry itself.

All along my route across the "Sucker State," I encountered, day after day, white hogs and black hogs, hogs of every grade and shade, my horse often stepping aside in equine dignity to allow a drowsy or pugnacious porker to pass.

As I had determined to reach Ottawa by nightfall, I was compelled to ride nearly all day in a drizzling rain which at noon was followed by a heavy thunder shower. This I took advantage of by stopping at Seneca for dinner, and then pushed forward. Was forced to halt again at three o'clock on account of rain, and being near a farm house was invited to "come in" while the good people took care of my horse.

Overtook a troop of boys on horseback near Ottawa and had their lively company into town. There I met an old acquaintance—Mr. Kean—who was among the first to greet me. My time was passed pleasantly here, and I would do injustice to the proprietor of the Clifton were I to forget the many courtesies politely extended to me while his guest.

One Hundred and Thirty-third Day.

Harrison House,
LA SALLE, ILLINOIS,
September Twenty-first.

Left the Clifton House, Ottawa, at two P. M. The weather was still in an unsettled condition which obliged me to make my way as best I could between showers in order to keep my lecture appointment at La Salle. I considered it fortunate that my route was now along the west bank of the Illinois, a stream in which I had long been interested owing to the important part it played as a convenient and favorite water course for the early explorers of the Valley of the Mississippi. Between its verdant banks, Joliet, Marquette, La Salle and others glided on their way to the great stream. How the lover of history and adventure thrills at the accounts of La Salle's Fort Crève-Cœur, and his colony scattered over this same region of country !

Probably none of these historic men paid a more flattering tribute to "La Rivière des Illinois" than Hennepin, the priest, who, when passing down it to the Mississippi was not too much oppressed with anxiety to admire its charms. What a different appearance its shores presented in 1680 to that of 1876! In place of the forest, waving corn fields under high cultivation attracted my attention on every hand, and in contrast to the wilderness inhabited by the savages whom Hennepin encountered, I saw an emigrant train peaceably moving along on its way from the East to the promising country west of the Mississippi.

One Hundred and Thirty-fourth Day.

Harrison House,
LA SALLE, ILLINOIS,
September Twenty-second.

The equinoctial storms were now at their height and as my lecture at Davenport was not to be delivered for some days, I decided to spend a day or two in this pleasant little city, until "Old Sol" had "crossed the line."

I found that this is the centre of important coal and lead mines, which I should have visited and examined, superficially at least, had not the inclement weather prevented. Through the courtesy of Colonel Stephens, editor of the *La Salle County Press* and a colonel in the volunteer service during the late war, I was introduced to many of the citizens who told me much of the history and enterprises of their town.

One Hundred and Thirty-fifth Day.

Harrison House,
LA SALLE, ILLINOIS,
September Twenty-third.

Rode down to Peru in the morning accompanied by Colonel Stephens, who wished to show me the pride of the county—the big plow works, which constitute the leading industry of the place. Was introduced to members of the firm and shown through the various departments of the establishment, which were certainly imposing in the way of machinery and in the evidence of mechanical skill. We returned to La Salle at four o'clock and my hospitable comrade proposed that we take a stroll through the city, to which I quickly consented.

Colonel Stephens introduced me to my audience in the evening, and made pleasant reference to the brave and chivalrous Custer. My entertainment here was most gratifying and I was warmly assured of the good will of the people through the local press.

I have proved that everywhere in this country the spirit of hospitality reigns. Whether in large cities or small towns, the utmost cordiality prevails, and the stranger can always rely upon a hearty welcome.

One Hundred and Thirty-sixth Day.

Farm House,
NEAR HOLLOWAYVILLE, ILLINOIS
September Twenty-fourth.

Upon leaving La Salle at three o'clock in the afternoon, I was told that I would have no difficulty in securing accommodations for myself and horse at Hollowayville, so, with the assurance of finding everything lovely here, I jogged along over the intervening
twelve miles at my leisure.

My feelings can better be imagined than described
when, on my arrival at the little hamlet, I was looked
upon with suspicion. The simple-minded inhabitants
hinted that I might possibly be a " highwayman " or a
" horse thief," or, for aught they knew, one of the
James or Younger brothers. These desperadoes were
then exciting the people on both sides of the Mississippi and my equipment, set off with high top boots
and gauntlets, with the peculiar trappings of my
horse, only made matters worse.

Finding it impossible to secure lodging in the village, I rode on into the country, stopping at a farm
house which looked inviting. I entered the front yard
slowly and with dignity to dispel the horse thief suspicion. The farmer's daughter, a young girl of seventeen or eighteen years, and a few farm hands, stood
about, of whom I asked if the master of the place was
at home. The girl took me within, and Monsieur
and Madame Croisant received me. They were both
in bed, ill, but looking quite comfortable with their
heads pointing in different directions. They carried

on a lively conversation in French, the daughter inter-
preting, and in conclusion, after assuring them that I
was a harmless person, very tired and hungry, they
decided, if the clergyman of the place thought it safe,
that I might stay with them. The dominie was called,
looked me over a few minutes, cross-questioned me,
and approved.

My room that night was unique in more ways than
one and would have been punishment enough for
Jesse James himself.

When I retired I detected a strong odor in the room
and found it due to a collection of *sabots*, or wooden
shoes, seemingly centuries old, which were arranged in
a row under my bed. What to do with them was a
question, as, under the circumstances, I did not think it
best to tamper with the feelings of my host and hostess. As my room was on the ground floor, I decided
to place the *sabots* carefully outside under the window
and take them in in the morning before the family was
up. Unfortunately it rained and I overslept, so the
shoes were discovered full of water before I appeared.
However, nothing was said and I ate my breakfast
in peace, the good people probably thanking their
stars that they and their house had not been robbed.

Before leaving in the morning the *La Salle County
Press* was handed me by Miss Croisant, in which I
read the following flattering notice of my lecture in
that city and which in some measure compensated for
my unpleasant reception at Hollowayville :

" We have not often met with a more agreeable and pleasant gentleman than Captain Willard Glazier, who entertained a very respect-
able number of our citizens at Opera Hall on Saturday evening by
delivering a lecture on ' Echoes from the Revolution.' The captain

has a fine voice and his manner of delivery is decidedly interesting, while his language is eloquent and fascinating. His description of the battles of the Revolution, and the heroes who took part in them, from the engagement on the little green at Lexington down to the surrender of Cornwallis at Yorktown, was grand indeed, and was received with frequent and enthusiastic applause. In conclusion he referred in an eloquent and touching manner to the 'Boys in Blue,' who took part in the late war for the Union, and all retired from the hall feeling that the evening had been spent in an agreeable and profitable manner.

"Captain Glazier served under Generals Kilpatrick and Custer during the late war, since which time he has devoted much labor to writing and is now making the attempt to cross the continent from Boston to San Francisco on horseback, for the purpose of collecting material for another work. He left Boston the early part of May, and will endeavor to reach the Sacramento Valley before the fall of the deep snow. His horse, *Paul Revere* is a magnificent animal, black as a raven, with the exception of four white feet. He was bred in Kentucky of Black Hawk stock, has turned a mile in 2.33, but owing to his inclination to run away on certain occasions, was not considered a safe horse for the track. The captain, however, has broken him to the saddle, and also convinced him that running away is foolish business; consequently, he and the captain have become fast friends, and with *Paul* for his only companion, the gallant cavalryman proposes to cross the continent. Success attend him!"

One Hundred and Thirty-seventh Day.

Ellsworth House,
WYANET, ILLINOIS,
September Twenty-fifth.

The equinoctial storms which had been raging since I left Ottawa, were, for a few days at least, at an end, and a bright autumn sun greeted me every morning as I rode onward. Rich cornfields stretched away on either side of the road, their monotony broken here and there by fine apple and peach orchards just coming into their glory. Another characteristic of Illinois—fine stock farms—were also noticeable, and thus for another stage of fourteen miles, surrounded by evidences of fertility and thrift, I passed on, reaching Wyanet early in the evening.

One Hundred and Thirty-eighth Day.

Private House,
ANNAWAN, ILLINOIS.
September Twenty-sixth.

Before leaving Wyanet I had *Paul's* bridle—a Mexican make—repaired, and when it was again used he chafed at the restraint of the curb. Not for long though, for we were soon on the prairie, he evidently enjoying it as much as his master. The roads were rougher than usual and there was a change here in the soil, its black clayey loam being very rich and productive, making Henry County noted for its fine farms. Eighteen miles of grass-covered prairie, diversified by cultivated fields, brought me to Annawan, where I was the guest of O. T. Buttermore, and while at this place I received the following gratifying communication from Colonel Stephens of La Salle—further proof of the good will to "the stranger within their gates," of the citizens of La Salle:

LA SALLE, ILLINOIS,
September 25, 1876.

TO CAPTAIN WILLARD GLAZIER:

I take pleasure in expressing to you on behalf of many of our citizens, the gratification afforded our people who listened to your instructive and entertaining lecture given at Opera Hall on Saturday evening last. While in conversation with several of our prominent citizens, among them, W. A. Work, superintendent of our public schools; A. J. O'Connor, clerk of the city court; W. T. Mason, Esq., and others, all of whom were present and heard your lecture, I was requested to write you and tender their hearty thanks for the enter-

A HAPPY FAMILY.

tainment and their good wishes for your success in your ride across the continent. Should you ever again visit our city you can rest assured you will be most cordially received.

Very truly yours,

R. C. STEPHENS,

Late Colonel U. S. Volunteers.

One Hundred and Thirty-ninth Day.

Farm House,

BETWEEN GENESSEO AND MOLINE, ILLINOIS,

September Twenty-seventh.

Started away from Annawan at nine o'clock but after riding about a mile and a half I discovered that I had left my journal and was obliged to return for it. All day I was on a seemingly endless prairie, dotted here and there with cornfields and apple orchards. Illinois takes the lead in stock-raising, and the horses and cattle seen in this day's ride were fully up to the best standard.

Had dinner at the house of a coal miner, whom I found very intelligent, and was well entertained by a talk on mining industries in Illinois from a practical point of view. This is a bituminous coal region and there are mines in operation all over the State.

My host, Pullman by name, had recently returned from the Pacific coast and to my eager inquiries was able to tell me much about the country between Omaha and Sacramento.

At night, after having made twenty-one miles, I reached this place and was domiciled with the family of Mrs. Charlotte Bills, who came formerly from Jefferson County, New York. As my native county of Saint Lawrence adjoins Jefferson, the Bills and I had a lively talk on "Old York State," and I became much interested in the work of this enterprising woman and her family.

Mrs. Bills has succeeded in a direction which has not generally been attempted by women; this is the management of a farm. She does a good business and supports herself and children by raising corn for which, in this stock-raising locality, she finds a ready market. The corn is generally bought for hog feed and as these animals quickly fatten upon it, it is profitable. The practical rather than the romantic has place with these Western people who are striving for a livelihood. Each day gave me new ideas of people and their occupations—but this woman-farmer was something unusual and certainly very praiseworthy.

One Hundred and Fortieth Day.

Milan House,
MILAN, ILLINOIS,
September Twenty-eighth.

Mounted my horse at eight o'clock and by easy riding reached a farm house in Rock River Bottom, where I passed the noon hour. After dinner I made good time as the weather had changed and become cold, reminding me of the necessity of hurrying on if I would avoid the deep snows which the traveller is sure to encounter in the elevated regions farther west and it was every day more evident that I could not well afford to allow my lecture appointments to conflict with the dispatch of my journey.

On starting from Genesseo in the morning it was

AN ILLINOIS VILLAGE.

my intention to make Moline the evening objective, but I was compelled to halt at Milan—twenty miles from the morning starting-point—where the bridge was torn up that crossed Rock River at this point. Being delayed, I sent a note forward to Davenport informing Babcock that I would cross the Mississippi the following afternoon at three o'clock ; in the meantime waiting, with what patience I could muster, for the bridge work to proceed.

CHAPTER XXI.

FOUR DAYS AT DAVENPORT.

LEFT the Milan House at two P. M., *Paul* being eager for the start. Before proceeding far I dismounted and ran ahead leaving him to follow me if he would. I ran over two or three small hills and the faithful animal broke into a gallop and was soon by my side mutely inviting me to remount. About four o'clock we crossed the Mississippi on the fine Government Bridge which unites Rock Island and Davenport, and proceeded to the Burtis House—since named the Kimball. Colonel P. A. J. Russell was one of the first to greet me. Moore's Hall having been engaged for my lecture, I spoke at the usual hour to a large audience, to whom General Sanders introduced me. The local band in full uniform volunteered their services for the occasion. The lecture was a financial success.

The next three days were occupied in making my acquaintance with the city. It is only fifty years ago that the first cabin was erected here by white men. By the side of the great river a bluff rises gradually to an elevation of about one hundred and fifty feet, and on its side and at its base the city of Davenport is built. Over a bluff we come upon a beautiful rolling prairie, and back as far as Duck Creek the land is covered with fruit, vegetable and flower gardens, and presents a picture of uncommon beauty. Views of the Mississippi are obtained from the summit of the bluff; also of Rock Island Arsenal and Rock Island City on the opposite shore of the river.

In 1832, General Winfield Scott made a treaty with the Indians of the Sac tribe for the purchase by the United States of the land occupied by them bordering on the west side of the river. The city of Davenport was named after Colonel George Davenport, the first white settler. Antoine Le Claire was the first to own land in Davenport. His mother was the daughter of a Pottawatomie chief and his father a French Canadian. At this time the Northwest territory was peopled entirely by Indians, with here and there one of a different race fearless enough to brave the dangers of a frontier life. . Le Claire purchased the claim upon which the city of Davenport was laid out for one hundred and fifty dollars. In 1835, he sold it to a company who commenced the building of the city. The first ferry between Davenport and Rock Island dates from 1835. It was a flatboat propelled by oars. At present a large steamboat is constantly employed in transferring passengers and freight between these cities. The river is about a mile in width at this point.

Davenport excels all the other cities of the State in the beauty and advantages of its location. The view from the hill-tops is scarcely to be equalled for picturesqueness by anything I saw during my journey.

The city has made great and rapid progress in its industries, wealth and population. The education of the young is well provided for. It has a high school built at a cost of $65,000. Griswold College—Episcopalian—occupies a very picturesque site, over-looking the river. The Catholic College is in a retired and quiet spot, surrounded by beautifully shaded grounds, the buildings being elegant and commodious. The churches are numerous, every denomination being represented. Grace Church, the protestant Cathedral, is a fine substantial edifice, erected at a cost of $80,000.

The Public Library on Brady street, founded by Mrs. Clarissa Cook, a lady of wealth, is a highly prized and flourishing institution. The Academy of Sciences embraces a most valuable and unique collection of rare curiosities, both ancient and modern, among others, relics from the mounds of Iowa and adjoining States, including skulls and skeletons of pre-historic man.

The population of Davenport is now about 20,000. On account of its being built on a declivity the drainage is perfect. It is surrounded by a most fertile country and possesses every element for the growth of a large city.

Recrossing the magnificent bridge spanning the river between Davenport and the Illinois shores, I found myself on Rock Island. The Island lies to the north of the city, the latter not being located on the Island but on the mainland of Illinois. Since 1804 the Island proper has been the property of the United States Government, although not occupied until 1812, on the breaking out of the war with England. The surface is very fertile, and coal and limestone are

THE ROAD TO THE CHURCH.

found in large quantities. It is about three miles long, covering nine hundred and sixty acres. An arsenal and armory are located here. A fort was erected in 1816, and named Fort Armstrong. It was garrisoned until May, 1836, when it was evacuated. An ordnance depot was established by the Government in 1840. In 1862, by Act of Congress, the Island was made a United States Arsenal. General Thomas J. Rodman was the first appointed to the command and held the position until his death. In 1869, Congress appropriated $500,000 for a bridge across the Mississippi uniting the Island with the city of Davenport. This fine structure is a railroad and wagon bridge and affords all necessary facilities for the movement of military stores. General Rodman was succeeded in the command of the Arsenal, in 1871, by Colonel D. W. Flagler of the Ordnance Corps, and the Island has become, under his management, the strongest military post on the Mississippi. Substantial quarters for the officers of the garrison and barracks for the soldiers, have been erected, also a bridge connecting the Island with the city of Moline.

Rock Island is connnected with Rock Island City on the Illinois shore and with Davenport on the opposite side of the river, and also with Moline on the east side about three miles above Rock Island.

In the spring of 1828, there were only nine white men and their families on the site now occupied by Rock Island City; the Indians of the Sac tribe were much aggrieved by the whites taking possession of their lands while the latter were away on their hunting expeditions. Black Hawk, chief of the tribe, took great offence and protested strongly against it, and as the number of white settlers increased the discontent of the Indians grew stronger. They were urged by the commanding officer of the Island and the Indian agent, Colonel Davenport, to move across to the west side of the river in compliance with their treaty with the United States Government; but Black Hawk refused to move and contended that the Island was his property. The Fox tribe crossed the river and established themselves there. The lands on the Illinois side were now surveyed and sold to the settlers by the Government, but Black Hawk and the Sacs still refused to leave. Depredations were committed by the Indians of which the whites complained, and in 1831 Black Hawk gave notice to the settlers to leave his lands. Some neighboring tribes it was now feared, would unite with the Sacs in an attack on the settlers, who petitioned the military authorities and the Governor of Illinois to protect them, and in this way what is known as the Black Hawk War originated.

In response to the complaints of the settlers, Governor Reynolds, of Illinois, called out sixteen hundred mounted volunteers and marched them to the Island and General Gaines at Saint Louis proceeded immediately to the scene of action with the Sixth United States Infantry. General Gaines ordered all the settlers to move to the Island, and then invited Black Hawk to talk over the situation. The military and settlers met in the Council House, and Black Hawk, with about one hundred warriors in their war paint, approached and entered and soon commenced shouting in an intimidating manner. It was thought that an attempt at a general massacre would be made. An Indian called "The Prophet" raised his voice very high, gesticulating and speaking rapidly in an angry tone as if he desired to excite the warriors to an attack. At length quiet was obtained and General Gaines spoke to Black Hawk, reminding him of the sale of the lands in dispute to the United States Government. Black Hawk and his followers claimed that the lands had never been sold. The treaty was then read and explained to the chief, which seemed to enrage him greatly. Black Hawk shouted : "The white people speak from paper, but the Indian always speaks from the heart." He further said that their lands had not been sold, that the men who signed the treaty had no authority to do so, or to sell their land. And even if it was sold, they were not paid for it. The General said that the Government had assigned him and his people land on the west side of the Mississippi. His only answer was that he would neither leave nor fight and if the whites attempted to drive him off, he would sit down in his wigwam and they might do what they liked with him. General Gaines understood by this that he would defend what he considered his rights.

Preparations for an attack were now made by the commanding officers and Governor Reynolds, and on June 19, 1831, troops were assembled near the mouth of Rock River. The next morning they moved upon the Indian village. Black Hawk, however, and all his people had left in the night, crossed the Mississippi and were camped a few miles below Rock Island. Ten days after, the chief presented himself on the Island with twenty-seven warriors and voluntarily signed a treaty of peace with General Gaines and the Governor of Illinois, the latter representing the

National Government. The terms of this treaty included a pledge on the part of Black Hawk not to return to the east side of the river or give any more trouble to the white settlers.

In the following winter, Black Hawk refused to keep the treaty any longer and in April, 1832, he and about five hundred of his braves crossed the Mississippi at Burlington and moved up the east bank of the river with his women and children, intending to drive out the settlers and return to their old village on the Island. The Winnebagoes and other Indians were to have assisted him in recovering the land. This news soon reached Saint Louis and Colonel Atkinson with a body of infantry left that city for Rock Island. Zachary Taylor, afterwards President of the United States, was in command of a company, and Lieutenant Jefferson Davis, afterwards President of the Confederate States, was attached to the same regiment throughout this campaign.

About two thousand volunteers were brought forward by Governor Reynolds of Illinois, assembling at Beardstown and marching to Yellow Banks, fifty miles below Rock Island. They moved to the mouth of Rock River where they were joined by Colonel Atkinson and his regulars. The volunteers were under the command of General Whiteside, and Abraham Lincoln, afterwards President of the United States, served under him as captain of a company. The Indians had ascended Rock River and halted opposite Rock Island, the women and children having been sent higher up the river in canoes. Black Hawk now made an attempt to capture Fort Armstrong. He crossed to the Island with his warriors in the night, but a violent storm arising interfered with his plans that night, and in the morning Colonel Atkinson's Infantry arrived and drove them from the Island. They followed their women up Rock River, pursued by Colonel Atkinson and the volunteers under General Whiteside.

Nearly the whole of Black Hawk's band was destroyed in the following months of May, June, July and August, and Black Hawk himself was captured and removed as a prisoner to the Island. He and his son Seoskuk, and other chiefs, were afterwards taken to Washington and other eastern cities. On his return from his eastern tour, Black Hawk settled down with a remnant of his own tribe on Des Moines River, where he died in 1838.

The Sacs and Foxes are believed to have originally come from the vicinity of Montreal, Canada, about the year 1700, and had lived on or near, Rock Island over one hundred and thirty years. After the close of the "Black Hawk War" there were no hostilities with the Indians at Rock Island.

During the late Civil War the Island was converted into a military prison and upwards of 12,000 Confederate prisoners were confined here. About 2,000 died and were buried on the Island.

A pleasant day may be passed in wandering over the Island, which is now an important United States Arsenal for the Mississippi Valley.

Rock Island City is situated on the mainland on the Illinois bank of the river. East of the city, stretching away to Rock River, are some picturesque bluffs and scenery of great beauty. On the sides of the hills are many comfortable residences of well-to-do citizens. The city is about midway between Saint Louis and Saint Paul, and immediately opposite the larger city of Davenport, Iowa. The iron bridge owned by the United States Government and connecting the two cities is open to the public free of toll.

The water power produced by the rapids has largely contributed to the growth of Rock Island City, and also of Moline—a city of factories—within an easy walk of its neighbor. In the latter I found many establishments for the manufacture of plows, cultivators and other farming appliances; also wagons and carriages, together with foundries and machine shops.

Rock Island City has a commerce and trade second to no city of its size in the Union. The centre of a system of railroads, the city has a busy aspect at all times. The population at the time of my visit was about 16,000.

Three miles from Rock Island City, inland, is a resort frequented by the residents of both sides of the river. Its traditions and associations are romantic. It is known as *Black Hawk's Watch Tower*. The *tower* consists of a rock and is the summit of the highest hill, overlooking Rock River and affording an extensive picture of the surrounding country. The rock derives its name from its having been used by Black Hawk as a point from which he could survey his lands for many miles. Tradition says it was se-selected by the chief's father and overlooked the tribe's first village on the banks of Rock River. Black Hawk gave the following account of the place to Antoine Le Claire in 1833: "The tower was my favorite resort and was often visited by me alone, where I could sit and smoke my pipe and look with wonder and pleasure at the grand scenes that were presented, even across the mighty river. On one occasion a Frenchman who had been resting in our village, brought his violin with him to the Tower to play and dance for the amusement of my people who had assembled there, and while dancing with his back to the cliff, accidentally fell over it and was killed. The Indians say that at the same time of the year soft strains of the violin can be heard near the spot." He further relates that in the year 1827, a young Sioux Indian, who was lost in a violent snow-storm, found his way into a camp of the Sacs, and while there, fell in love with a beautiful maiden. On leaving for his own country he promised to return in the summer and claim his bride. He did so, secreting himself in the woods until he met the object of his affection. A heavy thunder-storm was coming on at the time, and the lovers took shelter under a rocky cliff on the south side of the Tower. Soon a loud peal of thunder was heard; the cliff was rent into a thousand pieces and they were buried beneath them. "This, their unexpected tomb," says Black Hawk, "still remains undisturbed."

In the spring, summer and autumn many hundreds of visitors climb to the Tower, especially on Sunday and holidays, and while breathing the pure, healthful atmosphere, enjoy delightful views of the surrounding country and the majestic river at their feet. The Davenport family own the property, which, however, is accessible to all visitors.

CHAPTER XXII.

DAVENPORT TO DES MOINES.

One Hundred and Forty-fifth Day.

Farm House,
NEAR BLUE GRASS, IOWA,
October 3, 1876.

WEATHER cold, but clear and bracing. Mounted *Paul* at three o'clock P. M. and halted at the office of *The Democrat*, to say good-bye to Colonel Russell. On the road I overtook S. N. Garlock, a farmer, who invited me to spend the night at his house, which I agreed to do and was made very comfortable. I soon discovered that Mr. Garlock was a native of the Empire State, but came to Iowa twenty-seven years ago, and was now the owner of a prosperous farm near the village of Blue Grass. He spoke of visiting his old home in the East and his intention to proceed by way of Philadelphia and spend a day or two at the Centennial Exposition. He said that many Western people were making arrangements to go to the "Exposition" and at the same time visit their old homes and the old folks whom they had not seen for many long years.

One Hundred and Forty-sixth Day.

Iowa House,
M O S C O W , I O W A ,
October Fourth.

Moscow is a small agricultural hamlet twenty-nine miles west of Davenport, with a population of less than three hundred, but increasing in number as the surrounding region is occupied. On the road here from Blue Grass I found the weather becoming very cold and was compelled to dismount several times and walk some heat into my body. The country is rich in fertility of soil—generally rolling prairie. The villages along the road are said to be growing very rapidly.

One Hundred and Forty-seventh Day.

St. James Hotel,
I O W A C I T Y , I O W A ,
October Fifth.

Reached here at six o'clock P. M., fifty-five miles from Davenport. Weather, most of the day, cold, cloudy and generally disagreeable. I learn upon inquiry that the land about here for miles is, for the most part, settled by a thrifty, intelligent and enterprising people, and is well adapted to all the wants of the agriculturist. The railroad brings all the produce into market and farmers and manufacturers have their labors rewarded. The soil is a rich, black loam, and often, I am told, from five to ten feet in depth.

Had supper and retired to my room to attend to my correspondence.

One Hundred and Forty-eighth Day.

St. James Hotel,
IOWA CITY, IOWA,
October Sixth.

The weather continued extremely cold. Babcock completed necessary arrangements with the proprietor of Ham's Hall for my lecture the following evening. In the meantime I took a look at the city which was for many years the State capital. Its most salient feature appeared to be the State University, in which both sexes continue their education with commendable zeal, under competent professors. There are also a high school, a female college, a commercial college and several common schools. Four or five daily and weekly newspapers keep up the interest of the people in local affairs and national politics ; and four banks encourage the thrifty to place their spare cash with them at interest. Woollen and flax manufactures give employment to a considerable number of young people, and the mills are said to be in a flourishing condition.

The city has a large internal trade as well as with the several surrounding villages.

One Hundred and Forty-ninth Day.

St. James Hotel,
IOWA CITY, IOWA,
October Seventh.

The former State House is a fine and capacious building and an ornament to the city. On the removal of the seat of government to Des Moines, one hundred and twenty miles farther west, the building with its extensive grounds was granted by the Legislature to the State University.

I also noted several large places of business here, including dry goods, groceries and hardware. There are several lumber yards, flouring mills, plow factories, iron foundries, for manufacturing machinery; also due proportion to the population.

The newspapers published here are, according to all accounts, ably conducted and well sustained. The surrounding country is well adapted to all the wants of the agriculturist and is thickly settled.

In the evening I delivered my promised lecture to a very full house—Hon. G. B. Edmunds introducing me to the audience. The walls were covered with flags and a profusion of flowers greeted me on my arrival on the platform.

One Hundred and Fiftieth Day.

Tiffin House,
TIFFIN, IOWA,
October Eighth.

Mounted *Paul* in front of the Saint James to continue my journey and felt the need of an overcoat. Drew rein at Tiffin, a few miles from Iowa City. Of Tiffin little more can be said than that it has a rustic population of about fifty souls. The accommodations at the Tiffin House I must leave to conjecture, as any description would fall short of the reality. The only guests were a Methodist parson, two farmers on an expedition in quest of apples, and an overland tourist. The nabob of the village came into the public room in the course of the evening—a farmer and former State senator. This "Hon." gentleman engrossed our attention for about three hours by a long-winded description of the varieties of the "genus hog"—how to breed, how to feed and fatten, and how to drive him to market; all of which would probably have been edifying and elevating to the average Tiffinite, but it made me and the parson drowsy and I retired to dream of hogs and fat bacon until awakened by the daylight.

One Hundred and Fifty-first Day.

Grand Pacific Hotel,
MARENGO, IOWA,
October Ninth.

In my journey from Tiffin I found it necessary to dismount several times and walk in order to drive away the sensation of cold. Reached Marengo in the evening and registered at the Grand Pacific Hotel. Winter seemed to be approaching with rapid strides at this time and I was warned that it was necessary to lose as little time as possible at the different resting-points.

Marengo is eighty-five miles from Davenport. There is a good bridge crossing the Iowa River here, which adds much to the facilities for doing business. A thriving community of farmers occupy the surrounding land. Among the most important villages and towns in this and adjoining counties, are Newton, Grinnell, Montezuma and Millersburg, all growing in size and importance. Marengo is the county-seat of

AN IOWA VILLAGE.

Iowa County, and contains a population of nearly two thousand.

The State of Iowa, taken as a whole, is one of the most fertile in the United States. The native prairies are fields almost ready-made for the farmers' hands; their rich black soil returning him reward for his labor a hundred fold.

One Hundred and Fifty-second Day.

Skinner House,
BROOKLYN, IOWA
October Tenth.

My ride to-day from Marengo has been over fine prairie land with occasionally a farm in the distance like an oasis in the desert. Brooklyn is one hundred miles from Davenport and, as some evidence of its prosperous condition, has four hotels. I was fortunate in selecting the Skinner House, the proprietor of which knows how to make his guests comfortable. Paul also seemed happy to-night when I shut him in a clean and well-appointed stable with his supper.

Brooklyn is a village of over twelve hundred inhabitants, and wears the impress of success. There are several grain elevators, foundries, flour mills and business houses of all kinds; also graded schools, banks, and daily and weekly papers. The streets are clean and well paved, which is more than can be said for its Eastern namesake. The surrounding farms are large and well cultivated, and the country presents a most attractive appearance.

One Hundred and Fifty-third Day.

Moore House,
KELLOGG, IOWA,
October Eleventh.

In front of the Skinner House, *Paul* caused me some little anxiety by dashing up the street from the front where I had left him with loose rein for a moment while settling my bill. Coming back he gave me to understand, by a toss of his head, that he only wanted to shake a little dust from his feet. I was soon mounted and off at a gallop, covering thirty miles, when I stopped at a farm house for dinner.

On reaching the outskirts of Grinnell, I hailed a party of boys who were "playing *ball.*" One bright little fellow gave me the time, two o'clock, and the distance to Kellogg. I then pushed on without stopping at Grinnell. Amused myself with some little boys in front of a country school house who were "playing *horse.*" I inquired of the youngest if he went to school, and his brother answered for him in the affirmative. I then asked, "What does he learn?" "He don't learn nothin'," answered the youth. "Then why do you take him to school?" I inquired. "So, when the boys go out, he can 'play *horse*' with us."

Have seen some of the finest scenery and grandest farms to-day that I have encountered along my journey. The day has been unusually bright and pleasant, and the country looks lovely in the extreme. Reached Kellogg to-night, half an hour after dark. Caught a young snipe about a mile from the village and offered it to a young girl if she could name its species. She could not, and a boy claimed the prize.

Amused some of the guests in the evening with incidents of my journey, and they, in turn, gave me some useful information about the Far West, North Platte, Green River, and Humboldt Valley.

One Hundred and Fifty-fourth Day.

Pacific Hotel,
C O L F A X , I O W A ,
October Twelfth.

Arrived at Colfax in the evening after a glorious ride over the prairie. The grain on the farms waved in the breeze as the fields were passed and numerous streams crossed finding their way to the rivers that intersect the State. This prairie is not entirely devoid of timber, for groves dot the extended landscape like islands in a green sea; while from the higher grounds I viewed the prairie decked with wild hay and autumn flowers.

> ——" Broad on either hand
> The golden wheat-fields glimmered in the sun,
> And the tall maize its yellow tassels spun."

The prairie here is from twenty to forty miles in width. A variety of minerals are found and mined to a limited extent. Time will work many changes. A quarter of a century hence, Colfax will probably be known as an important mining town with large and varied interests. Its growth will be gladly noted by many who have faith in its future.

One Hundred and Fifty-fifth Day.

Jones House,
DES MOINES, IOWA.
October Thirteenth.

Mounted *Paul* at eight o'clock and rode twenty miles, which brought me to Des Moines. Most of the journey was over prairie land; the sun shone brightly and afforded me an agreeable warmth as *Paul* stepped out bravely—cheered, possibly by the prospect of entering a large city and resting for a day or two. We know nothing of a horse's prevision. The country along my route is rich in fertility of soil, but its resources are not yet fully developed. I am told that but little snow falls on this prairie, the winter being made up of cool, sunshiny days, and clear, frosty nights. There is nothing, I think, to hinder this part of Iowa from being one of the most healthy portions of the United States.

One Hundred and Fifty-sixth Day.

Jones House,
DES MOINES, IOWA,
October Fourteenth.

I have not seen a brighter or more stirring city in my line of march than Des Moines, the capital of the State of Iowa. Under the escort of Professor E. T. Bowen, city editor of *The Leader*, and two other well informed gentlemen, I visited the Iowa State Perpetual Exposition and was introduced to the secretary, who courteously showed me over the buildings.

The city stands at the mouth of the Raccoon River, is three hundred and fifty-eight miles west of Chicago and one hundred and forty-two east of Omaha. Its shape is quadrilateral—four miles long by two miles wide. The Des Moines River flows through its centre, dividing the East from the West Side. The city stands on a declivity, its highest part extending to about one hundred and sixty feet. The Post Office, Court House and city offices, the principal depots and hotels, and the greater portion of the business houses, are situated on a plateau about a mile long and half a mile wide, rising about fifteen feet above high water; and on the higher ground beyond are some of the handsomest and largest private residences.

On the East Side is another business locality. Capitol Square contains ten acres on an elevated site commanding a fine view. The State House was erected at a cost of nearly $3,000,000. The Public Library contains some 30,000 volumes. There are over twenty churches of all denominations in the city. The Post Office and Court House buildings are of marble and cost $250,000. There is also a State Arsenal, a large County Court House and many public improvements found only in first-class modern cities. Two daily and upwards of a dozen weekly papers are published here. In the vicinity are mines of excellent coal and a number of manufactories of various kinds are in operation.

Before leaving the Jones House it is but just that I should say that I was not more courteously treated during my journey than by Messrs. George W. Jones and Son. Professor Bowen and Captain Conrad with many others saw me off.

The next day a copy of the Des Moines *Leader*

reached me, in which the following notice appeared. I insert it here as one of many pleasant references to my journey.

"Captain Willard Glazier, the horseback traveller across the Continent, took in the Exposition on Saturday evening with intense gratification. He says he has seen no place on his route from Boston more promising than Des Moines. Among the calls he received at the Jones House was one from Captain Conrad, a prominent attorney from Missouri and now settled in his profession in this city, who was a fellow-captive with Captain Glazier in Libby Prison during the Rebellion. The Captain continued his journey westward yesterday with the best wishes of the friends he has made during his short stay here."

ON THE WAY TO MILL.

CHAPTER XXIII.

DES MOINES TO OMAHA.

One Hundred and Fifty-seventh Day.

Byers House,
A D E L , I O W A ,
October 15, 1876.

LEFT Des Moines with pleasant thoughts of the cordial reception I had met with, and pursuing my way westward over the prairies, reached this village in the evening after a twenty-five miles' ride over a section of the country strikingly beautiful. The soil of the prairie, I am everywhere informed, is almost invariably of the most productive character. No other State, in short, has finer facilities for growing all the cereals of the temperate zone than Iowa.

Adel is the county-seat of Dallas County, situated on the Raccoon River—generally called the "Coon." At the period of my visit the village had a population of less than one thousand, and although agriculture is the leading industry, considerable attention is given to manufacturing. The prairie land in the vicinity was, as yet, sparsely settled, but every inducement was offered settlers to establish themselves here. I noticed some broken fields, and blue smoke curling up from farm houses in the distance; and after eighteen miles of enjoyable exercise in the pure prairie atmosphere, reached this small village, where I concluded to halt for the night.

One Hundred and Fifty-eighth Day.

Private House,
DALE CITY, IOWA,
October Sixteenth.

Weather warmer, pleasant and more invigorating than during the past few days. Left Adel at eight o'clock A. M., and passed through Redfield at eleven, still on the great prairie which appears to have no limit. From the hilltops the valleys wear the aspect of cultivated meadows and rich pastures; and on the level spreads the wild prairie, decked with flowers, its long waves stretching away till sky and prairie mingle in the distance. Twenty years ago the red men chased the elk and buffalo where now are prairie farms and prairie homes. As I advance, I meet occasionally with trees skirting the streams that find their way to the rivers that intersect this beautiful State.

Had dinner at a prairie farm house and talked politics with the farmer, whom I found was an enthusiastic admirer of Peter Cooper. He did not expect his political favorite would be elected, but as a matter of principle would vote for him. I told him if he called himself a Republican, he should cast his vote for Governor Hayes, but my advice probably had little effect upon him. Reached Dale City about one o'clock. It

A NIGHT AMONG COYOTES.

was a small village in Lyon County, with about two hundred inhabitants.

One Hundred and Fifty-ninth Day.

A Night with Coyotes,
BETWEEN DALE CITY AND ANITA, IOWA,
October Seventeenth.

My journey to-day led me again over the seemingly endless prairie—extending beyond the range of human vision. Halted at a farm house for dinner, near Dalmanutha, an agricultural settlement in Guthrie County. Wishing to reach Anita before stopping for the night, I continued on the road after dark, contrary to my usual practice.

For some time before sunset I had not seen a farm house or even a tree as far as the eye could reach, and now could see nothing of road or trail. Accordingly I gave *Paul* the rein and left him to pick his way. He followed a sort of blind road which led to a haystack. I thought I could do no better than make my bed on the sweet hay, and decided to spend the night there supperless. I had scarcely settled myself when a troop of coyotes, or prairie wolves, came howling and barking in front of me. This made things uncomfortable, and I at once jumped to my feet and, revolver in hand, faced the enemy. Several were killed by my fire. The remainder, however, continued to threaten an attack. I was puzzled as to what was best to do when I was suddenly re-inforced by a friendly dog, who, attracted doubtless, by the report of the pistol and the barking of the coyotes, came to my rescue, and kept the animals at bay for the remainder of the night. At daybreak I was not sorry to bid adieu to the haystack and, neither, I believe, was *Paul*, who had also spent a restless night, notwithstanding the abundance of good fodder at his disposal.

It may be mentioned that the coyote seems to partake of the nature of the dog and the wolf. In the winter, when food is scarce, these animals will attack man, but, unlike the wolf, if a bold resistance is offered, they will speedily decamp. A pack of coyotes, however, are not pleasant company on a dark night.

One Hundred and Sixtieth Day.

Pacific Hotel,
ATLANTIC, IOWA,
October Eighteenth.

Was again all day on the prairie inhaling the pure, invigorating air as *Paul* and I faced a stiff breeze from the Northwest; and at four o'clock arrived at Atlantic, a thriving village of over three thousand inhabitants, dependent, like all the villages I had passed, upon the surrounding farms. These farms are mostly in a flourishing condition, are fenced and under good cultivation, divided into meadows and fields of every variety of grain. The village is delightfully situated. As an evidence of its prosperity it supported two ably conducted daily papers and three weeklies, three banks and several graded schools. I was now eighty-two miles from Des Moines. The prairie here is gently undulating and the soil composed of vegetable mould and sand. Atlantic, I infer from its busy appearance, has a destiny above that which it has attained.

One Hundred and Sixty-first Day.

Columbia House,
A̶voca, Iowa,
October Nineteenth.

Weather cloudy, threatening rain as I rode out of Atlantic in the morning at ten o'clock. Covered twenty miles and stopped for dinner at another farm, near Walnut. On my road saw a man at work in a large cornfield and, hailing him, inquired the distance to Avoca. After a few words had passed between us, I was surprised and pleased to discover that he was from my native county—St. Lawrence, New York, and knew many of my old friends and acquaintances in that quarter. Our conversation turned upon old localities and associations, much to our mutual enjoyment. The days of our youth were recalled, and although we had never met before, we parted after half an hour's chat as if we had been friends of many years' standing. My friend expressed perfect satisfaction with his rustic life on the prairie and was quite enthusiastic over the prospects of his farming operations. The soil he said was excellent, easy to cultivate and, in fact, second to none in the State.

Avoca is a purely agricultural village with a population of about 1,500, all, more or less, interested in the big farms within a radius of one to two miles of the busy town. Two weekly newspapers kept the citizens *en rapport* with the outside world and the hustling life of the large cities.

One Hundred and Sixty-second Day.

Neola House,
NEOLA, IOWA,
October Twentieth.

A drizzling rain on leaving Avoca made the prospect of my ride to this point somewhat gloomy. Over the interminable prairie again my journey lay, as it had done ever since I entered the State of Iowa, but a more magnificent sight I never saw than presented itself before me this afternoon on reaching the summit of an extensive table-land between Avoca and Minden.

Halted a few minutes for lunch at Minden, and met a gentleman there who had attended my lecture at Detroit, upon which he was pleased to compliment me. Neola is a small prairie settlement of about three hundred inhabitants and is surrounded by several good farms. Of the Neola House I can only say that I shall not easily forget it and its proprietor—especially the nocturnal serenade of all the cats of Neola—which deprived me of sleep throughout the night; and the extremely scant accommodations provided for the guests.

The soil here is inferior in quality to that of no other section of the State. The land is well watered and was gradually filling up with an industrious class of citizens.

One Hundred and Sixty-third Day.

Atlantic Hotel,
OMAHA, NEBRASKA,
October Twenty-first.

Left Neola at eight o'clock and reached Council Bluffs at three P. M. Found the road on approaching

OMAHA, NEBRASKA, IN 1876.

the city, in bad condition, but the splendid country through which I had passed since entering the State was perhaps equal to anything ever trodden by the feet of man. The surface of Western Iowa is very different from that of the prairie region in the eastern part of the State, being rougher and more hilly. The numerous streams proceeding from springs bursting from the hillsides, are clear and swift. Near the Missouri River, high and precipitous mountain bluffs are ranged, and the region contiguous is very hilly. The highest hills are covered with verdure—grass and timber. The soil generally is light and to appearance poor, but is loose and sandy, and found to be easily cultivated. Creeks and smaller streams of water occur frequently and afford power for mills and machinery, and furnish abundant supply for farming uses and stock.

The first white settlement in Western Iowa was made in the year 1847, by a company of Mormons or Latter-Day Saints, who had been exiled from Illinois in poverty and destitution. They passed through a part of the country then only inhabited by savages. They planted small colonies at places on the route, the main body pushing on to the bluffs near the Missouri River. A considerable number, unable to go farther, remained here, commenced clearing the land for farming, and two years later, in 1849, began the building of a town on the site now occupied by the city of Council Bluffs. Their new town they named Kanesville after one of their leaders. Several stores were built and opened, and the population was soon largely increased by people who were not Mormons and had no sympathy with them. The new settlers being greatly in the majority, virtually drove out the

"Saints," who finally left in a body to join their people at Salt Lake City.

Council Bluffs is now the most populous and flourishing city of Western Iowa. At the time of my visit, the inhabitants numbered only about 8,000, but it was then growing rapidly and bid fair to become one of the big cities of America. There is a large trade here employing an immense capital. The most important manufactures are the iron works and machine shops, the agricultural works, carriage factories, steam plows, and mills of various kinds, the city has ample railroad communication by means of several lines converging here. Omaha, on the opposite bank of the Missouri, is only four miles distant. The fine, substantial bridge connecting the two cities is 2,750 feet in length and has eleven spans. It has a railroad track, and accommodation for horse-cars and ordinary travel.

The most important public buildings are the County Court House, City Hall, High School building and the ward school houses. There were three banks and two daily and three weekly newspapers. The Catholics have a seminary for young ladies and a boys' parochial school. The State Institute for the Deaf and Dumb is near the city.

HIGH SCHOOL, OMAHA, NEBRASKA.

CHAPTER XXIV.

A HALT AT OMAHA.

OMAHA, the capital of Douglas County, the chief commercial city and metropolis of Nebraska, is the half-way station across the Continent. It is aptly called the "Gate City," seeming, as it does, a sort of opening to the great railroads, the great waterways, and the whole fascinating great beyond of western enterprise and western commerce.

As I rode into the city it seemed that it would be hard to find a more attractive place.

"A fine plateau nearly a mile broad, and elevated fifty or sixty feet above the Missouri, is occupied by the chief business portion of the city," while the beautiful bluffs, the low, rounded, tree-covered hills, forming a semi-circle on the west and south, are thickly dotted with tasteful and elegant residences and buildings surrounded by carefully laid-out grounds.

The streets cross at right angles. Most of them are one hundred feet broad; but Capitol avenue is one hundred and twenty feet in width.

On high grounds, just southwest of the city limits, is

Hanscom Park, a fine, natural grove, beautified by art for the delight of pleasure seekers.

Conspicuous on the west is the extensive Poor House Farm, containing the fine brick poor house.

To the north, on a high wooded hill, solitary, apart from the city, yet always within sight of its bustle and rush, lies, in its solemnity, Prospect Cemetery.

In the northern section of the city, also, we find the Douglas County Fair Grounds, the Omaha Driving Park, and Fort Omaha.

A bridge, the erection of which cost $1,500,000, spans the Missouri and connects Omaha with Council Bluffs.

I found Omaha not only fair to look upon, but also interesting in many ways. It is the key to the Rocky Mountains and the gold mines of California. Its wholesale trade amounts to about $15,000,000 annually and is constantly increasing. Its industries include smelting, brewing, distilling, brick making, machine and engine building and meat packing. The trade in the latter branch being only excelled by that of Chicago and Kansas City.

Its manufactures are constantly increasing. The Union Pacific Machine Shops alone employ about seven hundred men. Omaha has a linseed oil mill which turns out yearly millions of oil cakes and thousands of gallons of oil. One of the city's distilleries is so extensive that it pays the United States Government a tax of $300,000 per year.

The educational advantages of this metropolis are unsurpassed by any city of its size in the West. It has eleven fine ward school buildings and one high school. The latter occupies the former site of the old territorial capitol. It is a fine, large building, erected in 1872, at a cost of $250,000. Its spire is three hundred and ninety feet above the Missouri River, and its cupola commands a view embracing many miles of river scenery.

Creighton College is a Jesuit institution, endowed by Mrs. Edward Creighton to the amount of about $155,000. It will accommodate four hundred and eighty pupils and opens its hospitable doors to all students, irrespective of creed or race.

A four-story stone Post Office stands on the corner of Dodge and Fifteenth streets. That building, together with the furniture which it contains, is alleged to have cost $450,000 ; and Omaha people claim that it is one of the handsomest government buildings in all the land.

By the way, self-respect, humble pride, an appreci· ation, a love and admiration of every good thing the " Gate City " contains, is a characteristic of all honest, true-hearted Omaha men—God bless them ! They are even proud of their jail, which is universally conceded to be the handsomest and strongest penal institution in the West.

Omaha is headquarters for a military division known as the Department of the Platte. A great part of the financial supremacy of the city is due to the heavy purchase and distribution of military supplies. The General Government, some time since, acquired eighty-two and a half acres of land, two miles north of Omaha, christened it Fort Omaha, and spent over $1,000,000 in erecting military buildings upon it.

Statistics change rapidly in this Gate to progress and improvement. In the year 1877, improvements were added to the city amounting to about $800,000; in 1878, amounting to $1,000,000, and in 1879, to about $1,222,000.

Such was the Omaha which I rode into. How thought-compelling a place it was! How typical of the push, vigor, enterprise and pluck which have proved so masterful in the development of our once "Wild West." It is with pleasure that the mind runs over its history.

The first knowledge we have of the region in which Omaha is situated, comes to us, like many another crumb of information, from Father Marquette. He visited that tract in 1673, explored it and mapped out the principal streams. At that time the region was claimed by Spain, and formed a part of the great Province of Louisiana. It finally became a French possession, and was sold by that nation to the United States in the year 1800, for $1,500,000.

On the twenty-seventh of July, 1804, Messrs. Lewis and Clark came up the Missouri, and camped on the Omaha plateau, where the waters of the river then covered what is now the foot of Farnam street, and that part of the city where the Union Pacific Machine Shops are now located, also the smelting works, warehouses, distillery, extensive coal and lumber yards, and where numerous railroad tracks form a suggestive network.

In 1825, T. B. Roye established an Indian trading station on the present site of the city.

In 1845, a band of Mormons, driven from Illinois, settled slightly north of the Omaha of to-day. They came as "strangers and pilgrims," and called their .ittle settlement by the suggestive title of "Winter

Quarters." The Indians, however, insisted that the Mormons should not remain. So pressed, the saints divided their little party. A few families, under the leadership of Elder Kane, crossed the Missouri and started a settlement destined to become Council Bluffs.

The balance of the inhabitants of "Winter Quarters" placed themselves under the leadership of Brigham Young, and with one hundred and eight wagons migrated to Utah, where they immediately staked out Salt Lake City, and began to build their Temple.

By so slight a circumstance Omaha missed being next door neighbor to, or even becoming herself, the New Jerusalem of the Saints.

William D. Brown is conceded to have been the first white settler who staked out a claim on the plateau now occupied by Omaha. He started for the California gold fields. On his way it occurred to him how profitable it would be to establish a ferry across the Missouri to accommodate the thousands passing westward. Putting in practice his idea, in 1852, he equipped a flatboat for that purpose. He named this venture of his "Lone Tree Ferry," from one solitary tree on the landing, just east of where in Omaha to-day stand the Union Pacific Shops.

In the spring of 1853, Mr. Brown staked out a claim embracing most of the original town site of Omaha.

July 23, 1853, Brown became a member of the Council Bluffs and Nebraska Ferry Company, whose object was to open a steam ferry, and to establish a town on the west bank of the river. Despite protests from Indians and without consent of the

United States, in the winter and early spring of 1854, what is now Douglas County was nearly covered by staked-out claims of "sooners" and speculators.

May 23, 1854, Nebraska was admitted into the Union as a Territory, and in the same year Douglas County was created. Immediately, upon a beautiful plateau, a town site was selected, laid out, and christened Omaha.

The first house in Omaha was commenced before Omaha itself legally existed. It was built by Thomas Allen. It was a log house, was named the St. Nicholas, was used as a hotel, a store, or anything else which the public demanded.

In July of the same year another house was built— this one being of pine flooring. It was on the present site of Creighton College. Here, a few weeks after its erection, the first native Omaha boy first saw the light, and from this same house, a few days later, an Omaha citizen first passed out to that mysterious country

"From whence no traveller returns."

The third house was called "Big 6." Its owner opened "A general assortment of merchandise suitable. for time and place," and "Big 6" soon became a place of note.

House No. 4 was opened by a house warming, which was attended even by settlers from the adjacent State of Illinois.

In the same year, that of 1854, the so-called Old State House was built by the Ferry Company to accommodate the first territorial legislature. It was not an architectural beauty, and consequently, in 1857, it gave place to a large, brick Capitol.

In this, to Omaha, memorable year of 1854, the

SPORT ON THE PLAINS.

first doctor, the first lawyer and the first minister settled in her boundaries, also the first steam mill began running.

January 15, 1855, the large frame Douglas House was opened by a grand ball. It did an immense business for many years, and became notedly the headquarters for politicians and speculators.

The first territorial legislature convened January 16, 1855, and remained in session until March seventeenth of the same year. Where that legislature should meet became a question of vital importance to a number of Nebraska towns. The matter was hotly contested but the metropolis won the prize, acting Governor Cummings designating Omaha as the favored spot.

Traffic by steamboat did much to develop the " Gate City." Sometimes boats arrived seven or eight times a week, bringing new inhabitants, timber, machinery, provisions, furniture, and piling their cargo—human or inanimate—out upon the since washed away levees, to be taken care of as best the embryo city could.

The first boat of the season was the event of the year. Down the inhabitants ran to meet it, without regard to age, sex or race; down they trooped, laughing, shouting, rejoicing that communication with the great world was once more open. Many a " cotillon " was danced on the deck of that first boat, while the unloading was being vigorously carried on below.

There was little crime in the new city. In the three formative years only one murder is known to have been committed, and no criminal was legally executed until 1863.

There was never much Indian trouble in this vicinity. However, Omaha several times raised troops to protect the whites of Douglas County. In 1864, a large band of Indians appeared on the Elkhorn and so frightened the settlers that they poured into Omaha before daylight. Business was suspended, a meeting called in the Court House at two o'clock P. M., and before sunset every able-bodied man was armed. This promptness and efficiency so impressed the Indians that no outbreak took place.

In the late Civil War, Omaha responded nobly to the call of the General Government. The First Regiment of Nebraska Volunteers, the First Battalion, the Second Regiment Nebraska Volunteers, the First Nebraska Veteran Cavalry, and four companies of Curtis' Horse, came almost entirely from Omaha.

The first telegraph line reached Omaha in 1860.

The first breaking of ground for the Union Pacific Rail Road took place in Omaha, December 3, 1863.

The first train from the East reached Omaha by the Chicago and Northwestern route, January 17, 1867.

So Omaha grew and prospered. It took about twenty-seven years to bring it out of original wildness to the state of excellency in which I found it as I passed through on my horseback journey. Yet it seems but yesterday since no human dwelling occupied the place now covered by our young city. Here the Indian council-fires burned ; on the bluffs, with no more civilized weapon than his bow and arrow, he hunted deer, buffalo, elk, bear and wolf. Here his warwhoop rang out clear and unmolested. Here brave, free, unfearing, he dwelt,

"Monarch of all he surveyed."

And now he is completely effaced from this region.

PAWNEE INDIANS. NEBRASKA.

Gone and only remembered by some quaint name still attached to stream or mountain.

To-day "the moving millions, both in this country and Europe, are making earnest inquiry for Nebraska." 50,000 new inhabitants came to it in 1880. The close of the late war brought many ex-soldiers and their families here to claim land privileges near Omaha, and from "the four quarters of the globe the swelling thousands have come to settle with those that made their way thither. From Maine and Texas, and from every territory of the Rocky, Mountains, they came." "The rank and file, the bone and muscle, were men who came to stay, who counted the cost, who measured the sacrifice." Under their faithful hands the desert has been made to "blossom like the rose." "The dug-out and the log house have given place to the elegant mansion, and thousands of groves have sprung up almost as if by magic all over the prairies."

These brave pioneers knew it would be so. They believed in the embryo city. By faith they saw the fields blossoming for the harvest. "They heard the song of harvest home, they saw the smoke of the rising city, the highways of commerce, and some of them saw the highways of nations, so long a fable to the American people, stretching up through their valleys to the everlasting mountains and on to the broad Pacific. To-day the day-dream of these brave men is realized—

For lo ! it has all come true.

CHAPTER XXV.

OMAHA TO CHEYENNE.

AS winter was approaching and the days were now becoming considerably shorter, it was incumbent upon me to hasten my departure from Omaha, if I would reach my destination as contemplated at the outset. Having learned from frontiersmen that Eastern horses are not available in the Alkali Region of the Plains, I placed my faithful *Paul* in a boarding stable in Omaha, purchased a mustang of a Pawnee Indian and forthwith continued my journey westward.

Webster defines a *mustang* as the "Wild Horse of the Prairie." My experience with him has taught me that he is sufficiently docile under the restraint of a tight rein; will travel a longer distance over a rough road in a given time than the average horse, and scarcely ever shows fatigue even if the road is all up-hill. Of course, some of them are vicious, and will make things uncomfortable for the rider; but in this particular some civilized horses are not unlike them. I found the Mexican saddle more convenient than the "McClellan" which I had hitherto used, and thought much easier for the animal.

NORTH PLATTE, NEBRASKA.

453

My mustang proved tractable and made excellent time; and having obtained in Omaha all the information within my reach concerning the remaining half of my journey, I determined to use all despatch and avoid as far as I could the cold weather of the Rockies and Sierras.

I may here state that in consequence of the long rides I was now compelled to make, with very few stoppages except at night, the original plan of the journey was somewhat changed, and my journal necessarily fell into disuse; my chief object being to get over the mountains as quickly as possible. I was, therefore, unable during the remainder of my ride to refer so much to daily incidents, but confined myself to jotting down in a general way whatever I thought might prove of interest to the reader.

Over the Great Plains that lie between the Missouri and the Rockies my nerve was thoroughly tested, and not less so the mettle of my mustang which carried me a distance of five hundred and twenty-two miles in six days. Halts at this time were few and far between, except for necessary food and sleep. The weather had become very cold since leaving Omaha, and the ascent had been gradual but continuous.

The surface of Nebraska is extremely varied. There are no elevations that can be dignified with the name of mountains, but in its northern and western parts there are lofty hills. Along the Niobrara and White Rivers, extending into Dakota, there are sand-hills with a very scanty vegetation and very difficult to traverse on account of the loose sand. The gently rolling lands of three-fourths of Nebraska appear very much like the suddenly petrified waves and billows of the ocean. Minerals had not yet been found to any con-siderable extent, and the scarcity of coal rendered more valuable the extensive beds of peat found in some parts of the State. The *salt* basins of Nebraska are rich and extensive. The principal one is located in Lancaster County, covering an area of twelve by twenty-five miles. Fossil remains, of great interest to geologists, have been discovered in great quantities. Indian hiero-glyphics, which ante-date the traditions of all living tribes, are cut deep in the bluffs along the Missouri River, in places now inaccessible.

The Platte or Nebraska River, from which the Ter-ritory received its name, is a broad and shallow stream. It is claimed that there is not a foot of land in Eastern Nebraska that is not susceptible of cultivation. High winds sweep over the plains, and the storms are some-times of terrible severity. The climate is dry and exhilarating, and the nights generally cool throughout the summer. There is no part of the United States better adapted for stock-raising than the prairies of Nebraska.

There is a well-equipped university at Lincoln, a normal school for the training of teachers and an insti-tution for the blind at Nebraska City.

After a fifty miles' ride from Omaha a halt was made at the Sherman House, Fremont, Dodge County, for supper and lodging. The journey had been pleasant and the landscape charming in its quiet beauty. The south wind was neither too warm nor too cold for per-fect comfort, and my mustang looked as if he could carry me another fifty miles without any inconvenience to himself.

Fremont had a population of nearly 3,000, and has

a large trade in grain, cotton and lumber. It has a court house, a high school, three banks and four news-papers.

Left early the following morning and at night slept in a wigwam with Pawnee Indians, in the absence of other shelter, and they gave me of their best. At Lone Tree, a post office in Nance County, I stopped at the Lone Tree House for the night, and next morn-ing at dawn, the weather being very fine, hurried for-ward on my journey. Reached Grand Island, where I was accommodated at a private house with bed and board.

Grand Island is in the Great Platte Valley on Platte River, one hundred and fifty-four miles west of Omaha. It stands 1,800 feet above sea level. The Island, on which the town is built, is fifty miles long.

Wood River, my next resting-place, is a township in Hall County with a population not exceeding one thousand. On the following day good headway was made, but I could find no better accommodation for the night than at a Pawnee camp. On the suc-ceeding night, after a hard day's ride, I stopped at Plum Creek, two hundred and thirty miles west of Omaha, and was accommodated at the Plum Creek House. A bridge spans the Platte River at this point. The population was only three hundred, but a weekly paper had been started and was well supported. The next evening, the McPherson House, McPherson, received me and my mustang and treated us hospitably. Then followed North Platte, one hundred and thirty-seven miles from Grand Island, where I lodged for the night at a private house, the home of a pioneer. The repair shops of the Union Pacific Railroad were located here; also a bank and two enterprising newspapers. The population of the township was nearly three thousand. At Sidney, which is a military post, I stopped at the Railroad Hotel. Sheep-farming is a leading industry of Sidney and its vicinity. My last stopping-place in Nebraska was at Evans Ranche, Antelope, a small village on the Elk Horn River.

Crossing the boundary into Wyoming Territory and reaching Cheyenne, I made my entrance into this most interesting region—a great plateau of nearly 100,000 square miles, its lowest level 3,543 feet, its highest altitude more than 13,000 feet above the sea. Some one has said that it seems "a highway, laid out by the 'Great Intelligence,' in the latitude most favorable, at all seasons, for great migrations to the shores of the Pacific."

Shales bearing petroleum, iron, limestone, soda, sulphur, mica, copper, lead, silver and gold, are all there for the taking.

There, volcanoes are still at work.

There, great mountains, great canyons, and great cataracts make the face of Nature sublime.

There, in past centuries, "at some period anterior to the history of existing aboriginal races," lived a mysterious, to us unknown people, traces of whom we still find in neatly finished stratite vessels, "knives, scrapers, and sinkers for fish lines made of volcanic sandstone or of green-veined marble. Such is the tract of territory called Wyoming."

Beginning at the south-east corner of this tract, we encounter, not far from the boundary, a semi-circular range, about 2,000 feet above the general level, known as Laramie Hills. The north branch of the

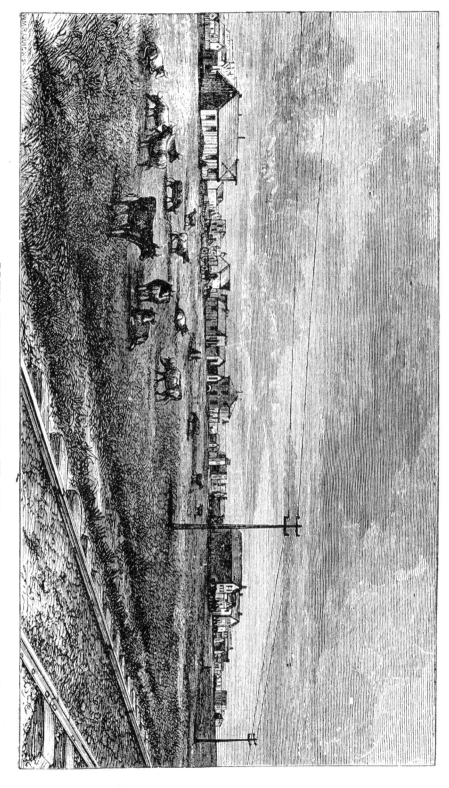

PLUM CREEK, NEBRASKA, IN 1876.

459

Platte, coming from the south, sweeps in a long curve about it; and just at the base of this Laramie range nestles the so-called "Magic City," Cheyenne, the capital of Wyoming.

White men first explored this region in 1743, and in 1744, when Sieur de la Verendrye and his sons came down from Canada, lured by the then unexplored Rocky Mountains. But the region was fearfully wild. Not only was the face of Nature most strange, but the whole tract was overrun by belligerent savages.

In 1804 a few brave white men began hunting beaver there. But it was many long years before civilization took possession of the spot. Not indeed until mining was begun on the summit of the Rocky Mountains in Dakota.

Then the fact of railroad construction brought great crowds to the North Platte country, crowds composed of two diametrically opposed elements, namely workers and loafers. These two elements joined hands for once, strange as it may seem, and together they settled Cheyenne. They located it near several military posts, and just as close to Denver as they could get it, and still keep it in Wyoming. At Denver was a bank. They wanted to be near that institution, and so came within one hundred and six miles of it. Such were a settler's ideas of propinquity!

Several items contributed to making this young settlement a success. The most important of these items was that, in 1867, the Union Pacific Railroad Company began to locate its shops there. That was rarely fine bait for mechanics. The coal and iron mines in the suburbs proved good bait for miners.

So, from these humble beginnings, Cheyenne came into existence, awoke, bestirred herself, became fired with ambition, and made the summer of 1867 one never to be forgotten in her boundaries.

On July first of that year, the agent of the Union Pacific Railroad erected in Cheyenne the first structure belonging to that company.

In August, the city government was formed, H. M. Hook being chosen mayor.

On September nineteenth, the first issue of the Cheyenne *Evening Leader* was published.

September twenty-seventh, a meeting was held for the purpose of organizing a county to be called Laramie.

On October eighth, an election was held to vote for a representative to Congress, to elect county officers, and to locate the county-seat. It was decided that every citizen of the United States, who had been in the territory ten days, might vote. One thousand nine hundred votes were cast, and Cheyenne was declared the county-seat.

On October twenty-fifth, telegraphic communication with the East was opened.

November thirteenth, the first passenger train came through from Omaha, and one month later the track was laid to Fort Russell.

About July first of that year, a Mr. Post bought two lots in Cheyenne for six hundred dollars. He then went to Denver on business, stopped to stake out his claim in a coal mine, and returned to find that city real estate had become so inflated in his absence that he was enabled to sell a fractional part of his six hundred dollar lots for five thousand six hundred dollars.

CATTLE RANCHE IN NEBRASKA.

About July first, the Union Pacific Railroad sold lots for one hundred and fifty dollars per lot. A month later, they were worth one thousand dollars apiece, increasing in price at the rate of one thousand dollars per lot each month for some time after.

On July 1, 1867, Cheyenne was simply a little corner of the wilderness.

On January 1, 1868, it was a city of six thousand inhabitants.

Was it not indeed a "Magic City," which could furnish a six months' record like the above?

However, this was but the *Quatre Bras* before the Waterloo.

Cheyenne's real struggle for life, for advancement, for culture and permanent prosperity, was to begin with this new year of 1868. We know how grandly the young city conquered, not by "magic" this time, but better still, by patience, pluck, and indomitable will. But to her honest and law-abiding citizens, at the outset of 1868, things looked dark indeed.

Cheyenne was the terminus of the Union Pacific Railroad that winter, and the scum of the floating Western population drifted thither.

Houses were insufficient, and many wintered in tents and dugouts.

To make things worse, great numbers of squatters came, and began seizing town lots.

"Shootings were frequent, and every manner of vice abounded. A canvas saloon would answer as well as another for gambling, drinking, and the purposes of the dives. Various men and women made the place intolerable. It was never disputed that this town exceeded in vice and unwholesome excitement any of the new cities of the West." The police were overwhelmed. Crime, theft, and assault were rampant. Patience ceased to be a virtue.

The commander at Fort Russell was appealed to, and a battalion was sent by him to escort the squatters beyond the city limits.

After that, the good people of Cheyenne took matters into their own hands, deciding to

> "Take up arms against a sea of troubles,
> And by opposing, end them."

A vigilance committee, that *dernier* resort of the order-loving Westerner of that period, was formed.

On January 11, 1868, this committee arrested three men for robbery. The criminals were bound together and placarded with the following notice:

"$900 stole. $500 returned! Thieves F. St. Clair, W. Grier, E. D. Brownell! City authorities please not interfere until ten o'clock A. M. Next case goes up a tree! Beware of Vigilance Committee!"

Comparatively gentle measures, like the above, were useless. Authority in that wild land had to be made of "sterner stuff." Not until the vigilants had hung and shot a dozen men did comparative order prevail. There was many a dark day for the well-wishers of Cheyenne; yet they lost

> "No jot of heart or hope,
> But pressed right boldly on,"

and gradually peace came out of strife, order out of confusion, and civilization reigned supreme.

In 1869, Cheyenne became the great *entrée* port of the vast regions north and west.

On September seventh of that year the first term of court was held in the city.

A MOUNTAIN VILLAGE.

In that same month of September, an election for members of the first Territorial Legislature took place.

That Legislature held a sixty days' session. Some of its *dicta* were as follows:

Gambling was allowed.

Taxes were placed upon all property, real or personal, excepting only United States and public property; and in cases of individuals, exempting clothing and furniture, amounting to one hundred dollars.

Jails were to be placed in every county.

And, "last but not least," Cheyenne was declared the seat of the territorial government, and an appropriation was asked for with which to build a capitol.

Surroundings change rapidly in the rush of a new community, and 1870 saw Cheyenne established, strengthened, purified, settled.

The floating riff-raff had passed away, leaving a solid, intelligent population of sixteen hundred.

The city had at that time one public school and two private ones; the latter containing about sixty pupils. It had five well built and well furnished churches. The orders of Masons, Knights Templar, Odd Fellows, and Good Templars were all represented in Cheyenne at that time. The city had two large banks, three tobacconists, three hardware houses, two shoe stores, one confectionery, two bakeries, one livery stable, two first-class hotels, many common ones, a daily newspaper, two weeklies, a well organized fire department, and "an acqueduct, nearly completed, for bringing water from a source seven miles away into the city."

Cheyenne was now well governed, orderly, at peace, and only three years old.

She has not stood still—the brave little "Magic City!"

She keeps on growing, becoming more beautiful, more prosperous. The best we can wish for her is that her future may prove as phenomenal and brilliant as her past has been.

CHAPTER XXVI.

CAPTURED BY INDIANS.

CHEYENNE was at length left behind, and, with the object of securing companionship in my journey across Wyoming and Utah, I made the acquaintance of two herders—rough men and plain of speech, but apparently reliable and trustworthy. During the few days spent with these pioneers of the Plains, I learned but little of their past lives, yet I was thoroughly satisfied from the first that they would prove invaluable guides in my otherwise lonely ride over the Rockies.

My new companions, Israel Gordon and a Mexican with unpronounceable name, were on their way to Salt Lake City with a few mustangs and Indian ponies, and we at once arranged to journey together as far as our respective routes carried us.

On our first day out from Cheyenne we were much favored, having a clear sky and a southwest wind, which tempered pleasantly the usual chilliness of the season. A ride of thirty-three miles on an up-hill road brought us to Sherman, the highest point touched in the Rocky Mountains by the Union Pacific Railway. Here we halted for the night, had supper, and slept under our blankets in the open air.

After a light breakfast the following morning, November first, we continued our journey along the line of the Union Pacific. Still favored with fine weather and our mustangs being in excellent condition, good progress was noted in the march westward. I had now become quite well acquainted with my new-made friends, and, as our ponies shook the dust of many miles from their feet, we talked of the strange region through which we were passing, and of the routes which led to objective points beyond the mountains. During these conversations I learned that Gordon was born in Vermont, and lived in that State until the close of the Civil War, when he emigrated to Nebraska, and later to Wyoming, where for several years he led a wandering life among the hunters and cow-boys of the Far West. My other companion told me that he began life in New Mexico, and at the age of twenty-one drifted into Colorado, from which Territory he migrated to Cheyenne, in 1867. Both men were robust, strong of limb, and thoroughly accustomed to the habits and practices of the mixed population of the Plains.

As the reader may have observed, I have undertaken from the outset in this chapter to give some idea of the life and habits of my fellow-travelers, for, as will be discovered on another page, they were destined to share with me the most trying ordeal of my journey from Ocean to Ocean.

On reaching a point about a mile east of Skull Rocks, on the Laramie Plains, we were surprised to find our-

CAPTURED BY INDIANS.

473

selves confronted by a band of Indians—thirteen in number. This caused no uneasiness at first, as Indians are often seen on these Plains. We soon discovered, however, that they were on no friendly errand, and, upon a nearer approach, the herders pronounced them a raiding party of Arrapahoes. They were evidently in pursuit of plunder, were decked in war-paint, and as soon as we came in range of their rifles sounded the war-whoop and bore down upon us, in a manner that betokened anything but a peaceful visit, and left no doubt in our minds as to the motive of their attack.

The Arrapahoes were at this time the friends and allies of the Sioux, and the chief objects of their raid were doubtless revenge for white men and horses for their warriors, who were then rendezvoused in the Black Hills.

Fully convinced that we were in the presence of an enemy determined to kill or capture our little party, no attempt was made to parley. The ponies were hurriedly drawn together so as to form a barrier against the assaults of the Indians, who were now in short range and gradually closing in upon us. As they galloped around us, the Indians formed a circle and kept up an incessant fire, to which we replied over the backs of our ponies, but with little effect, as from their mode of attack they were a constantly shifting target and difficult to reach, even with the best weapons in use. My own equipment consisted of a carbine, such as I had used in the cavalry service during the Civil War, and a 22-calibre Colt's revolver. Gordon and the Mexican were each provided with a Winchester rifle and navy revolver, while nearly all the Arrapahoes were armed with Winchesters and revolvers.

But few moments were required to settle the unequal contest. Four of our horses fell in rapid succession, including my own mustang; in the meantime we br ught down one Indian and three ponies. The Indian was instantly killed by a shot from the Mexican.

On seeing one of their number fall, the Arrapahoes rushed upon us with deafening yells, and with such force as to render resistance useless. Our arms were taken from us, our horses quickly seized, and, in much less time than it takes to tell it, we were mounted and riding at a rapid pace to the northward, under a guard of six well-armed Indians, who were carefully instructed as to their duties by their chief, Lone Wolf. The remainder of the band were more or less occupied in scouring the country for horses and other plunder, wanted for their encampment in the Black Hills.

We rode at a trot or gallop until about ten o'clock at night, when a halt was ordered by the chief, and all dismounted; a fire was built and some antelope meat, secured during the day, was partially roasted and distributed among the Indians and their captives. We were for some time squatted around a big fire—our captors engaged in earnest conversation. Gordon understood enough of their language to interpret that the discussion related to their prisoners—that the friends of the Indian killed at Skull Rocks, and who were in the majority, were in favor of putting all of their prisoners to death for having shot one of their number. Lone Wolf, however, interposed, saying it would be enough to take the life of him who had killed their brother. Supper over, four Arrapahoes approached us and seized the herder who had fired the fatal shot. They led him to a stake which had been

DECIDING THE FATE OF THE CAPTIVES.

driven in the ground about fifty yards from the bivouac; to this stake he was firmly bound by lariat ropes. All of the Indians then began dancing around and torturing their victim in the most brutal manner conceivable. Arrow-heads were heated in the fire and held against his naked person. Three or four of the Indians made a target of their captive, and amused themselves by hurling at him their sharp-pointed knives, which, penetrating his body, remained imbedded in the flesh until he was nearly exhausted with pain and loss of blood. These tortures were continued until our unfortunate comrade lost consciousness, when one of the Arrapahoes, more humane than his associates, advanced and ended his sufferings by a pistol-shot in the head.

In the meantime Gordon and I were seated on the ground, bound together, and unable to offer any relief to our suffering companion, who bore his tortures with a greater degree of composure and fortitude than I ever witnessed on the battle-field or within the walls of the dungeon, and, while no stately column or monumental pile marks his resting-place, he deserves to sleep beside the heroic martyrs of the border who have risked life and suffered privation and hardship for the advancement of a higher civilization.

Having disposed of the Mexican, several of the Indians now approached Gordon and myself, and, separating us, seized me roughly by the arms, and, dragging me to the stake, bound me to it and commenced a series of dances, accompanied by much gesticulation and taunting, which they doubtless intended as a sort of introduction to tortures which were to follow. Lone Wolf, who had from the first seemed friendly, but who was at this time some distance from the camp-fire, now rushed to my rescue and dispersed our inhuman captors, who were loath to desist from their devilish work. A few minutes later a brother of the Indian killed at Skull Rocks removed the scalp of the Mexican, and, after he had fastened it to his belt, all began dancing around the fire, singing and shouting until they were thoroughly exhausted, when they squatted upon the ground, apparently regretting that they had not been permitted to put more trophies in their scalp locks.

An object of interest to us at this time was the horses which were tethered by long lariat ropes to stakes which had been driven in the ground at a convenient distance from the encampment. Could we but elude the guard and mount the mustangs we were riding when captured, our chances for escape would be all we could wish. As usual, we were bound together, with two stalwart Indians in charge. The other Indians disposed themselves around the fire and slept. I and my companion slept very little, but pretended to do so. We were always on the alert and seeking opportunities to escape. About two o'clock in the morning our guards were relieved by two others, and all was again quiet around their camp-fire. At the first streak of dawn, the Indians were up and had a scant breakfast of dried buffalo meat and venison, which had been secured from the ranches of frontiersmen during their raid of the previous day; of this they gave us barely enough to satisfy hunger.

As soon as all were ready for the trail, Gordon and I were each given a pony, which we mounted under the close scrutiny of the guard, and the entire party

ESCAPE FROM THE ARRAPAHOES.

started northward at a brisk trot. No real attempt to escape had thus far been made and the watch became somewhat relaxed, the attention of the Indians being devoted chiefly to foraging. When opportunity seemed favorable for the capture of horses or cattle, a halt was called by the leader, and three or four of the party were detailed for this purpose. These foragers were expected to keep themselves and their prisoners supplied with meat and such other rations as could be found in the straggling cabins of frontiersmen, but, as their raids often proved fruitless, we were, at best, scantily provided for, and many times entirely without food.

We were now skirting the Black Hills, and I had discovered by this time that our captors were making their way to the Arrapahoe rendezvous, about one hundred miles from Deadwood.

At the end of the second day the routine of the previous night was repeated: the Indians built a fire, cooked and ate some antelope meat, which had been brought in by the foragers during the afternoon, and then lay down around the fire for the night, their two prisoners being again bound together, with a guard on each side. Notwithstanding these precautions, however, on the part of the Arrapahoes, I was quietly on the alert, and, although feigning sleep, was wide awake and prepared to take advantage of any circumstance which might prove favorable to an escape. I passed the fingers of my right hand over the cord that bound the left to my fellow-prisoner and felt sure that with patience and persistence the knot could be untied and our liberty regained.

While the guards dozed and slept, as on the previous night, our eyes steadily sought the arms and ponies. We were quite certain that any attempt to escape, if detected and defeated, would result in immediate torture and death; but were, nevertheless, firmly determined to make the effort, let the consequences be what they might, for by this time we were thoroughly convinced that, if taken to their encampment in the Black Hills, the Indians would be most likely to detain us as hostages for a long period, and in the end possibly, should the inclination seize them, subject us to brutalities that only savages can devise. With such reflections and but indifferent opportunity to put our plans for escape to the test, we passed our second night in captivity.

At dawn of the third day, November second, after the usual breakfast of antelope, Lone Wolf called his band together and, mounting, continued his march northward, halting occasionally for rest and refreshment. About eight in the evening all dismounted and bivouacked for the night. The weather was now extremely cold in this high altitude, and was keenly felt by the Arrapahoes and their white captives.

Shivering with cold and without blankets, Gordon and I, still bound together at the wrists, lay down to sleep with our captors around a smouldering fire. The Indians sought sleep—their prisoners thought only of possibilities for escape.

With the experience I had gained in Southern prisons during the Civil War and the herder's thorough knowledge of the Plains, I felt confident that we could make our escape if we were constantly on the alert for the opportune moment. During the early hours of the night we had each fixed our eyes upon a pony.

These animals were grazing near the camp-fire, with their saddles on, ready for immediate use if required. Under the pretence of being asleep we began snoring loudly, and the guards, feeling at ease concerning their prisoners, slept at intervals, although restless until midnight, when we found them sleeping soundly.

I now worked at the cord which bound me to my white companion and ascertained that I could untie it. While making the attempt one of the Indians moved in his sleep and I ceased my efforts for the moment, and all was quiet again. The opportunity arrived at length, the knot was loosened, and the noose slipped over our hands, which gave us liberty. We quickly took possession of two revolvers, but the guards, being awakened by our movements, were about getting on their feet, when we dealt them stunning blows with the butt of the revolvers, forced them to the ground, and gained needed time for our escape. Each rushed for a pony, leaped into the saddle, and, before Lone Wolf and his band had shaken off their slumber, we were urging our mustangs to their utmost speed southward.

But a moment elapsed before all of the Indians were mounted and in pursuit of their escaping captives; but this had the effect only of spurring us to still greater speed. Finding several of our pursuers in short range I turned in my saddle and sent a bullet among them; another and another followed. One Indian fell from his horse, but the darkness prevented our seeing if the other shots had told. The Arrapahoes returned the fire, but luckily without any worse result than increasing the pace of our flying ponies.

Away we tore over hill-top and through canyon until but three or four Indians could be seen in pursuit, when Gordon, saying it would be much better for both to take separate routes, at once dashed off through a ravine to the right. One Indian considerably in advance of his companions was at this time closing upon me, but I sent a bullet into his horse, which put a temporary stop to pursuit and would have enabled me to distance my pursuers in the saddle had not my own horse fallen an instant later through a well-directed shot from the Indian I had just dismounted.

I now dropped into a gulch, remaining hidden until morning. With the coming light I found the coast clear, and, emerging from my place of concealment, set out in a southwesterly direction, which brought me to a cattle ranche late in the afternoon, grateful, indeed, for liberty regained and for the freedom which enabled me to continue my journey toward the shores of the Pacific. After listening to my story the generous ranchmen whom I here met supplied me with food and a fresh mustang. Again facing westward I pursued my course over the Rockies, striking the Old Government Trail near Fort Steele at the end of three days.

CHAPTER XXVII.

AMONG THE MORMONS.

IN my ride across the Territory of Utah amid its snow-capped mountains, hot sulphur springs and its great Salt Lake, I met no hostile Indians, but on the contrary many hospitable Mormons; in fact, my reception by both Mormon and Gentile was invariably kind and generous. I saw something of the social life of Utah as well as the wonderful country through which I passed, and was favorably impressed with the material development of the latter, as witnessed in its farms and mechanical industries. The men I conversed with were fairly intelligent— some exceptionally so; and hesitated not to explain and justify their peculiar faith and domestic life. They are certainly neither monsters nor murderers, but men possessing good manners and many of them refined tastes. In short, I found much good human nature among this people as well as social culture. Business intelligence and activity is a marked feature in their intercourse with strangers.

In Utah agriculture is the chief occupation of the people. The long dry summers and the clayey character of the soil insure defeat to the farmer, unless he helps his crops by artificial means. Irrigation is therefore universal, and the result—the finest crops to be found anywhere in the West.

The Territory of Utah covers the region drained by the Great Salt Lake and many miles more, both in length and breadth, but the Mormon settlements extend one hundred miles further into Idaho on the north and two hundred miles into Arizona on the south. These settlements are mostly small, but there are some places of considerable importance, as, for instance, Provo at the south and Ogden at the north.

On July 14, 1847, Brigham Young, a Mormon leader, and his followers entered the valley of the Great Salt Lake. The lake itself is one of the most remarkable bodies of water on the globe. It is seventy miles long and forty-five miles broad, and stands 4,250 feet above the sea-level. It bears a strong resemblance to the Dead Sea of Palestine, but, unlike that sea, it abounds in animal life. When Young entered the valley Utah belonged to Mexico, and the leader believed he could found whatever character of institution should suit him and his people best. It has been alleged that Brigham Young had "chains on men's souls." There is no doubt that superstition and the machinery of the Mormon Church were in some degree the secret of his irresistible power over his followers; but back of the superstition and the marvellous church organization stood the brain of a great and masterful man. His power, he knew, must rest upon something material and tangible, and this something he reasonably discerned to be the prosperity of the people themselves. He proved himself to be an organizer of prosperity, and this was the real source of his strength.

Mormonism is the religion of 250,000 of the world's inhabitants. The Territory of Utah has a population of 160,000, and of these, probably, 110,000 are Mormons. Their doctrines may be explained in a few words:

They believe that both matter and spirit are eternal, and both are possessed of intelligence and power to design.

The spiritual realm contains many gods, all of whom are traced back to one Supreme Deity.

This Supreme Deity and all the gods resemble men and differ only in the fact that they are immortal.

In form they are the same as men, having every organ and limb that belongs to humanity. They have many wives, and are as numerous as the sands upon the sea-shore.

Among the gods, Jesus Christ holds the first place, and is the express image of the Supreme Father.

A general assembly of the gods, presided over by the Supreme Deity, is the creating power.

When this world was created, Adam and Eve were taken from the family of gods and placed in it. In the fall they lost all knowledge of their heavenly origin, became possessed of mortal bodies, and only regained what they had lost by the quickening of the Holy Spirit and continuous progress in knowledge and purity.

Among other creations of the gods are innumerable spirits which can only attain to the rank of gods by the rugged road of discipline and trial trod by our first parents. These spirits are constantly hovering over our earth waiting for fleshy tenements in which to begin the steep ascent.

As soon as a child is born, one of these spirits takes possession of it and is then fairly launched forth upon its heavenly voyage.

Those who do not listen to the teachings of the church here will, at death, enter upon a third estate or probationary sphere, when they will have another opportunity, when, if they improve it aright, they will, with all the faithful, enter upon the fourth estate, which is the estate of the gods.

The Holy Spirit is a material substance filling all space, and can perform all the works of the Supreme Deity. It is omnipresent; in animals it is instinct, in man reason and inspiration, enabling him to prophesy, speak with tongues, and perform miracles of healing and many other wonderful things. The Holy Spirit can be imparted by the laying on of hands by a priesthood properly constituted and duly authorized.

The two prominent features of Mormonism are polygamy and lust for power. Salvation is not so much a matter of character as of the number of family.

Such is the teaching of Brigham Young in his sermons, and of George Q. Cannon, Heber Kimball, and of all the leading Mormons.

Social life among this people may be judged of from the Mormon estimate of woman. She exists only as a necessity in man's exaltation and glory. Her only hope of a future life depends upon her being united in " celestial marriage" to some man. Thus joined, she will have a share in her husband's glory. In marrying her, her husband confers upon her the greatest possible honor, and for this she must be his obedient slave. In order that she may be contented with her lot as a polygamous wife, she is taught from childhood to look upon conjugal love as a weak and foolish sentiment, and upon marriage as the only way to secure a future life.

The Mormons have been largely recruited in numbers by immigrants who have been brought into Utah through the efforts of missionaries sent by the church to other parts of America and to Europe. About six thousand missionaries are thus employed. They leave their homes in Utah and go to any part of the world to which they may be assigned by the authorities of the church, paying their own expenses, or collecting the money for their sustenance from their converts. These missionaries usually travel in pairs, and preach, for the most part, in ignorant communities. It is estimated that about 100,000 immigrants have gone to Utah under their leadership. The organization of the missionary force is very complete and effective. The immigrants, though for the most part ignorant, are always able-bodied, and are usually industrious, frugal, and obedient to discipline. The average yearly immigration is about 2,000 persons.

Mormonism has lately spread into the State of Nevada, and into Montana, Idaho, Wyoming and Arizona.

The sect was founded by Joseph Smith at Manchester, New York, in 1830. Smith was born December 23, 1805, at Sharon, Vermont. When only fifteen years old he began to have alleged visions, in one of which, he asserts, the angel Moroni appeared to him three times and told him that the Bible of the Western Continent—a supplement to the New Testament—was buried in a certain spot near Manchester. Four years after this event he visited the spot indicated by the angel, and asserts that he had delivered into his charge by another angel a stone box, in which was a volume, six inches thick, made of thin gold plates, eight inches long by seven broad, and fastened together by three gold rings. The plates were said to be covered with small writing in the Egyptian character, and were accompanied by a pair of supernatural spectacles, consisting of two crystals set in a silver bow and called "Urim and Thummim." By aid of these the mystic characters could be read. Joseph Smith, being himself unable to read or write fluently, employed an amanuensis to whom he dictated a translation, which was afterward, in 1830, printed and published under the title of the "Book of Mormon." The book professes to give the history of America from its first settlement by a colony of refugees from the crowd dispersed by the confusion of tongues at the Tower of Babel. These settlers having in the course of time destroyed one another, nothing of importance occurred until 600 B. C., when Lehi, his wife and four sons, with ten friends, all from Jerusalem, landed on the coast of Chili, and from that period, according to the Mormon theory, America became gradually peopled.

OGDEN.

Having heard much of the city of Ogden in Northern Utah—of its peculiar origin and rapid progress—I resolved to rest there for a day or two before proceeding to Corinne and other points in my route toward the Sierras.

AN INDIAN ENCAMPMENT, WYOMING.

The pretty city of Ogden has had one of the wildest and most thrilling of birthplaces.

To-day it reminds the stranger of one of the peaceful little cities of old Massachusetts, nestled among the Berkshire Hills, wide of street, stately of architecture, redolent of comfort and refinement.

But in reality Ogden is the child of Utah. Mines of precious metals are its neighbors. It has been the scene of daring explorations, of Indian raids, and of many murders and massacres. Its original inhabitants were fanatics, so enthused with, so overwhelmed by their tenets, as to believe themselves of all the world the favorites of the Almighty; the only original handful of His saints, the small remnant of the human family to which constant revelations from Heaven were vouchsafed.

Upheld by this fanaticism, drawn with it as by a magnet from all over the United States, from Canada, from the countries of Europe, proselytes came to join the Mormons. They journeyed by mule trains over the Plains, or they walked perhaps, pushing their all in hand-carts before them. They encountered persecution, suffering, and even death, undaunted. Some of them, on their perilous journey to the Promised Land, subsisted on roots. Some boiled the skins of their buffalo robes and ate them. Some pushed their little carts on the last day of their lives and then laid down to freeze before the land of their desire was in sight. Graves or skeletons frequently marked their route of march, but still they came, and having come they prospered.

Their farms throve; their boundaries increased; their settlements became many.

With foolhardiness, but also with desperation, with dauntless effrontery, with infinite pluck, they defied the United States and her army, using the tiny handful of Mormon soldiery in a way that makes one's mind run back to the story of Thermopylæ.

Such was the blood that settled Ogden.

It was such inhabitants that Brigham Young, in 1850, advised to "put up good dwellings, open good schools, erect a meeting-house, cultivate gardens, and pay especial care to fruit raising," so that Ogden might become a permanent settlement and the headquarters for the Mormons in the northern portion of the Territory.

So well was his advice carried out that in 1851 the city was "made a stake of Zion," divided into wards, and incorporated by act of legislature.

From the very first, everything connected with the city seemed to have a spice and dash about it.

Away back in 1540, Father Juan de Padilla and his patron, Pedro de Tobar, went on an exploring expedition. On his return the priest spoke of a large and interesting river he had found in that "Great Unknown," the Northwest.

The account so fired the hearts of his brother Spaniards that Captain Garcia Lopaz de Cardenas was sent to explore further into that wonderland. He returned telling of immense gulches, of rocky battlements, and of mountains surrounding a great body of water. Many believe that in that far distant time, about the time that Elizabeth ascended the throne of England, before Raleigh had done himself the honor of his discoveries and settlements in Virginia, Signor Cardenas was simply taking a little vacation trip through Utah.

But however fabulous that may be, we know of a surety that on July 29, 1776, two Franciscan friars set out from Santa Fé to find a direct route to the Pacific Ocean. In their wanderings they strayed far to the north, where they came across many representatives of the Utes, who proved to be a loving, faithful, hospitable people. From their lips the Spaniards heard the first description ever listened to by white men of the region of country containing the present site of Ogden. "The lake," the Utes said, "occupies many leagues. Its waters are injurious and extremely salt. He that wets any part of his body in this water immediately feels an itching in the wet parts. In the circuit of this lake live a numerous and quiet nation called Puaguampe. They feed on herbs, and drink from various fountains or springs of good water which are about the lake, and they have their little houses of grass and earth, which latter forms the roof."

So the Great Salt Lake makes its entrance into comparatively modern American history.

In 1825, Peter Skeen Ogden, accompanied by his party of Hudson Bay Company trappers, pursued his brilliant adventures, and left behind a record which induced the naming of the city after him.

In 1841, the country around the spot where the city now lies was held, on a Spanish grant, by Miles M. Goodyear, who built a fort and a few log-houses near the confluence of the Weber and Ogden rivers.

On June 6, 1848, a man named James Brown came from California with his pockets stuffed with gold dust; nearly five thousand dollars' worth of the precious thing had he. With part of it he bought this tract of land from Goodyear. It proved to be a most fertile spot. Brethren came to it from Salt Lake City. Gentiles came from everywhere. The settlement grew and prospered.

In 1849, people began to talk of locating a city right there at the junction of the two rivers.

In 1850, Brigham Young, Heber C. Kimball, and others, laid out the settlement and called it Ogden, after Peter Skeen Ogden, the explorer, long since dead, but whose dashing, daring, brilliant adventures were still charming to the men of that wild land. Every time the city's name is mentioned it is another proof that although,

"The man might die, his memory lives."

Before a year was over a school house was built in the city.

Then came that un-American sight, a wall of protection built around a city. It cost $40,000, which amount was raised by taxation.

About this time several suburban settlements were formed, but bears, wolves, and Indians soon drove the venturesome suburbanites within city limits.

Just then a party of immigrants encamping on the Malade River shot two Indian women. By way of reprisal the savages killed a pioneer named Campbell who was building a sawmill near Ogden, and threatened to massacre the entire population of the town. Matters began to look serious, and the commander of the Nauvoo Legion gave the Indians chase, and so overwhelmed them that they at once retreated, taking with them no captives more important than many horses and cattle belonging to the white settlers.

October 23, 1851, the first municipal election was held in Ogden.

1852 found one hundred families living within city boundaries.

In 1854, a memorial was addressed to Congress, by the territorial legislature, urging the construction of an overland railroad. But it was May, 1868, before a contract was made between Brigham Young and the superintendent of construction of the Union Pacific Railroad for grading between Echo Canyon and the terminus of the line. At Weber Canyon there was blasting, tunnelling, and heavy stone work for bridges to be done. This work earned 1,000,000 or perhaps 1,250,000 dollars' worth of wages. The labor was splendidly done, but the remuneration came slowly. Finally, however, the Union Pacific Railroad turned over 600,000 dollars' worth of rolling stock, and other property to the Mormons. On May 17, 1869, ground was broken for a railroad between Salt Lake City and Ogden. So the city grew and flourished.

Ogden has an elevation of 4,340 feet. The ground plan of the city is spacious, the drainage good, the climate exceedingly healthy.

About the time I rode through, the population numbered 6,000 souls. The city contained one of the finest schools in Utah, a hotel which ranked among the best in the Union, a daily paper, a theatre, three banks, numerous Gentile churches, a 16,000 dollar bridge across the Weber, a reservoir, and a Court House, which was such an architectural beauty that all Utah may well be proud of it.

So Ogden came through narrow ways to broad ways! So she

> " Climbed the ladder, round by round ! "

She has won the respect and admiration of all who have watched her. May her industry never fail, her enthusiasm never lessen, her pluck remain indomitable, and may good fortune perch forever on her banners !

SHEEP RANCHE IN WYOMING.

CHAPTER XXVIII.

OVER THE SIERRAS.

SIERRA is the Spanish word for 'saw' and also for 'mountain,' referring to the notched outline of the mountains as seen against the sky."

My main object now was to push on to Sacramento. At Kelton, in Utah, where I remained only a few hours, I was still seven hundred and ninety miles from my destination. Stock is extensively grazed here and cattle shipped to the Pacific coast in very large numbers. Leaving Kelton, I rode thirty-three miles to Terrace, a small settlement in the midst of a desert; thence to Wells in the adjoining State of Nevada.

Nevada belongs to the "Great Basin," a table-land elevated 4,500 feet above the sea. It is traversed, with great uniformity, by parallel mountain ranges, rising from 1,000 to 8,000 feet high, running north and south. Long, narrow valleys, or canyons, lie between them. The Sierra Nevada, in some places 13,000 feet in height, extends along the western boundary of the State. The only navigable river is the Colorado, but there are several other streams rising in the mountains and emptying into lakes which have no visible outlet. Lake Tahoe is twenty-one miles long, ten miles wide and fifteen hundred feet deep. Although it is elevated 6,000 feet above the sea level, the water of this lake never freezes and has a mean temperature of 57° for the year. Nevada has its hot springs, some of which have a temperature of two hundred degrees.

A heavy growth of timber, particularly of pine, fir, and spruce, covers the eastern slopes of the Sierra Nevada, many of the trees attaining enormous size. There are numerous alkaline flats, and extensive sand plains, where nothing grows. The first discovery of silver ore was made on the Comstock lode in 1859, from which more than $100,000,000 have been taken. This has been the most valuable silver-bearing lode ever discovered in the world, exceeding in wealth the mines of Peru and Mexico. It is now exhausted and yields only low-grade ores.

Wells, my first resting-point in the Sierras, stands at an elevation of over 5,600 feet, and had a population of less than 300. Farming and stock raising are its principal industries. Formerly it was a watering and resting-place for old emigrant travel, where pure water was obtained—a luxury after crossing the Great Desert; and an abundance of grass for the weary animals. Some of the wells here are 1,700 feet deep.

Stopped next for the night at Halleck, a small village—over 5,000 feet elevation—thirteen miles from Camp Halleck, where United States troops are occasionally stationed. Leaving Halleck after a night's rest and a hearty breakfast of ham and eggs, I rode twenty-four miles to Elko, six hundred and nineteen miles

MINING CAMP IN NEVADA.

from San Francisco. This important town stands at an elevation of 5,063 feet above sea-level and is on the Humboldt River. The State University is situated here. Silver smelting works and manufactures of farming implements were the principal industries. One daily and two weekly papers were well supported. There were also three large freight depots for the accommodation of the railway business. I noticed several Indians about the town. The hot mineral springs of Elko are considered of great value for bathing. Population at the time of my visit, about 1,700, but the town is destined to develop into an important city. The money paid for freights consigned to this place, averaged $1,000,000 a year.

Leaving Elko, I pushed on for thirty miles. The pastures and meadows, with isolated cottages, were soon passed and I reached Palisade in the evening, a village of 250 inhabitants. Remained here for the night. For the last two hundred miles the road had been a gradual descent and the change of temperature was very perceptible. Palisade is a growing little place with a population of about 400 souls. It is located about half-way down a canyon, whose rocky, perpendicular walls give it a singular but picturesque appearance.

My mustang carried me forty-one miles next day, to Argentina, where I rested. This village is located in the midst of alkali flats and seemed to me an unattractive place for a residence. Continuing my journey along the foot of Reese River Mountain, I soon found myself at Battle Mountain, at the junction of Reese River and Humboldt valleys. The town of Battle Mountain has several stores, a public hall, a good school house and an excellent hotel; with increasing trade. The mountain from which the town derives its name is about three miles south of the latter and is said to have been the scene of a conflict between a party of emigrants and a band of Indians.

Golconda was reached on the evening of the following day—four hundred and seventy-eight miles from San Francisco. Here are gold and silver mines, but the place was small and calls for no further remark. Remounted at sunrise the following morning and rode to Winnemucca, the county-seat of Humboldt County. The town has a fine brick Court House, together with several stores, a hotel, shops and a school house.

Reached Humboldt the following day, where I was reminded that I was still in the land of civilization. Stopped at the Humboldt House, a most comfortable hostelry, its surroundings recalling my home in the East. Humboldt is the business centre of several mining districts and has a bright prospect before it.

Lovelocks, the next point reached, is also on the Central Pacific Railroad. It is a grazing region, and large herds of cattle are fattened upon the rich native grasses. Leaving Lovelocks, I found myself again on a barren desert, covered in places with salt and alkali deposits. Another station in the midst of this desert is Hot Springs. Pushing forward I reached Desert, three hundred and thirty-five miles from San Francisco. The village is rightly named, for it is, in truth, a dreary place. I was much relieved on reaching Wadsworth, a town of about 700 inhabitants, and only three hundred and twenty-eight miles from the end of my journey. Some large stores here do a flourishing business. There are also several good hotels, in one of

which I was soon comfortably housed. For several
days I had seen nothing but dreary, monotonous plains,
and now, almost another world opened to my view—a
world of beauty and sublimity. It was with reluc-
tance I left Wadsworth and crossed the Truckee River.
The trees, green meadows, comfortable farmhouses, and
well-tilled fields, were pleasant to look upon, and with
the prospect of soon reaching my final destination, I
rode on, and crossed the boundary into California.

Truckee, although within the State of California, is
in the Sierra Nevada, one hundred and twenty-one
miles from Sacramento. The village is handsomely
built, the surroundings picturesque and finely timbered,
and there is a line of stages running to the beautiful
Lakes Tahoe and Donner.

CHAPTER XXIX.

ALONG THE SACRAMENTO.

FROM Truckee I rode along the line of the Central Pacific Railroad, stopping for the night at villages intermediate between Truckee and Sacramento, the principal of which were Summit, Colfax and Auburn. Summit is the highest point of the pass through which the railroad crosses the Sierra Nevada, its height above sea-level being 7,042 feet. The population was only a little over one hundred. Colfax, fifty-four miles from Sacramento, had a population of nearly six hundred, mostly employed in the gold mines in the vicinity. Auburn, thirty-six miles from Sacramento, is also a gold-mining village. Its population was given me as over 1,200. Two weekly papers are published here, and three hotels offer good accommodations to tourists and others. Sacramento was reached November twenty-first, and here I found myself within a hundred miles of my destination.

California has the Pacific Ocean for its western boundary. Along the seaboard lies the Coast Range of mountains, while for an eastern boundary of the State stretch the Sierras. Between these two chains lies many a hill, yet, in the main, the whole interior of the

A ROCKY MOUNTAIN RIVER.

State is a great depression, called the **Valley of Cali-fornia**. The northern portion is called again the Sacramento Valley; the southern, the Valley of San Joaquin, both named for the streams that water them.

The inhabitants are a motley set; English, Celts, Spaniards, Mexicans, Indians, and above all the man from the eastern part of the United States, leaving his impress on all, Americanizing all.

Sutter's Fort, as already explained, was founded in 1839, very near the junction of the Sacramento and San Joaquin valleys, by a Swiss named John A. Sutter. It stood on a small hill, skirted by a creek which falls into the American River near its junction with the Sacramento, and overlooked a vast extent of ditch-enclosed fields, and park stock ranges, broken by groves and belts of timber. The settlement consisted of the Fort and an old adobe house, called the hospital. A garden of eight or ten acres, filled with vegetables and tropical fruits, surrounded the Fort, cattle covered the plains and boats were tied to the wharves.

Sutter's confirmed grant contained eleven leagues.

The Fort, so called, was a parallelogram. Its walls were of adobe, its dimensions five hundred by one hundred and fifty feet. It had loop-holes, bastions at the angles, and twelve cannon.

Inside of the walls were granaries, warehouses, storehouses, shops, and in the centre of it all the house of the commander, the potentate, Sutter. His house was rough, " Bare rafters and unpanelled walls." Many of the rooms were roughly furnished, crude benches and deal tables. Fine China bowls did duty for both cups and plates, and silver spoons were the only luxury which marked the service of the meals.

For his private apartments Sutter obtained from the Russians a clumsy set of California laurel furniture.

In front of his house, yet within the stockade, was a tiny square containing one brass gun, by which, day and night, paced a sentry, stopping only at the belfry post to chime the hours.

The Fort was a business centre. In it was located a blacksmith, a carpenter, and a general variety and liquor store. Prices were booming. Four dollars were charged for shoeing a horse. Wheat sold for one dollar per bushel, peas for a dollar and a half per bushel.

A sort of gravel road led to the spot, over which horses galloped, and heavy wagons rolled.

Sutter owned twelve thousand cattle, two thousand horses and mules, from one thousand to fifteen hundred sheep, and two thousand hogs.

This unique Fort was "the capital of the vast interior valley, pregnant with approaching importance."

In 1846, Sutter staked out the town of Sutterville, three miles below the Fort on the Sacramento, and built the first house there. His example was shortly followed by a man named Zims, who erected the first real brick structure in the State.

The Fort and town kept up regular communication with San Francisco by means of a twenty-ton sloop owned by Sutter, and manned by a few savages in his employ.

There was a ferry at the Fort, which consisted of a single canoe handled by an Indian.

The strangest of populations gathered about the settlement. Emigrants were there, many Mormons among them. Native Californians were there, wear·

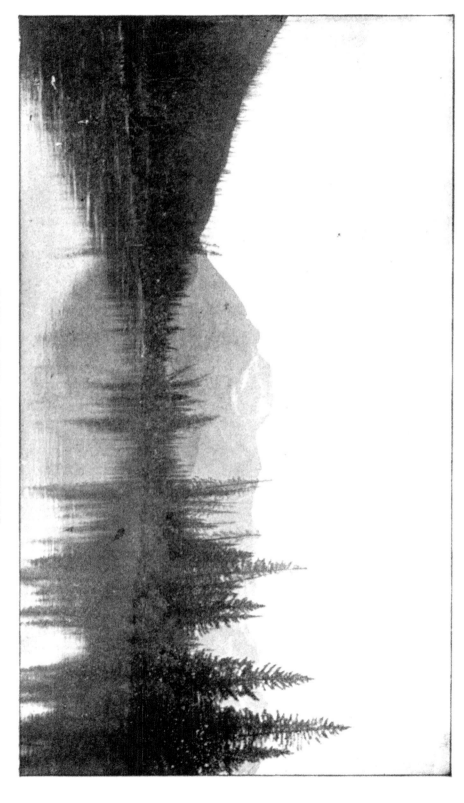

A LAKE IN THE SIERRA NEVADAS.

ing sombreros, sashes, and jingling spurs. Half-subdued Indians abounded, wrapped in their blankets, and decked with beads and feathers. While here and there appeared a shrewd Yankee, come across mountains of snow and rocks to seek his fortune.

The climate of Sacramento is charming, the average temperature in winter being 45°; that in summer 69°. The thermometer does not vary ten degrees between night and day. The sea breezes are constant, leaving rarely an uncooled night. Rainfall is a tenth less than on the Atlantic Coast. Early autumn finds this region dry and arid; its small streams dried up, the green fields sere, the weeds snapping like glass.

The winter rain begins in November, after six months of clear weather, and under its grateful ministry the region "buds and blossoms like the rose."

John A. Sutter, potentate of the region, in 1847, needed lumber, and therefore needed a saw-mill. His neighbors wanted lumber, too, and there would be a good market for it in San Francisco. Therefore a saw-mill would be profitable; but no trees suitable for this purpose could be found short of the foot-hills. Consequently the foot-hills were selected as the spot upon which he would build.

He engaged a motley company of all nationalities to erect his mill, appointing James Wilson Marshall, a native of New Jersey, as superintendent of the venture.

In August they started for their new field of enterprise, taking their belongings in Mexican ox-carts, and driving a flock of sheep before them for food.

By New Year's day, 1848, the mill frame was up.

On the afternoon of January twenty-fourth, Superintendent Marshall was inspecting the tail-race of the

mill. There had been a heavy flood, which had previously retreated, and to his surprise Marshall found
the ground thickly strewn with a peculiar yellow dust.
He stooped down and gathered some of it, remarking
quietly, "Boys, I believe I have found a gold mine!"
Then he began some simple tests upon the metal.
Gold must be heavy. He weighed it. That was all
right. Gold must be malleable. He bit and pounded
it, and it stood the test. Then he applied *aqua fortis*
to it, and it responded as it should. And so the truth
was known at last. It was gold, and the ground was
full of it.

Marshall saddled his horse, and dashed over to consult with Sutter, and together they agreed to keep the
matter quiet, and if possible to buy up the surrounding
land. But how to buy it. That was the question!
They leased it from its semi-barbaric owners, paying
for it in hats and trinkets, but that title seemed in-
secure. The Mexican government could no longer
give grants. The United States government was appealed to in vain. The answer came that California
was held as a conquered province, and no title deed
could be executed.

And meantime the precious secret leaked out. Sutter was impelled to write the wonderful news to friends
at a distance. All the men at the saw-mill knew of
the discovery. One of them, named Bennett, while in
a store near Monte del Diablo, pulled out of his pocket
a bag of gold dust, exclaiming, "I have something
here which will make this the greatest country in the
world." The same man took a specimen of the precious
metal and showed it at San Francisco. A few days
later an intoxicated Swede offered, at a store, to pay

for his drink in gold dust. Then a Mormon must tell his fellow-saints of the discovery. So the secret was out, and the precious mystery became public.

Both Sutter and Marshall were backwoodsmen, unsophisticated, child-like, trustful, slow. They hesitated, they faltered, they delayed mining, and they were lost! Before they fully comprehended the matter, the great world had rushed in, and taken possession of the treasure.

In the last issue of *The Californian* appears this only too true statement: "The whole country from San Francisco to Los Angeles, and from the seashore to the base of the Sierra Nevada, resounds to the sordid cry of gold! GOLD!! GOLD!!! while the field is left half planted, the house half built, and everything neglected but the manufacture of shovels and pick-axes, and the means of transportation to the spot where one man obtained one hundred and twenty-eight dollars' worth of the real stuff in one day's washing, and the average for all concerned is twenty dollars per diem."

In the rush Marshall and Sutter were crushed.

Marshall had little or no money to invest. He was particularly unfortunate in locating his small claims. Worst of all, the miners, knowing him to be the great discoverer, followed him *en masse*, believing that he knew the secrets of the hills and rivers. The crowds so overwhelmed him, that he had no chance to mine. They even threatened to hang him if he did not lead them to the finest diggings. In a few years after, he died, miserable, broken-hearted, poverty-stricken.

Sutter fared but little better. True, he sold a half-interest in his saw-mill for six thousand dollars, and he gained something from the mining of his Indians, but Sutter's Fort was, for the time being, ruined. Let him tell the story in his own words. He says:

"My grist mill was never finished. Everything was stolen, even the stones. There is a saying that men will steal everything but a mile-stone and a mill-stone. They stole my mill-stones. They stole the bells from the Fort, and gate-weights; the hides they stole, and salmon barrels. I had two hundred barrels which I made for salmon. Some of the cannon at the fort were stolen. * * My property was all left exposed, and at the mercy of the rabble, when gold was discovered. My men all deserted me. I could not shut the gates of my Fort, and keep out the rabble. They would have broken them down. The country swarmed with lawless men. Emigrants drove their stock into my yard, and used my grain with impunity. Expostulation did no good. I was alone. There was no law."

In face of all these disadvantages he struggled on until farm helpers demanded ten dollars per day, then, a hopeless old man, he gave up the struggle, and in 1849, with his Indians, he moved into Hock Farm, little dreaming that his Fort was to be the nucleus for Sacramento, the second city as to size in California.

He retired, but his son took the reins out of the father's feeble hands, and staked out a town around the Old Fort, down to the embarcadero, and along the river front, naming the settlement Sacramento. The streets were laid out eighty feet wide, except the centre one, M street, which was one hundred feet in width. The purchasing of more than four lots by one person was discouraged.

At first Sacramento was a "city of tents, with its

A CASCADE BY THE ROADSIDE.

future on paper;" but by April of that year, 1849, building lots were selling at from one thousand to three thousand dollars a piece; at that time there were twenty-five or thirty stores upon the embarcadero, and, in the vicinity of the Fort, eight or ten more. There was a hotel, a printing office, bakery, blacksmith's shop, tin-shop, billiard room, and bowling alley.

In that month of April, the city had the honor of becoming a port of entry.

By June of the same year, one hundred houses graced the city.

A few months later the city hotel was completed at a cost of one hundred thousand dollars, and rented to Messrs. Fowler and Fry for five thousand dollars per month.

In 1850, the scourge of cholera broke out, carrying off one-fifth of those remaining in Sacramento. The city was full to overflowing with a transient population. Accommodations were scant and primitive, vice and disorder prevailed. The disease became rampant. Patients at the hospital were charged sixteen dollars per day. Then it was that the order of Odd Fellows came nobly forward, setting to that plague-stricken district an example of charity and philanthropy long to be remembered, and accenting the fact "that simple duty has no place for fear!"

On February 25, 1854, Sacramento was designated as the seat of government of California. The dignity of being the State capital gave new life to the city. Her growth is instanced by the assessment on real estate, which rose from $5,400,000 in 1854, to $13,000,000 in twenty years.

When I rode through, the population was 21,400.

In 1853 the streets were planked, and provided

with sewers. In 1854 a gas company was formed. The street railroad came in 1870. There were ten churches in the city as I found it.

The first public school came in 1855, the high school in 1856.

When I was there the city had sustained from time to time about forty daily papers and twenty-four weeklies.

The State Library is a brilliant feature of the place. Various large manufacturing interests thrive in the city. Its commerce is awe-inspiring.

Sacramento sent to the east in one year 90,000,000 pounds of fruit, her entire east-bound shipments being over 130,000,000 pounds.

The annual manufacturing and jobbing trade is over $60,000,000.

Looking at these statistics, one is reminded of the magic tent of Prince Ahmed. At first it was no bigger than a nut-shell. Surely it could hold nothing; but it did. People flocked to it. Surely it could not cover them;—but it did! it did!! The army flocked to it;—but the tent was elastic. It covered all; it sheltered all; it welcomed all.

Has not Sacramento proved itself the magic tent of the Golden Age, ready to cover, shelter, welcome the whole world should occasion require?

From Sacramento to San Francisco my route lay along the eastern shore of the river, and few halts were made between the two cities. I was anxious to reach my final destination, as a feeling of fatigue was now overcoming me, which, however, only served to stimulate and urge me forward. I passed several places that strongly tempted a halt for refreshment and rest, and finally entered the Western Metropolis on the twenty-fourth of November, registering at the Palace Hotel.

CHAPTER XXX.

SAN FRANCISCO AND END OF JOURNEY.

AN FRANCISCO, the chief city on the Western Coast of North America, is in every respect a wonderful city, not least so in its origin and development. Not very long ago—less than a century—the Pacific Coast was almost an unexplored region. The great State of California—next to Texas, the largest in the Union—now teems with populous cities and new settlements, and produces meat and grain abundantly sufficient for the supply of a large portion of the country. It has a coast line on the Pacific Ocean of seven hundred miles and, extending from the coast, a breadth of three hundred and thirty miles. California has also the most wonderful gold fields of the world. They were discovered in the middle of the last century by the Jesuits, who kept the knowledge a secret.

In 1848, as previously stated, Captain Sutter found gold on the land of one of his farms, and the news of the discovery at once spread. The excitement extended throughout the Union and the " Argonauts of '49 " came swarming to the gold fields. People ran about picking up the precious lumps as " hogs in a forest root for ground-nuts." The golden product of 1848, was $10,000,000; 1849, $40,000,000; and that of 1853, $65,000,000.

Silver mining has been attempted in many localities in the State, but generally with poor results. There are valuable deposits of iron ore, coal, copper, tin, platinum, manganese, asphalt, petroleum, lead and zinc. Fruits are abundant, of great size, and are sold in all the Eastern markets.

The constitution of California requires a free school to be supported in each district six months in each year, and the system includes primary and grammar schools, high schools, evening schools, normal schools, technical schools, and the State University, which is free to both sexes, and is a perpetual public trust. The schools of California are justly famous.

Upper California was discovered in 1538 by a Spanish navigator. In 1578, Sir Francis Drake visited it and gave it the name of New Albion. The Spaniards planted the first colony in 1768. The territory was purchased from Mexico by the United States in 1847 for $15,000,000. A constitution was adopted in the same year, and in 1850, California, without ever having been under a territorial government, was admitted into the Union as a State.

The progress of California has been of the most substantial character. Gold mining has become a staple industry, but in the agricultural capabilities of her soil lie the possibilities of her greatest wealth. Among the most valuable of her industries in the future will be those of the orchard and the vineyard. The grape growers of the State can now sell their grapes with as much certainty as the farmer his wheat.

There is sent to the Atlantic coast more wine than is imported from France, the heretofore wine market of the world.

In Central California a little peninsula juts out from the main land, a great harbor is on one side, a great ocean on the other. The lofty mountains, lower just here, form, as it were, a natural gateway to the great interior beyond.

Here, in 1836, an American named John P. Lease settled, and here, in time, a little town called San Francisco grew up around him. Two miles to the south loomed up the antiquated building of the Catholic Mission Dolores, with its pretty old gardens. The opposite shores of the bay presented a most beautiful park-like expanse: the native lawn, brilliant with flowers and dotted by eastward bending oaks, watered by the creeks of the Alameda, San Lorenzo, San Leando, and their tributaries, and enclosed by the spurs of the Diablo Mountains.

San Francisco was on the soil of Mexico, under the flag of Anàhuac, governed by an Alcalde and a sapient council, yet the spirit of the United States breathed in it, built its stout wooden houses, and thronged its busy wharves. Animated by this spirit, it was destined to become the metropolis of the Pacific, one of the noted cities of the globe.

Before the " Golden Age," while California was a peaceful settlement, of no especial importance, it was said that around San Francisco Bay there was raw material enough, of different types, to develop a new race.

San Francisco was not in the gold region, but it was the gate to that region.

Two weeks after Marshall first discovered the precious metal, a bag of it was brought to the city for analysis, and one day early in May, 1848, "Samuel Brennan, the Mormon leader, held a bottle of gold dust in one hand, and jubilantly swinging his hat in the other, passed through the streets of San Francisco shouting, 'Gold! Gold!! Gold!!! from the American River!'"

This started the enthusiasm, the fever, the madness for gold.

Carson writes his sensations when first looking upon a well-filled bag of gold dust. He says:

"A frenzy seized my soul, unbidden my legs performed some entirely new movements of polka steps. * * Houses were too small for me to stay in. I was soon in the street in search of necessary outfits; piles of gold rose up before me at every step."

All yielded more or less to the subtle influence of the malady. Men hastened to arrange their affairs, dissolving partnerships, disposing of real estate, and converting other effects into ready means for departure.

Stores were rummaged for miners' tools.

One man offered as high as fifty dollars for a shovel. By the middle of June, San Francisco was without male population. The once bustling little town looked as if struck by a plague. Sessions of the town council were at an end. There were no church services. Stores were closed. Newspapers dropped out of existence. Merchandise lay unhandled on the docks. The sailors deserted the ships that lay at anchor in the bay.

One day a Peruvian bark came to anchor in the port. Amazed at the desolation which he beheld, the captain inquired the cause. He was answered, "Everybody has gone northward, where the valleys and mountains are of gold." Instantly upon hearing this marvellous assertion his own crew joined the innumerable throng.

The San Francisco *Star* of May 27, 1848, says:

"Stores are closed and places of business vacated, a large number of houses are tenantless, various kinds of mechanical labor suspended or given up entirely, and nowhere the pleasant hum of industry salutes the ear as of late. * * Everything in San Francisco wears a desolate and sombre look; everywhere all is dull, monotonous, dead."

Apparently the Californian of that day was thoroughly imbued with the saying of the Cyclops, "The wise know nothing worth worshipping but wealth."

The Pacific Mail Steamship Company was incorporated in 1847, to sail from New York to New Orleans and Chagres, and from Panama to such Pacific port as the Secretary of the Navy might designate. Later, when the existence of gold in her mines made California the cynosure of all eyes, San Francisco was decided upon as the western terminus of the route.

On October 6, 1848, the "California," the first vessel of this line, steamed out of New York harbor, with but a small number of passengers. As this ship was intended for use on the Pacific coast alone, she was obliged to take the tedious and perilous route through the Strait of Magellan to reach her destination. Arriving at Panama, she found the Isthmus apparently turned into pandemonium. The one time dingy, sleepy city of Panama appeared to have fallen entirely into the hands of the gold-seekers. Cholera had broken out with terrible malignity on the banks of the Chagres. The panic-stricken travellers were fleeing from the disease, some trying to reach the land of their desire by an old trail, others were trying to make some progress in boats called "longos," poled by naked negroes. The mass of the worn, weary, eager wayfarers, however, were waiting as best they might, for that vision of hope and comfort, the "steamer." At last she reached them, with accommodations for about one hundred. She was mobbed by the frantic men, and at last when she left port, over four hundred of them had embarked upon her, many a man braving that adventurous voyage, with only a coil of rope or a plank for a bed.

Steerage tickets for the trip are said to have cost one thousand dollars, or over.

After spending four months in her passage, the "California" steamed into the Bay of San Francisco, February 29, 1849, a day never to be forgotten at the Golden Gate! The town was crowded with miners wintering there; the ships in the harbor were gay with bunting; the guns of the Pacific Squadron boomed out a salute to the new-comers. Bands of music played, handkerchiefs waved, and men cheered in their enthusiasm, as the first steamship of a regular line entered the Golden Gate, in pursuit of the treasures of the "Golden Age."

That ship bore to California the new military commander, General Persifor F. Smith.

So high ran the fever for treasure, that before the passengers had fairly left the steamer, she was deserted by all belonging to her, save one engineer, and she was consequently unable to start on her return trip.

VIEW IN WOODWARD'S GARDENS, SAN FRANCISCO.

Nor was it alone the "California" which was deserted. Five hundred ships lay in the San Francisco
Harbor deserted, the crews, wild for gold, carrying off
the ship's boats in their eagerness to reach land; very
often the commander leading, or at least joining in the
flight. Many vessels that year were left to rot; many
were dragged on shore and used as lodging houses.

In the spring, San Francisco seemed deserted, only
two thousand inhabitants being left. The heart of the
city began to quail. Thousands thronging through
her harbor, yet so few to stay! But winter brought
the miners back to civilization again, and the population swelled to twenty thousand.

San Francisco was at this time mainly a city of
tents, although there was a sprinkling of adobe houses,
and a few frame buildings. It was a community of
men. The census of 1850 showed that only eight per
cent. of the population were women. It was, moreover, a community of young men; scarcely a grey
head was to be seen in it.

Men were there from all the European nations,
together with Moors and Abyssinians from Africa,
Mongols, Malays, and Hindoos from Asia and Australia. Turks, Hebrews, and Hispano-Americans
jostled the ubiquitous Yankee, in the new streets of
San Francisco.

The predominant dress, we are told, was "checked
and woollen shirts, mainly red and blue, open at the
bosom which could boast of shaggy robustness, or
loosely secured by a kerchief; pantaloons tucked into
high and wrinkled boots, and belted at the waist,
where bristled an arsenal of knife and pistols. Beard
and hair emancipated from thraldom, revelled in long

and bushy tufts, which rather harmonized with the slouched and dingy hat. * * The gamblers affected the Mexican style of dress, white shirt with diamond studs, chain of native golden specimens, broad-brimmed hat, with sometimes a feather or squirrel's tail tucked under the brim, top-boots, and a rich scarlet sash or silk handkerchief thrown over the shoulder, or wound around the waist."

They were a buoyant race, brave, intrepid, light-hearted—above all things free from restraint.

They had braved all hardships and dangers to reach the land of their desire. They had reached there safely, however, and they exulted. They overflowed with activity; they worked jubilantly and untiringly.

They shouted, they fought, they gambled, in their moments of recreation, intoxicated with the bracing climate, with their excitement of success, and with that rollicking freedom which threw off all shackles of custom or self-restraint.

They worshipped success, and greatness with them meant "fitness to grasp opportunity!"

In their eyes the unpardonable sin was meanness.

Fifty cents was the smallest sum which could be offered for the most trivial of services.

Laborers obtained a dollar an hour, artisans twenty dollars per day. Laundry expenses exceeded the price of new underwear.

They loved grandeur. Bootblacks carried on business in prettily fitted up recesses furnished with cushioned chairs, and containing a liberal supply of newspapers.

It was over such a San Francisco that the frightful plague of cholera swept in 1850, carrying with it a lesser plague of suicide.

THE PACIFIC OCEAN—END OF JOURNEY.

Doctors' fees were from sixteen to thirty-two dollars per visit, while for a surgical operation one thousand dollars was the usual price.

In spite of plague and death, that part of San Francisco which escaped continued to be jubilant.

Bull fights were in high favor, and the stage, though crude, was very popular, but the great, enchanting delight of the city was gambling. Money, gold, jewelry, houses, land and wharves were all put up to be gambled for. The city abounded with men of elegant manners and striking dress, who were professional gamblers. It was indeed an advance in civilization and morality when in September, 1850, a law was passed forbidding this pastime on the Sabbath day.

The news that California had been admitted as a State in the Union reached San Francisco on the morning of October 18, 1850, when the "Oregon" entered the harbor, flying all her bunting, and signalling the good news. Business was suspended; courts were adjourned; and the whole population, frenzied with delight, congregated on Portsmouth Square to congratulate each other. Newspapers containing the intelligence from Washington sold for five dollars each! The shipping in the harbor was gaily dressed with flags; guns boomed from the heights; bonfires blazed at night; processions were formed; bands played; and the people in every way expressed their joy. Mounting his box behind six fiery mustangs lashed to highest speed, the driver of Crandall's Stage cried the good news all the way to San José—"California is admitted!!" while a ringing cheer was returned by the people as the mail flew by.

The awaking of San Francisco during the five or

six years following the discovery of gold was wonderful. "Hills were tumbled into the bay, and mud flats were made solid ground." Streets were graded, handsome buildings were erected, and San Francisco began to rank among the first cities of the land. So valuable was her water-front that, in 1853, four small blocks on Commercial street sold for over 1,000,000 dollars. The assessed valuation of property that year was about 10,000,000 dollars over that of the previous year.

The population was then estimated at about 50,000 ; that being about one-seventh of the then population of the State.

The city had, at this time, 1856, seventeen fire companies, twelve military companies, and a number of social clubs, four hospitals, seventeen public schools, thirty-two church organizations, thirteen daily newspapers, and as many weeklies published in half a dozen different languages.

From that time she has continued ever increasing, ever justifying her title of the metropolis of the Pacific.

Her City Hall is one of the grandest buildings on the Continent. Its construction cost 6,000,000 dollars. It stands five hundred and fifty feet on Larkin street, seven hundred on McAllister street, and eight hundred and sixty feet on Park avenue.

The Mint at San Francisco is the largest one in the United States. Its architecture is Doric, and it is constructed of freestone and California granite.

San Francisco is supplied with water from several large reservoirs, having a united capacity of seventy billion gallons. Her harbor could accommodate the shipping of the whole world.

Her commerce is immense. The trade of the Western Coast from Chili to Alaska is her natural heritage, and she can justly claim a fair, large share from China, Japan, India, Australia and the islands of the sea.

She has eighty-one public schools, sixty-nine clubs, nine public libraries, one hundred and fourteen churches, and thirty public parks and ornamental plazas.

What words could more aptly describe the career of San Francisco than those lately written by Governor Markham?

"Originally San Francisco consisted of wind-swept hills, the shifting sands of which seemed to defy either stability or cultivation. Now those hills, graded by pick and shovel, are gridironed by streets and railways, and crowned with the magnificent buildings of a populous city, or transformed by the magic of water and patient tillage into miles of verdant park, dotted by miniature lakes, ribboned with gravel drives, crowded with grottoes, statuary, conservatories, and ornamental buildings, enriched by luxuriant shrubbery and brilliant flowers, the wonder of the tourist, and a delight to her contented people."

There are larger and more populous cities in America than San Francisco, but few more deserving the designation of a Great City. The energies of her people, the prodigal wealth of her territory, and her singularly equable and temperate climate, form a sufficient guarantee of the increasing greatness of her future.

———

Finding my quarters at the hotel comfortable and restful after the strain I had endured as the result of two hundred days of rough riding, I deferred terminating my journey until two days later. It will be remembered that I undertook to ride from the Atlantic to the Pacific in the saddle, and hence my tour would not be literally completed before I reached the shores of the Pacific. Accordingly on the twenty-sixth of November I remounted and rode to the Cliff House, a romantic resort built on a rocky prominence overlooking the ocean. From here I descended the Toll Road to the sandy beach. A westerly breeze rolled the breakers up to the feet of my horse, and I forthwith walked him into the waters of the Pacific. My self-imposed task—my journey from OCEAN TO OCEAN ON HORSEBACK—was accomplished.

Other books from CGR Publishing at Amazon.com

1939 New York World's Fair: The World of Tomorrow in Photographs

San Francisco 1915 World's Fair: The Panama-Pacific International Expo.

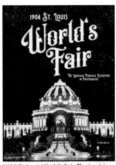

1904 St. Louis World's Fair: The Louisiana Purchase Exposition in Photographs

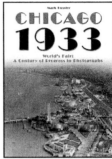

Chicago 1933 World's Fair: A Century of Progress in Photographs

19th Century New York: A Dramatic Collection of Images

The American Railway: The Trains, Railroads, and People Who Ran the Rails

The Story of the Ship

The World's Fair of 1893 Ultra Massive Photographic Adventure Vol. 1

The World's Fair of 1893 Ultra Massive Photographic Adventure Vol. 2

The World's Fair of 1893 Ultra Massive Photographic Adventure Vol. 3

World War 1: A Dramatic Collection of Images

The White City of Color: 1893 World's Fair

Ethel the Cyborg Ninja Book 1

Ethel they Cyborg Ninja 2

How To Draw Digital by Mark Bussler

The Kaiser's Memoirs: Illustrated Enlarged Special Edition

Other books from CGR Publishing at Amazon.com

Ultra Massive Video Game Console
Guide Volume 1

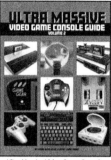

Ultra Massive Video Game Console
Guide Volume 2

Ultra Massive Video Game Console
Guide Volume 3

Ultra Massive Sega Genesis Guide

Discovery of the North Pole: The
Greatest American Expedition

Chicago's White City Cookbook

Official Guide to the World's
Columbian Exposition

How To Grow Mushrooms: A 19th
Century Approach

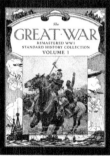

The Great War Remastered WW1
Standard History Collection Vol. 1

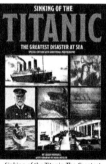

Sinking of the Titanic: The Greatest
Disaster at Sea

The Illustrated History of the 1876
Centennial Exhibition

Old Timey Pictures with Silly Captions
Volume 1

The Art of World War 1

The Kaiser As I Know Him: As Told by
his Dentist

Captain William Kidd and the Pirates
and Buccaneers Who Ravaged the Seas

The Aeroplane Speaks: Illustrated
Historical Guide to Airplanes